Overhead Cost Control

BOOKS BY PHIL CARROLL

Overhead Cost Control

PHIL CARROLL
Professional Engineer

M c G R A W - H I L L   B O O K   C O M P A N Y

New York　　*Toronto*　　*London*

OVERHEAD COST CONTROL

Preface

Overhead is a word we use every day in most industrial plants. Yet, many managers and foremen have only a vague understanding of its meaning. Many speak of overhead as something accountants tack onto costs up in the office. Their confusion increases when overhead rates rise after many method improvements have been made in conscientious cost reduction drives.

This lack of knowledge bothers me. I think supervisors, who make the costs what they are, should thoroughly understand them.

On the other hand, much of the mystery about overhead could be eliminated. All we have to do is abandon the silly habit of treating it as a per cent of direct labor.

Our practice is wrong for a couple of reasons. Primarily, the fallacy lies in the concept of a fraction. Actually, labor plus overhead is a sum. Their total is conversion cost. This is the value added by the process we call industry. In this conversion effort, we make improvements continually by adding to overhead and subtracting from so-called direct labor. When these transfers are judiciously made, the new total conversion cost is less than the old one. That's progress.

The second error is in using the per cent or overhead ratio as a measure of performance. This is negative. From one view, an increase in overhead ratio calls for criticism of methods improvements that cost money classified as overhead expense. From the opposite view, a drop in overhead ratio elicits applause. This can happen when monies are wasted in declines of direct labor productivity.

v

We should straighten out our "communications" as one step toward gaining control of overhead costs.

Secondly, we should measure correctly the work we class as overhead. It is not directly related to volume. Much indirect labor costs about the same whether the customer orders 10 or 1,000. It is like setup on a machine in the shop.

Correct measurement is necessary to control. Managers who do whatever controlling is done will work toward goals only when they appear to be fair. That is why budgets should represent work required.

Further, control in this book is interpreted to mean reductions in waste. There is waste. It is chiefly in two forms. One is in the same types of habits that were improved upon in the plant years ago.

The other waste is in unprofitable systems adornments. These exist because we do not figure overhead operation costs and compare these with values. More than that, we keep on adding to systems, thinking that systems control costs.

All in all, there are major reductions and realignments to be made in overhead costs. We should get back to the basic purpose of "serving the customer at a profit."

This is the direction my book is pointed toward. The emphasis is placed on profit improvement. Analysis, assignment, and control of overhead costs are explained means for achieving this necessary result.

My hope is that you, Mr. Reader, will find some ideas here that will be useful in getting better overhead cost control. Most of these have been drawn from my long and varied experiences.

Also, many ideas were taken from writers in the field. Proper credit has been given for these, and I am indebted to their authors.

I am greatly pleased to include here two chapters written by my son. Phil, Jr., is Controller-Treasurer of Brock Candy Company in Chattanooga. Before locating there, he had worked with 30 some companies as a consultant. So he is not an amateur in the field of cost control.

Finally, I want to acknowledge the help of Virginia Secor who did all the work of putting the book into readable form. Despite our best efforts, you may find some errors, especially in the thoughts expressed. When you do, please let me have the benefit of your suggestions for improvement.

Phil Carroll

Contents

PART THREE. *How Managers Should Apply Controls to Improve Profits*

PART ONE

How to Develop Measures
for Controlling Overhead Expense

Major overhead costs are caused by factors that are not proportional to output volume—our generally used measure of expense. Thus, to improve control, you should determine more correct relations between causes and costs.

CHAPTER 1

Question Overhead Excess

"Our overhead is too high. We have to cut down. We can't compete with burden cost as high as it now is."

Probably, you have often heard such comments. You may even have concluded there is a record player somewhere that is running with its needle tracking in one groove.

Continuing repetition of this same tune may have prompted you to think, "All we do is talk about high overhead costs." Or you may have said to yourself, "I guess Parkinson was right." Instead, you may have wondered, "How do we know overhead is too high?"

For overhead to be too high, you must have applied some basis for gauging. Do we say overhead is too high because

Its ratio to direct has gone up?
The number of white-collared people has increased?
Our costs are higher than our competitors'?
Net profits are lower than they should be?

Maybe your answer is "Yes" to one or more of these questions. Many managers will agree with you, if I judge correctly from the comments I hear and read. Unfortunately, however, their conclusions may be right or wrong depending upon the yardsticks they use for measuring.

Overhead Ratio

For instance, too many managers gauge by overhead ratios that are rising. Maybe they were taught by accountants to think in these terms. Even so, the premise is wrong. The granddaddy of this notion is the overhead "rate" or burden per cent computed for costing purposes. It is the result of dividing an amount of expense called overhead by a volume of production. The volume may be measured in tons, labor dollars, piecework earnings, labor hours, or standard times. The ratio can be correct as an exercise in arithmetic, but it is wrong as a measuring stick.

One error is shown by Fig. 1a. There you see that expense at any volume contains a large constant amount. The constant is what some folks think of as the cost of "keeping the doors open." I call it the cost of the "nucleus of the organization." It is a very

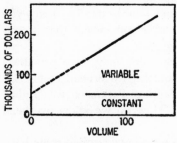
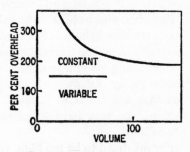

a. Overhead costs are made up of constants and variables.

b. Constant costs as per cents increase as volume declines.

Fig. 1. Overhead cost includes an important amount that is relatively constant regardless of volume.

real cost in a successful company. It amounted to 25 per cent of the total cost of operations at normal volume in one company I worked with. Probably, it is a much larger per cent in companies that have utilized automatic machinery.

You shouldn't set aside this constant by calling it "period costs," as the advocates of direct costing urge. That method does not relieve you of the necessity for controlling this major cost. Nor does it enable you to escape adding its proper proportion into your product costs.

But prorating this constant into an overhead ratio, as portrayed in Fig. 1b, makes for a faulty yardstick. One big change in ratio or overhead per cent is a result of simple arithmetic—the spreading of a constant cost over a varying volume. Thus, the effect of the constant cost on an overhead per cent is that of any reciprocal $(1/x)$.

Increased Productivity

A similar change in overhead ratio occurs where progress is being made. Every time we increase productivity, we whittle a piece off the end of the yardstick we call direct labor.

This measure is reduced in length about 3 per cent each year

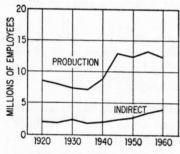
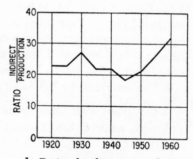

a. Millions of employees in manufacturing for the years 1920 to 1960 at 5-year intervals.

b. Ratio of indirect to production employees figured as many now calculate overhead.

FIG. 2. Total employees and the relation of indirect to production include all sorts of variables such as war production, new business, and consumer demands.

according to our newspapers—3 per cent being the commonly mentioned increase in productivity. A 3 per cent improvement in each of five successive years shortens the measuring stick from 100 per cent to about 86 per cent in length. Thus, an overhead ratio may appear to have climbed about 16 per cent (100/86 − 100) in five years, if there were no change in the amount of overhead or in the actual volume of production.

Recent figures show more rise. In Fig. 2 are numbers of employees in manufacturing as reported by the National Industrial Conference Board in *The Economic Almanac*. Figure 2*a* reflects the growths in millions of production and indirect employees. Figure 2*b* depicts the ratio. This rose from 26.8 in 1955 to 32.4 in 1960—an increase of 21 per cent.

Management Tools

Also we raise overhead ratios whenever we make progress by utilizing better management tools. To emphasize by example, "Why introduce Production Control?" That is overhead. Your answer may be, "It's good business." The reason you say it is "good" is that you expect it to pay for itself. You figure that Production Control will reduce delays. If these delays are buried in so-called direct labor, as many are, labor time and cost will be reduced. This divisor used to compute your overhead ratio becomes smaller. And your overhead ratio takes another hike.

From this viewpoint, I think a manager should be more concerned about a low than a high overhead ratio. For example, how should he interpret the following comparative figures?

"A U.S. plant with 1200 hourly workers needs 912 salaried employees, while a U.S. owned plant abroad with 1300 hourly workers needs only 221 salaried employees." [1]

These figures indicate that the U.S. plant has 1.3 and the plant abroad has 5.9 hourly employees for each salaried employee. These ratios suggest that the people part of overhead is 4.5 (5.9/1.3) times as large in the U.S. plant.

More Progress

Such comparisons assume that underlying conditions are alike. That "ain't necessarily so," as you and I know. What bothers me more is that attempts to control overhead costs by ratio has the effect of stifling many forms of progress.

Take a simple example. Your operating people learn of a more efficient machine. Should you buy it? If you do, its cost will increase your overhead. Even if you save money in maintenance costs, chances are the new depreciation costs will be substantially more than on your old machine.

[1] "Indirect Labor: Our $7 Billion Opportunity," *Steel*, p. 54, April 10, 1961.

Actually, we must continue to make improvements. Probably, we will have to step up our rates of change when the squeeze of competition from abroad becomes more intense. To lessen such pressures, usually we add and extend the uses of better "tools" of all kinds. It follows that overhead ratios will climb arithmetically. As I have said many times, "Come the millennium, when we are fully automated, everybody will be overhead and the rate will be infinity." [1]

Conserving Cash

Seeing overhead ratios climb will prompt some managers to "trim fat" from overhead payrolls. This kind of reaction is not cost control. It is conservation of cash. It is a form of "crisis engineering" that may be necessary in order to relieve the profit squeeze. But no control is established that will prevent the return of excess costs.

Cutting 20 per cent from the payroll of an indirect department does not in any way assure you that the work will be done at an improved rate of productivity. More than likely, the work will be piled in a corner and not done at all. Thus, payroll cutting, as Henry Hazlitt stresses, is but

". . . the persistent tendency of men to see only the immediate effects of a given policy, or its effects only on a special group, and to neglect to inquire what the long-run effects of that policy will be, not only on that special group but on all groups." [2]

Conversion Process

To get control of overhead costs, we have to think differently. For example, Frederick Taylor suggests,

"No greater mistake can be made than to assume that economy is realized by cutting down the so-called overhead expense.

[1] Carroll, Phil, "Profit Control: How to Plug Profit Leaks," p. 76, McGraw-Hill Book Company, Inc., New York, 1962.
[2] Hazlitt, Henry, "Economics in One Lesson," p. 3, Harper & Row, Publishers, Incorporated, New York, 1948.

Just the opposite is true in the very best managed companies." [1]

What he says broadly describes my understanding of overhead cost control. This may be made more clear by taking a look at our industrial process. In this we apply our efforts to change arrangement, size, shape, and color of incoming materials into some products that customers are willing to buy. Our changeovers are made by using two kinds of people skills. These are (1) the trade skills of those we call blue-collar employees and (2) the technical skills of the white-collar employees, plus managers and, of course, plant facilities. You may prefer to think of three divisions. You might call the skills utilized (1) manual, (2) mechanical, and (3) managerial. However we view the industrial operation, it should not be described in terms like hourly and salary employees. Such classifications are simply methods of payment.

Whatever names are used, our industrial progress has resulted, in part, from the transfer of work from people to machines—from manual to mechanical. This has been a steady process since 1798 when Eli Whitney invented the "thing-a-ma-jig." Whitney's development of what we now call jigs for making 10,000 muskets was the beginning of our country's interchangeable parts manufacture. Ever since, we have been doing what I describe as "taking money out of our left and putting it in our right pockets." We have been reducing what we call labor costs by spending money that increases so-called overhead costs. Pictorially, this series of steps is shown in Fig. 3.

Scientific Management

In the same way, we have shifted work from the shop to the office following a basic principle Taylor advocated. This is,

"The great gain that comes under scientific management consists of the new and absolutely unheard of duties and burdens which are voluntarily assumed by the men on the management

[1] Copley, Frank Barclay, "Frederick W. Taylor," Vol. 1, p. 422, Harper & Row, Publishers, Incorporated, New York, 1923.

side, new things that the management never dreamed of, new duties and obligations in the performance of the work that the management has to take over." [1]

Supposedly, in both types of changes, we go through the process of break-even thinking to determine beforehand whether or not changes will pay off. The premise in nearly every such decision is that labor cost will be reduced more than overhead

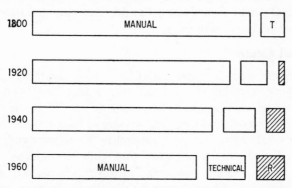

FIG. 3. Our industrial progress has been made by shifting costs from our left to our right pockets with reductions in total effort shown as darkened blocks at the right. The dates shown are decorative only.

cost will be increased. Overall reductions are indicated by the darkened blocks at the right of the lower three bars in Fig. 3.

Two Loopholes

But there are two big loopholes in this deciding process. One is that we do not know our costs. To illustrate, suppose we were thinking about a new die, jig, or fixture. When we estimate the cost to the company, chances are we include only the materials, tool-room labor, and perhaps tool-room overhead. We omit such expenses as managerial discussions, industrial engineering computations, and cost accounting calculations. In contrast, were we to buy this on the outside, the price quoted would include material, labor, and all the overhead of the supplier plus a profit.

[1] "Industrial Relations," Vol. 1, p. 775, Government Printing Office, 1916.

Overlooking the errors in estimating, we do fairly good jobs in making break-even analyses before increasing overhead costs for tangible things. But very few managers make the same critical judgments about the costs of staff functions.

The other loophole is in the lack of follow-up or justification. Commonly, some report is required of the savings made by improvements in shop methods. Rarely, however, are costs compared with results achieved by additions to overhead personnel. Maybe that is why Henry Margolis said, "American industry is the most over-managed in the world." [1]

Overhead Control

Regardless, very few companies have made anything like the same intensive studies of overhead costs as they have been carrying on to reduce plant costs for many years. To begin sorting cost facts from overhead figures, we should take a closer look at Webster's definition. He says, control is "to exercise restraining or directing influence over." Note that while "restraining" means curbing or suppressing, "directing" means regulating activities or courses of action. Thus, to exercise directing influences on overhead costs can mean increasing them. That is exactly what smart managers do when they elect to spend money for better managerial tools of all kinds with the expectations of cutting other costs by larger amounts.

Increasing overhead costs should be two-directional. One is internal. For example, you should raise the cost of time and method study if you expect to get control of other overhead costs. Reasons why will be given in Chap. 7. The other is external in that there are many overhead costs now reported as direct labor. This phase of control will be explained in our next chapter.

Underlying Influences

But there are more problems. Perhaps the most important are that both volume and overhead are mixtures of unlike quantities. These are suggested by the combinations of odd shapes in Fig. 4.

[1] "Elgin Gets a New Mainspring," *Business Week*, p. 133, November 25, 1961.

No, this is not a surrealist's picture. It is my attempt to sub-divide ". . . a perplexity into smaller segments, each of which can be separately explored and understood." [1]

As we examine more closely this complex called overhead, we will find that it results from many causes. Some are major and some are minor. Those of misreported amounts and of diversified

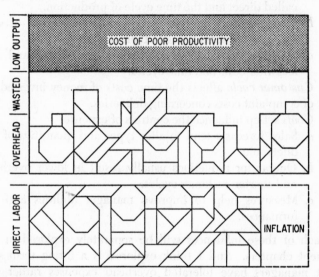

FIG. 4. Conversion cost consists of labor plus overhead, but both are mixtures of unlike amounts including excesses.

products have been mentioned. These six are listed below, how-ever, to get all the major influences together that I think should be analyzed.

1. *Definitions* of what is direct labor modify amounts of expense charged to and reported as overhead cost.
2. *Diversities* of products have important influences on the amounts of overhead expenses.
   a. Complexities of products affect the extents of overhead costs.

[1] Van Fange, Eugene K., "Professional Creativity," p. 3, Prentice-Hall, Inc., Englewood Cliffs, N.J., 1959.

      b. Quantities on production and sales orders establish the number of overhead setup costs.

3. *Systems* of all kinds determine types and amounts of overhead.

4. *Productivities* of people establish degrees of overhead cost.

      a. Rates of shop output determine the amount of payroll called direct and the time cycle of production.

      b. Efficiencies of indirect people influence costs of overhead and process times of their operations.

      c. Methods of making and marketing products and services alter costs and time cycles.

5. *Customer cycle* affects the time costs of money invested and of complaint costs concerning deliveries.

6. *Goals* set up influence the controls of expense.

      a. Sales forecasts tend to alter types and quantities of products sold.

      b. Quotas for reductions usually result in lower overheads and shorter customer cycles.

      c. Measures help to improve manager abilities and performances.

Each of these influences will be separately explored in subsequent chapters. And I think explored is a fitting term since most managers have tolerated overhead expenses rather than looked at them through high-powered glasses.

CHAPTER 2

Separate Salable Pieces

"Your new car is 215 inches long overall," the salesman replied to my question, "Is this car longer than my old one?" His was a precise measurement. Trouble was I couldn't use it. I did not know the exact inside length of my garage. It was built before the advent of fantails.

I knew that my old car did fit into the garage. I had removed battens from the doors to gain another inch. Hence, what I needed was a relative measurement. I had to make use of the yardstick available, as the Paris tax collectors did, of course, for a different reason. They

". . . discovered several years ago that they could often get an accurate measure of a restaurant's turnover by finding out how many tablecloths it sent to the laundry—rather than simply accepting the proprietor's accounting at face value. In a surprising number of cases little restaurants reporting a couple of dozen luncheons a day were for some reason inundating the laundry with 40 or more tablecloths a day." [1]

We use relative measures in industry to gauge overhead costs. We say, "Overhead costs are too high," generally, because they are higher than they were. As one wit explains, "We try to drive forward by looking into a rearview mirror." Many managers compare expenses for this month with the same month last year, or with budgets made up from past performances.

[1] "The Latch String," Vol. 54, No. 5, pp. 19–20, The W. S. Tyler Company, Cleveland, Ohio.

Volume Bases

In such comparisons, our first concerns should be with volumes. Are they the same? Often, they are not and that's why "flexible budgets" were devised.

Usually, volumes are taken as totals. This is common practice, probably, because functional expenses are not related, as they should be, to the several products made and sold. Volumes for manufacturing expenses are usually totals of labor—hours or dollars. Totals mix together greatly differing work contents of diversified products. The result is exemplified by the varied shapes shown at the bottom of Fig. 4, Chap. 1. In addition, there are included types of indirect labor reported as direct. This inflation is indicated by the dotted extension at the right in the lower part of Fig. 4.

Commonly, volume measures of sales expenses are sales dollars. Further, many reports show all expenses as per cents of sales dollars. This is the most misleading measure we use. Not only do sales dollars mix diversified products, and perhaps services, but they also include material costs and profits or losses.

NAILS					BOLTS					NUTS
40	60	80	100	120	40					40
	40		60		80		100		120	60
		40		60		80		100	120	80
			40		60		80	100		100
				40		60	80		100	120

SCREWS

40	60	80	100	120	14	15	16	17	18	20	21	22	23	24	25	27	28
40					15	16	17	18	19	21	22	23	24	25	26	28	29
60	40				16	17	18	19	20	22	23	24	25	26	27	29	30
	60	40			17	18	19	20	21	23	24	25	26	29	28	30	31
80		60	40		18	19	20	21	22	24	(25)	26	27	28	29	31	32
	80		60		19	20	21	22	23	25	26	27	28	29	30	32	33
100		80		60	20	21	22	23	24	THOUSANDS					31	33	34
	100		80		21	22	23	24	25	OF HOURS OF					32	34	35
120		100		80	22	23	24	25	26	PRODUCTION					33	35	36
	120		100		23	24	25	26	27	29	30	31	32	33	34	36	37
		120		100	24	25	26	27	28	30	31	32	33	34	35	37	38
			120		25	26	27	28	29	31	32	33	34	35	36	38	39
				120	26	27	28	29	30	32	33	34	35	36	37	39	40

FIG. 5. Chart shows how volume of shop hours will vary according to types of products sold. Road map with arrows on the chart shows how to pick off volumes in thousands of hours.

Total Sales	Product Mix				Hours Production
	Nails	*Screws*	*Nuts*	*Bolts*	
$280,000	$120,000	$ 40,000	$ 80,000	$ 40,000	20,000
280,000	40,000	80,000	120,000	40,000	22,000
280,000	80,000	100,000	40,000	60,000	24,000
280,000	40,000	120,000	40,000	80,000	26,000
280,000	40,000	80,000	40,000	120,000	27,000

Fig. 6. Changes in mix of your product sales may cause major shifts in overhead work loads.

Work Volume

Even if the internals of these two volumes were alike, their relations to each other and to overhead expenses are different. The lack of relation is portrayed in Fig. 5.

This chart shows ranges in sales of four products. It is a great over-simplification in two respects. First is that it includes only four products whereas many companies turn out more. Second is that it assumes only one form, size, or style for each product. In this regard, you could read the chart as if you made only one product in four types.

Anyhow, note how volume of shop hours varies for a given total of sales. Five examples read from Fig. 5 are shown in Fig. 6. The change in work load from low to high is 35 per cent (27/20 − 100) in this series of product mixes. Yet the sales volumes are all $280,000. Thus, the first fundamental to remember is

> *Direct labor work load in manufacturing is not proportional to sales dollars.*

Inflated Labor

Within our so-called direct labor measure of volume there is concealed another variable. To explain, the hours shown in the examples in Fig. 6 are treated as though they were all the same. This is not the case, especially when timestudy standards are lacking. The hours are inflated because several overhead costs are concealed in totals labeled direct labor. Often, delay times, machine setups, and extra work are buried in direct labor in varying degrees.

Even where work standards are set, "unavoidable delays" are included in the times set by many timestudy men. Such items of labor cost do not represent salable pieces produced. Therefore they cannot earn overhead. Yet, when they are included in "direct" labor, the inflation brings about lower overhead ratios.

Another inflation occurs when allowances are made in the form of "temporary rates." The extra work may be caused by material that is too thick or too thin, too hard or too soft. The extra work

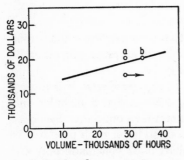 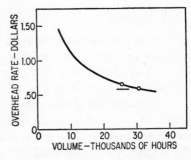

a. Inflated volume permits more expense allowance in budgets than is intended.

b. More apparent volume causes a drop in overhead rate or ratio that is unreal.

Fig. 7. Hours or dollars buried in so-called direct labor that do not represent added salable pieces cause inflation in volume.

does not result in more pieces. Actually, it is higher cost required to turn out the pieces that were produced. It is indirect labor—not direct. But its inclusion in "temporary rates" mixes it inseparably with direct labor and it becomes a part of the denominator used in computing overhead rates or ratios.

If the inflation were a relatively constant per cent, the error would be constant in degree. But it fluctuates appreciably in shops I know about. For that reason, it causes variances in the apparent performances of control of budget expenses. When there is a rash of poor material going through production, the inflation in apparent production allows more expenses in variable budgets. Thus, as can be seen in Fig. 7*a*, poor performance illustrated correctly by point *a* appears to be satisfactory as shown by point *b*. Similarly, there might be some patting on the back because the overhead rate dropped as suggested by Fig. 7*b*. Consequently, we should keep in mind that

Inflations in apparent volume cause increases in allowable budget expenses and other control measures based on volume.

Other Inflations

Similar types of inflation occur in the production of many items made in small lots. Usually, these are produced without the benefit of tools as efficient as those built for larger quantities. To illustrate with arithmetic, the time required to make item *A* with good tools may be 10 minutes per piece. For item *B*, without tools, more time is required. Suppose 15 minutes is required?

Assume one day's production to be 1,000 of item *A* and 200 of item *B*. Then by the usual methods of accounting, the day's production is summarized as 13,000 minutes (1,000 × 10 + 200 × 15). In reality, however, the extra 5 minutes required to produce item *B* is tool-room labor spent on the production floor because it was decided that the smaller quantity did not warrant the expense of better tooling. In comparison with item *A*, the 5 minutes extra required to make item *B* is indirect labor.

Similar inflations occur regularly when production is turned out on "old" machines. The time required is longer than that taken on the "new" machine. The extra time is equivalent to depreciation we haven't spent. Inflation happens also when added operations are performed and when "if necessary" operations are listed on production sheets.

Inflation creeps in from over-reporting, in two ways. One is because employees help to catch errors that reflect unfavorably upon their performances. The other is in failures to deduct all the labor losses in scrap.

Inflation is introduced when compromises are made in time standards, either to settle disputes or as a result of arbitration rulings. Perhaps worst of all is the inflation in those plants where direct labor is carried in dollars. To emphasize this distortion, I ask workshop groups, "Will we absorb more overhead when we give everybody raises?"

Salable Pieces

To make my point more understandable, let's go back to items A and B. Suppose they are almost identical parts. Then the 10 minutes of labor needed to make item A represents one piece in inventory and, eventually, in sales. In relation to A, only 10 of the 15 minutes required to make item B is direct labor. Said the other way, the 15 minutes for item B is not equivalent to one and one-half pieces completed in production.

This is not "straining at a gnat." It is not simply a fine technicality of timestudy. It is an underlying distortion in measurement that causes errors in control. It is more easily shown by a simple example in erroneous assignment of overhead cost.

Using items A and B, suppose $175 were spent for tooling the operations on item A. Then for simplicity, we will consider the $175 to be the only overhead expense. Now, following common practice, let's compute an overhead rate and figure overhead costs for items A and B as follows

Usual Method:

$$\frac{\text{Overhead}}{\text{Labor}} \quad \frac{\$175 + \text{zero}}{1,000 \text{ pcs} \times 10 \text{ min} + 200 \text{ pcs} \times 15 \text{ min}} = \$.01346 \text{ per min}$$

| Item A | 10,000 min × $.01346 | = $135 Tool overhead |
| Item B | 3,000 min × $.01346 | = $ 40 Tool overhead |

We know that both overhead allocations are wrong. For instance, we have charged only 77 per cent of the known tool costs to item A. And remember, the errors would have been magnified if the overhead dollars we used had included the costs of Vice-Presidents and postage stamps.

To reduce this type of error, we must think of the extra 1,000 minutes (200 × 5) as additional overhead because we got only 200 pieces. When we do, our arithmetic works out this way.

Correct Method:

$$\frac{\text{Overhead}}{\text{Labor}} \quad \frac{\$175 + \$35\,(200 \times 5 \times \$.035)}{1,000\text{ pcs} \times 10\text{ min} + 200 \times 10\text{ min}} = \$.01750 \text{ per min}$$

Item *A*   10,000 min × \$.01750   = \$175 Tool overhead
Item *B*   2,000 min × \$.01750   = \$ 35 Tool overhead

Look at this example as typical of distortion in any of the forms of inflation previously mentioned. It is inserted to emphasize a simple fact of arithmetic applied to costing.

> *Inflated parts of direct labor cause overhead costs to be shifted onto the inflation and away from standard operations, thus creating two sets of erroneous costs.*

Overhead Separation

From the discussion thus far, it should be apparent that we do not have consistent separations of overhead from direct labor. Relative amounts of mixtures I have seen in job shops are sug-

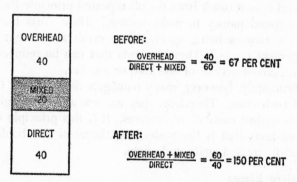

FIG. 8. Overhead amounts and per cents depend, to a considerable extent, upon how you define and measure them.

gested by Fig. 8. The point is that one cause of overhead cost is the definition you use for "direct labor."

You can look at the variations that result in two ways. One way is to say, "It doesn't make any difference." This is partially true if you think of conversion cost as labor plus overhead. Total conversion cost is the sum of monies in both left and right pockets, as depicted in Chap. 1. That's how we compute it. We add labor to labor times an overhead per cent.

You do control total conversion costs. However, the mechanics are such that control has to be exercised on the parts rather than on the total. For instance, manufacturing and selling are usually out of time phase with each other. Hence, a common measure is not used for a total of overhead expenses.

The other way of looking at the definition is the one I prefer. My first reason is not very logical. It plays upon the misconception of overhead ratio. Yet it works. You can see why if you look again at Fig. 8. The overhead ratio is more than doubled by the change in reporting. Such an increase will cause the average manager to jump out of his chair.

My second reason comes from another kind of experience. I find that progressive managers do more to reduce "labor" costs formerly buried in direct when they are correctly reported as indirect costs.

My real reason stems from the oft-repeated principle that "You have to spend money to make money." These costs buried in direct are monies being spent. They result from what I call "management errors." They are costs that can be reduced only by management actions of one kind or another.

Unfortunately, however, many managers do not know the extent of such costs. Therefore, they are not able to weigh their amounts against costs of alternatives. It is this principle of getting cost facts that is the underlying theme of this book. You will find it stressed again and again.

Equivalent Pieces

So the first step in our efforts to gain control of overhead costs is to recognize the basic fundamental of industrial operation. Our primary purpose is to turn out *salable pieces*. Only good pieces that our customers send us checks to pay for can *earn* overhead. It follows that the overhead per cents we use in costing are only convenient methods of application. To get these per cents, we add together amounts we call direct labor to divide into overhead expense, simply because we cannot logically add together our different kinds of pieces.

We can, however, correct the major errors in our measurements of volume for control purposes and in our costs by applying the following rule.

Direct labor is the consistent equivalent of good salable pieces. All other conversion costs are overhead.

The second step in the control of overhead costs is to find out how much they are. The overheads differ markedly for our several diversified products. The variations are indicated by the second story in Fig. 4, Chap. 1. The major differences will be discussed in our next chapter.

CHAPTER 3

Analyze Order Setups

"The only realistic costing of a given product is one which assumes that costs other than raw material are total costs for a period of time divided by the number of items, without regard for the volume of each item." [1]

Drucker's statement is startling. It was intended to be, I think, because he writes in the same article,

"Every product in the line should be put on trial for its life. If it does not offer prospects that would lead you to start making it now, it should be dropped."

Unfortunately, most of the managers I know can't put a product "on trial for life." They do not have realistic costs. Sure, "We carry out labor and material costs to the fourth decimal place. But we spread on the overhead with a shovel." [2]

Three Errors

The errors in costing result largely from two causes. One is that overhead is applied as an average to products that are not average. This error is only partially reduced by subdividing shop overhead into cost centers. Or by building separate plants, as some managers have done.

[1] Drucker, Peter F., "Product Scatter," p. 101, *Nation's Business,* March, 1962.
[2] Carroll, Phil, "Profit Control: How to Plug Profit Leaks," p. 182, McGraw-Hill Book Company, Inc., New York, 1962.

The second error is in applying overhead percentages of expenses like Sales and Administrative to factory cost. This figuring not only compounds the errors of averaging. It also puts overhead on top of overhead and worse, it applies overhead to the direct materials included in the factory cost. The distortions created in this step are perhaps best illustrated by the errors in pricing found by Edward Schleh. He told me that restaurant managers compute their costs by adding percentages for both labor and overhead to their material (food) costs. You can see why, for instance, profits in certain restaurants fell off when they put on drives to bring in the volume of business arising from functions put on by Ladies' Aids and Women's Auxiliaries.

The third error is in assigning overhead cost as though it were proportional to direct labor. The use of an overhead rate or per cent assumes that the overhead cost is the same for each unit of labor. It isn't. Overhead cost is much like the setup on a production machine. It is fairly constant. It is so much per "item," according to Drucker.

$$\frac{\text{Total costs} - \text{Material}}{\text{Number of items}}$$

Changing this fraction to terms of conversion cost or value added, it reads as follows

$$\frac{\text{Labor} + \text{Manufacturing overhead} + \text{Selling}}{\text{Number of items}}$$

This expression clearly indicates that overhead cost is a constant amount regardless of quantity. It even permits us to stretch our imaginations far enough to say that overhead cost is the same for a spare part as for a complex machine. This, I'm sure, is going too far in our assumptions. Regardless, my purpose is not to discuss costing. Proper costs for diversified products can be determined as outlined in another book.[1]

---

[1] Carroll, Phil, "How to Control Production Costs," McGraw-Hill Book Company, Inc., New York, 1953.

Overhead Causes

Here we are concerned with controlling these overhead costs. Even so, we can't get very far in this effort until we understand causes.

What causes overhead? One answer lies in the division of work between men and managers developed by Taylor. For instance, he says

> ". . . as a general rule I can say that the more men you can have working efficiently in management . . . the greater will be your economy." [1]

You will agree that many managers have taken his statement literally. They do have the *more* men in management. And some have skipped right over the "working efficiently" part of his principle.

Joking aside, the basic idea of dividing work is sound. Many duties are performed more cheaply in the office than in the shop. Too, many functions are carried out by overhead people that cannot be done by shop men. Contrariwise, and this has always been a sore point with me, expensive production equipment often stands idle when mechanics do work that should have been completed by overhead people. It follows, then, that one cause of overhead is its definition. This was discussed in Chap. 2.

Four Factors

Another is diversity of product. This is the only cause of overhead, if you use one interpretation of Drucker's statement. But such a definition will not give you a sound basis for the control of your overhead costs. You have to dig deeper.

As you analyze in more detail, you may find there are at least four major factors that affect overhead. These are Customer Cycle, Volume, Sales Orders, and Products. A diagram of your analysis might look like Fig. 9. This shows how overhead costs may be caused in an enterprise that turns out both assemblies

---

[1] Copley, Frank Barclay, "Frederick W. Taylor," Vol. 1, p. 422, Harper & Row, Publishers, Incorporated, New York, 1923.

and spare parts. It typifies, also, the overhead cost relations in a company making basic products that are sold in large and small lots.

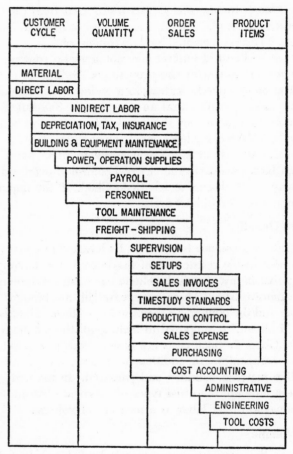

CUSTOMER CYCLE	VOLUME QUANTITY	ORDER SALES	PRODUCT ITEMS
MATERIAL			
DIRECT LABOR			
INDIRECT LABOR			
DEPRECIATION, TAX, INSURANCE			
BUILDING & EQUIPMENT MAINTENANCE			
POWER, OPERATION SUPPLIES			
PAYROLL			
PERSONNEL			
TOOL MAINTENANCE			
FREIGHT – SHIPPING			
SUPERVISION			
SETUPS			
SALES INVOICES			
TIMESTUDY STANDARDS			
PRODUCTION CONTROL			
SALES EXPENSE			
PURCHASING			
COST ACCOUNTING			
ADMINISTRATIVE			
ENGINEERING			
TOOL COSTS			

Fig. 9. Overhead expenses are caused by different factors in the business, and some are affected by more than one.

Turnover Costs

The first factor is the time-customer cycle. This represents the costs of money tied up in inventories during "turnover." These are suggested chiefly by material and direct labor.

There are many other time costs. Those most directly connected are floor space used in storing product in process and maintenance of buildings. Indirect labor is shown also for two reasons. One is for the many costs transferred from direct into this overhead account. The other is because of material handling and janitorial excesses created by shop congestion.

The overhead cost of interest may not show on your reports if you operate entirely with company funds. Still, such costs are there. You cannot overlook them as a widow friend of ours did when she said, "I can't afford an apartment." She failed to include interest on the money she invested in a six-room home she had bought when making her comparison of costs.

By whatever account labels you apply to these profit leaks, they must be reckoned with in any real control of overhead costs. That's why I will discuss at length in Chap. 16 the importance of shortening your "customer cycle."

Volume—Quantity

Alongside in sequence is Volume. Its location in second place is due solely to the restrictions of making up this diagram.

Notice that in my portrayal, volume has related to it only nine of the expenses listed. These, except freight, are brought about by people and the equipment they use to produce. The first one, labeled "Indirect," is supposed to include all the inflations mentioned in Chap. 2. Such costs are now recorded as direct labor by many companies. In addition, of course, are included expenses like material handling and janitorial. In the main, however, these nine are the usual types of overhead that are closely proportional to direct labor as a measure of volume.

Order Volume

Next are the expenses caused largely by Sales Orders. These are typical of per item costs. They are the kinds mentioned in the *Factory* study of short runs. One quote explains.

"Management costs of short-run manufacturing are higher, too. For example, a proliferation of short runs tends to build up indirect costs in the form of larger planning, scheduling, and inventory control staffs. But even more costly are the time demands on supervision and engineering at all levels."[1]

One way to rephrase the foregoing is to say, "Short runs create more paper work for a given volume." I prefer a more general conclusion.

There is no consistent relation between paper work and volume.

To demonstrate this inconsistency, Fig. 10 was developed. The chart is simple in that it assumes only four products. To

					10		15		20		25		30	BOLTS		10	N
						10		15		20		25		30		15	U
	NAILS						10		15		20		25		30	20	T S
								10		15		20		25		30	25	
10	15	20	25	30					10		15		20		25	30	30
10		SCREWS			24	27	30	33	36	39	42	45	48	51	54	57	60
	10		10		25	28	31	34	37	40	43	46	49	52	55	58	61
15		10			26	29	32	35	38	41	44	47	50	53	56	59	62
	15		10		27	30	33	36	39	42	45	48	51	54	57	60	63
20		15		10	28	31	34	37	40	43	46	49	52	55	58	61	64
	20		15		29	32	35	38	41	44	47	50	53	56	59	62	65
25		20		15	30	33	36	39	42	45	(48)	51	54	57	60	63	66
	25		20		31	34	37	40	43	46	49	52	55	58	61	64	67
30		25		20	32	35	38	41	44	47	50	53	56	59	62	65	68
	30		25		33	36	39	42	45	48	51	54	NUMBER				69
		30		25	34	37	40	43	46	49	52	55	OF SALES				70
			30		35	38	41	44	47	50	53	56	ORDERS				71
				30	36	39	42	45	48	51	54	57	60	63	66	69	72

FIG. 10. Chart showing the absence of any definite relation between volume of shop hours and number of orders, invoices, and similar overhead operations.

read it, you start at the upper left with Nails of 20 hours' shop work. Drop down to 20 hours of Screw work, then move to the right. The answer is in this row somewhere.

Enter at the upper right with Nuts equal 20 hours and move left to 20 hours of Bolts. Drop down this column to intersect the row previously determined. The answer is 48 sales orders.

[1] "Short-run Production," *Factory,* p. 93, November, 1962.

Shop Hours	Product Mix				Sales Orders
	Nails	Screws	Nuts	Bolts	
80	30	30	10	10	36
80	30	20	15	15	41
80	20	20	20	20	48
80	15	15	25	25	54
80	10	10	30	30	60

FIG. 11. Consistent volumes of hours of shopwork do not necessarily mean that overhead work loads are proportional.

This appears with four other readings on the chart in Fig. 11. There you see that for identical shop loads of 80 hours, there is a range in created overhead operations from 36 to 60. This is 67 per cent variation.

Order Setup

If Fig. 11 makes the point, let's move on to look more closely at one of the chief causes of overhead. To underline, we could even say that sales orders are the life blood of business. But our control problem is not that simple.

For instance, there are several kinds of orders. These are represented by the three columns on Fig. 12. At the left is a list of overhead operations caused by customer orders. Probably, your list will differ. Further, the operations done are not likely to occur in such neatly arranged groups. That's why I included "long-distance phone calls" and "high-priced expediting."

These lists show the relative constancies of sales order costs. Operations performed with dollar amounts like "Type invoice" and "Post Accounts Payable" will cost about the same whether for $.35 or $3,500 orders. To stress this fact, I can go on to say that it may take half an hour to schedule an order, 2 hours to figure a cost, 15 hours to develop a design, whether your customer orders 3 or 300 pieces. These time costs are merely suggestive.

Probably, each of your classes of orders will have different

Order of Operations	Orders, Special	Spare Part	Stock Item
Sell......................	x		
Interpret order.............	x	x	x
Long-distance phone calls.....	x	x	
Check credit...............	x	x	x
Type order.................	x	x	x
Check design...............	x	x	
Design.....................	x		
Purchase...................	x		
Record Accounts Payable.....	x		
Receive raw materials........	x		
Receive finished materials.....	x		
Inspect incoming materials....	x		
Issue production order........	x	x	
Order tools.................	x		
Set work standards...........	x		
Schedule production..........	x	x	
High-priced expediting.......	x	x	
Set up machines.............	x	x	
(Manufacture)...............	*	*	
Inspect.....................	x	x	
Put in Inventory............	x	x	x
Take from Inventory.........	x	x	x
(Assemble)..................	*		
Test.......................	x		
Pack.......................	x	x	x
Deliver.....................	x	x	x
Type invoice...............	x	x	x
Post Accounts Receivable.....	x	x	x
Collect.....................	x	x	x
Compute cost...............	x		

Fig. 12. Overhead operations will differ for your several kinds of sales orders.

costs. Some of these variations will be brought out later. The fundamental to keep in mind at this point is

Overhead cost of a sales order for a specific type of product is fairly constant.

Special Orders

Admittedly, there can be wide ranges in costs of processing orders through their overhead operations. Yours may be low because you sell through agents. On the other hand, they may be high for the reason that your company is more like an agent than most are. You may buy many of your products for assembly.

Still differently, you may have many orders for special products. Their degrees of variety may be extensive. Their complexities will influence expenses like engineering, purchasing, and manufacturing setups.

Engineering has been a major cost of the tailor-made products I have seen so often. That is why I placed it so far over in the Product column on Fig. 9. For the same reason, regular orders and specials are combined in one column on Fig. 12. One reason is that most companies turning out many specials utilize basic product designs. Generally, the differing features of special orders are additions, modifications, or subtractions. In such cases, engineering for sales orders would be costs of adapting basic designs to special needs. While costly, the expenses would ordinarily be substantially less than those of creating new designs.

Products—Items

On the other hand, if your specials are mostly products instead of orders, a different separation can be made. One way to distinguish between the two is to think in terms of first orders and repeat orders. Another is to look upon Engineering as product development cost. Many companies do. In this view, it is like Tool Cost and Administrative. Such costs are created more by products than by orders. It is for such reasons that I have listed these three costs together, overlapping the last column on Fig. 9.

Some such analyses as those preceding are necessary in order to get a basis for the control of overhead costs. Misleading conclusions can be reached if you follow our long-time habit of gauging by ratios or per cents. There are too many setup costs in overhead expenses for ratios to have meaning.

Yet, real control is not secured by getting counts that reveal the numbers of setups. For instance, how would you count a back order? Count alone could lead to multiplying the arrangements of overhead operations. Instead, you want improved results. You can get these by utilizing the several methods to be described in the following chapters.

CHAPTER 4

Compute Process Costs

"In every indirect area, people are poorly managed, poorly equipped, poorly scheduled, and poorly motivated." [1] Do you agree? Are all of these findings descriptive of all of your overhead operations? Probably, your answer is "No."

The fact remains, nevertheless, that most managers have given little of their urgings to the productivity of indirect people. They have been too busy getting out salable production. That's natural. They know that their paychecks and those for their employees come from the sales of good pieces. No, one can't find fault with seeing to it that "first things come first."

Control Neglected

Yet, we tend to think of managers as being short-sighted when they fail to look at the "whole picture." Some have simply accepted or tolerated overhead as a necessary evil. One reason may be that overhead is looked on as "the great unknown" by too many managers. For instance, when I ask, "What is overhead?", the common answer is, "Machines, buildings, taxes, and the like." Also, many people I talk with are confused between overhead as an amount and overhead as a rate.

Part of the seeming mystery lies in the technical explanations made by accounting people. As Fred White put it, "I get lost 'long about the sixth proration." He spoke as a president with financial training. Since one with his background and long ex-

---

[1] "A Decade of Debility," *Factory,* p. 79, December, 1961.

perience was confused, we need not wonder why the usual manager lacks understanding.

Cost Complex

More likely, our basic problem of misunderstanding lies in the grouping of a hodge-podge of accounts. The mixture is vividly portrayed by Fig. 13. This picture was carried over from Fig. 4

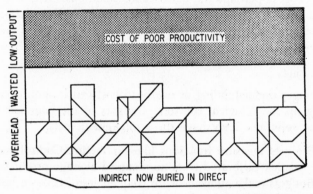

Fɪɢ. 13. Diagram represents all the overhead cost shown initially on Fig. 4.

to show altogether the overhead we are discussing. Hence, the indirect labor described as inflation in Chap. 2 has been added at the bottom.

The figures drawn in the lower portion were made irregular on purpose. They are supposed to indicate combinations of assorted costs. Their amounts differ greatly depending upon the

    Type of industry
    Degree of internal fabrication
    Complexity of products
    Method of marketing

To further obstruct understanding, there are several major influences acting upon the amounts. One is the constant cost of the organization explained in Chap. 1. A second is the indirect part of direct labor charged to overhead. This, to the foreman, is perhaps the most confusing part. His understanding is blocked by the answer he gets to, "Why?" Usually, it is no more explicit than, "Oh, that is overhead." This reply comes from rote, not reason. It arises from an arbitrary classification instead of resulting from a sound definition of direct labor. The need for clear distinction was brought out in Chap. 2.

A third roadblock is in the presence of constant sales order costs. This is perhaps the most troublesome one. It is not consistent with the volume measure generally used to determine budget performance. What is worse, the work loads in certain overhead departments may increase with declines in business.

More Facts

Manager understanding of overhead cost can be improved by setting up more logical controls. Budgets of the common type are not suitable. They have three inherent defects.

1. Budgets measure functions like Production Control with a yardstick calibrated from an assumed average product mix.
2. Budgets make allowances for frequencies of tasks to be performed only as related to volume.
3. Budgets compare current expenses with gauges based upon past history—prior errors, if you prefer.

By correcting some or all of these defects, you can build budgets that will be better understood. Getting better understanding is not the purpose. You aren't running an educational institution.

Work Types

You want to get control of overhead costs. To achieve this result, you must break totals into smaller sums. This procedure is a simple problem in arithmetic carried out with a large amount of common sense. I state it that way because you can't get accuracy in any control system I know of. But you sure can reduce the errors. A start can be made by looking at the similarities between plant operations and office work. Work done in the shop is reported in piece counts, job changes, and miscella-

neous times. In general terms, the comparisons might be shown
as outlined on Fig. 14.

At the left are the three influences discussed in Chap. 3 and
shown on Fig. 9. Alongside Volume is "Produce pieces"—the
factor we all recognize as direct labor. Corresponding for Accounting is the work of "Make paychecks" and for Engineering
is "Update drawings."

Cost Causes	*Shop Employee*	*Accounting*	*Engineering*
Volume	Produce pieces	Make paychecks	Update drawings
Sales Orders	Make setups	Type invoices	Interpret orders
Products	Talk with foreman	Figure costs	Develop designs
Maintenance	Oil and clean machinery	Compute P & L	Analyze quality

Fig. 14. Chart indicating similarities of overhead operations with work
done in the shop and reported on time tickets.

For Sales Orders are "Make setups" in the shop, "Type invoices" in Accounting, and "Interpret orders" in Engineering.

In the row labeled "Products" is "Talk with foreman" in the
shop. This is suggestive of getting instructions about making
new parts or assemblies. Similarly, Accounting may "Figure
costs" and Engineering will "Develop designs."

Last on the chart are similarities classified as Maintenance. I
use that term rather than overhead to avoid injecting another
meaning. But it does represent a general expense applicable to
the first three—overhead in overhead departments.

Three Degrees

Using some such designations as these, you can take apart the
costs in overhead departments. Several methods and degrees can
be used. Three are suggested by Fig. 15. They are suggested as
approaches for two reasons. One is to emphasize the possibili-

ties of cutting overhead costs. The other is to separate the reduction from the administrative phase of control.

Correctly or not, my plan is to show first how to get administrative control. With this established, you can then move on to raise and lower overhead costs so as to get reduced conversion costs with increased profits.

Guesstimates.........	Gauges set up for existing operations based upon current practices
Work standards.......	Measures established from timestudies for normal work pace
Minimums...........	Work standards determined for indirect operations you can afford

Fig. 15. Three degrees of time cost you may use to gauge indirect output.

Toward that goal, one first step is to make lists of operations performed. Such lists are better when they have more subdivisions rather than less groupings.

In the process, you want to get counts and times. Times will be changed to dollars later. But times give you a better basis to work from in subsequent analyses.

Next, you need to determine how many of each count are caused by each type of work. Then you want to find out whether each unit of count has about the same time costs. Your study should get results that appear somewhat like Fig. 16. It was made from an analysis of work done by people in a Timestudy Department.

Typical Orders

I would expect timestudy men to have such figures readily available. But other overhead departments may never have made such breakdowns. To get these, you should talk with each department manager. It will take time to build up the answers you need.

You can get facts in two stages. You can start with estimates. Educated guesses may be the best you can get if you are in a hurry. Then set the second stage by requesting that counts and overall times be recorded.

Your general approach is to make a study of the time costs of typical orders. I repeat the term "orders" because our overhead costs are primarily initiated by customer orders.

WORK DONE	HOURS PER MONTH	VOLUME QUANTITY	SALES ORDERS	PRODUCT ITEMS	DEPARTMENT OVERHEAD
SET EXPENSE STANDARDS....	90		200 STANDARDS		
CALCULATE MACHINE WAIT....	230		2,500 SHEETS		
CHECK TIMEKEEPING..........	2,200		280 EMPLOYEES		
REVISE STANDARDS............	90		160 STANDARDS		
APPRAISE METHOD CHANGE..	50		40 PROPOSALS		
IMPROVE METHODS............	150		40 METHODS		
AUDIT STANDARDS.............	10		20 STANDARDS		
INVESTIGATE GRIEVANCES..	150		50 PROBLEMS		
WORK WITH FOREMEN..........	70		20 FOREMEN		
MANAGE INCENTIVE PLAN.....	90		30 IE PEOPLE		
SET NEW STANDARDS..........	600			800 STANDARDS	
COMPILE ELEMENT DATA......	300			200 ELEMENTS	
MODIFY STANDARD DATA......	55			90 ELEMENTS	
REVISE STANDARD RECORD..	170			4,000 SHEETS	
MAKE ESTIMATES–SALES.....	70			360 ESTIMATES	
DEVELOP OTHER REPORTS..	60				20 REPORTS
MAKE PROGRESS REPORTS..	30				9 REPORTS
PREPARE ARBITRATION.......	20				1 CASE

Fig. 16. Counts and times for overhead operations will enable you to sub-divide overhead costs by causes.

These will be of several kinds. Three broad types were suggested by Fig. 12. These were

Orders, specials   Spare parts   Stock items

Pick names similar to these that are already in use in your plant. In any event, choose names that everyone will understand.

Cost Ranges

Analyses such as these may reveal major variations. For instance, we know that there are large differences in shop operation times and in setup times. Such variations in work required will be found in overhead operations. Typical differences were suggested by the several paths your orders might follow through overhead departments as marked on Fig. 12.

To average these variables will create the same kinds of errors I have stressed repeatedly. Consequently, you want to be on the lookout for ranges in time costs. I would expect to find them in both sales orders and product types. To uncover these ranges, you should continually ask, "Does each one of these take about the same time?" For instance, on Fig. 16 is "Set new standards —800 standards." Maybe each one will cost a like amount. I would suspect different costs.

Then comes the next question, "How many standards do you set for one type of sales order in contrast with another? Or how many more do you set for Product A as compared with Product B?"

"And how about those 200 Expense standards? How many do you set for production runs, how many for sales orders? How many are caused by each type?"

Range Limits

As you review these time costs, you will see some big differences. Ranges will be found within department costs. Greater variations may be observed when you compare costs of work done in several departments for a given type of product.

Don't become upset. If yours is the usual company, you were never aware of these major differences before. Then, too, you can't afford a system of control that will be accurate. The solution to this problem requires a decision as to degree of error. The question then is, "How much error can you tolerate?"

One approach is to pick some nice number out of a hat. Another way is to work backwards from per cent profit on cost or per cent return on investment. I suggest these as measures for one simple reason. It is that any error in cost carries over to become a variation in profit. Such errors you should hold to minimums. You want your profit to be reported correctly. That is your primary purpose for controlling overhead costs.

This theory can be put into numbers. Suppose you were to say, "I want the cost error to be no more than half my profit." With this premise, you can make a chart like Fig. 17. There you see, for example, you can have an error of 30 per cent in an overhead cost if it is only 25 per cent of total cost, provided this error is in a product group having 15 per cent profit.

Overhead Per Cent of Total Cost	Profit Per Cent					
	5	10	15	20	25	30
10	25	50	75	100	125	150
15	17	33	50	67	83	100
20	13	25	38	50	63	75
25	10	20	30	40	50	60
30	8.3	17	25	33	42	50
35	7.1	14	21	29	36	43
40	6.2	13	19	25	31	38
45	5.5	11	17	22	28	33
50	5.0	10	15	20	25	30

Fig. 17. Numbers in the chart are per cents of error in overhead costs equal to half the profit per cents.

Group Exceptions

Some such guides are necessary in order to determine your product and sales order groups. In different words, "How many piles do you break up an average into?" Notice, I used *an* instead of *the* before my word average. This is our first compromise. Chances are you will not follow a rule in arithmetic that would cause you to group unlike products.

Our second compromise is that, most likely, you will simply pick a per cent error for small order groupings. I say that because, usually, there is little if any profit made on them. A third grows out of any new development or major change. For instance, a new product design will increase Engineering, Time-study, and Cost Accounting expenses for the time being. Such increases must be considered in a sound control plan. But they should not be buried in the group averages you seek.

One exception to this caution will occur when new products are typical of your operations. Another exception can lie in a better method of handling major expenses like Engineering costs for special orders. That is to treat them as direct charges like tools, patterns, or molds. They are like a distinct form of setup that is created by first orders. Note also, the direct charge method gets away from allocating an erroneous average amount of Engineering to specially designed products. Too, direct charging of such variable costs will narrow the range of expenses between low and high, thereby reducing the number of order classes.

Operation Costs

Either way, you are trying to find costs or ranges of costs that typify your different order processes. Operations performed with dollar amounts, like Invoicing, may have costs that are almost the same for all types of orders.

A per cent error guide helps you to decide how many types of orders you should recognize. To make an illustration, refer to the 30 per cent error example drawn from Fig. 17. This means a range of plus and minus 30 per cent. Applying this ±30 per cent to a range of order costs like $.53 to $4.80 might prompt you to choose four classifications.

In making such choices, I save time in decision making by looking at a 10 per cent chart like Fig. 18. On this are circles indicating the spread of the four groups. The rectangles suggest the central points of these groups. These may not equal the average costs you should use.[1]

The spreads are not 60 per cent for two reasons. One is that 30 per cent plus and minus comes closer to 69 per cent total spread ($130 \times 130 - 100$). The other is that the numbers on my chart (Fig. 18) are slightly less than 10 per cent apart. How-

[1] Carroll, Phil, "How to Chart Data," Chap. 14, McGraw-Hill Book Company, Inc., New York, 1960.

100	110	120	132	145	158	174	191	209	229	251	275	302	331	363	398	437	479	525	575	631	692	759	832	912
110	120	132	145	158	174	191	209	229	251	275	302	331	363	398	437	479	525	575	631	692	759	832	912	100
120	132	145	158	174	191	209	229	251	275	302	331	363	398	437	479	525	575	631	692	759	832	912	100	110
132	145	158	174	191	209	229	251	275	302	331	363	398	437	479	525	575	631	692	759	832	912	100	110	120
145	158	174	191	209	229	251	275	302	331	363	398	437	479	525	575	631	692	759	832	912	100	110	120	132
158	174	191	209	229	251	275	302	331	363	398	437	479	525	575	631	692	759	832	912	100	110	120	132	145
174	191	209	229	251	275	302	331	363	398	437	479	525	575	631	692	759	832	912	100	110	120	132	145	158
191	209	229	251	275	302	331	363	398	437	479	525	575	631	692	759	832	912	100	110	120	132	145	158	174
209	229	251	275	302	331	363	398	437	479	525	575	631	692	759	832	912	100	110	120	132	145	158	174	191
229	251	275	302	331	363	398	437	479	525	575	631	692	759	832	912	100	110	120	132	145	158	174	191	209
251	275	302	331	363	398	437	479	525	575	631	692	759	832	912	100	110	120	132	145	158	174	191	209	229
275	302	331	363	398	437	479	525	575	631	692	759	832	912	100	110	120	132	145	158	174	191	209	229	251
302	331	363	398	437	479	525	575	631	692	759	832	912	100	110	120	132	145	158	174	191	209	229	251	275
331	363	398	437	479	525	575	631	692	759	832	912	100	110	120	132	145	158	174	191	209	229	251	275	302
363	398	437	479	525	575	631	692	759	832	912	100	110	120	132	145	158	174	191	209	229	251	275	302	331
398	437	479	525	575	631	692	759	832	912	100	110	120	132	145	158	174	191	209	229	251	275	302	331	363
437	479	525	575	631	692	759	832	912	100	110	120	132	145	158	174	191	209	229	251	275	302	331	363	398
479	525	575	631	692	759	832	912	100	110	120	132	145	158	174	191	209	229	251	275	302	331	363	398	437
525	575	631	692	759	832	912	100	110	120	132	145	158	174	191	209	229	251	275	302	331	363	398	437	479
575	631	692	759	832	912	100	110	120	132	145	158	174	191	209	229	251	275	302	331	363	398	437	479	525
631	692	759	832	912	100	110	120	132	145	158	174	191	209	229	251	275	302	331	363	398	437	479	525	575
692	759	832	912	100	110	120	132	145	158	174	191	209	229	251	275	302	331	363	398	437	479	525	575	631
759	832	912	100	110	120	132	145	158	174	191	209	229	251	275	302	331	363	398	437	479	525	575	631	692
832	912	100	110	120	132	145	158	174	191	209	229	251	275	302	331	363	398	437	479	525	575	631	692	759
912	100	110	120	132	145	158	174	191	209	229	251	275	302	331	363	398	437	479	525	575	631	692	759	832

PATENT 2295497

FIG. 18. Chart of "10 per cent" numbers, sometimes called preferred numbers.

ever, this per cent is compounded over any spread. You can see this effect if you look at any number in the top row or left column and compare its increase over 100 with its position number times 10 per cent less 100.

Collect Results

Using the approach just outlined, Fig. 19 was made up. It is a chart that provides spaces for collecting your results. It shows at the left side of each column the Counts for "Set expense standards," the top entry on Fig. 16. From these counts and their respective time costs, the dollar costs were computed. These are recorded at the right on lines labeled "Expense." Under these are dollars of departmental supervisory or like applicable overhead costs shown as "Maintenance."

Using some such chart, you can set down the different kinds and degrees of costs your analyses reveal. You should record your findings in time rather than dollars. One advantage is that your end results are easier to revise later when either the work or the wage changes.

Product		Volume	Order Cost			Total
			Type 1	Type 2	Type 3	
Nails.....	Count	10		20		30
	Expense	$ 8		$26		$34
	Maintenance	3		10		13
	Total	11		36		47
Screws....	Count	20	30			50
	Expense	26	$39			65
	Maintenance	9	14			23
	Total	35	53			88
Bolts.....	Count	30	20	10	20	80
	Expense	22	15	13	$46	96
	Maintenance	8	5	5	17	35
	Total	30	20	18	53	131
Nuts......	Count	20		10	10	40
	Expense	16		23	40	79
	Maintenance	6		8	15	29
	Total	22		31	55	108
Set Expense Standards	Count	80	50	40	30	200
	Expense	72	54	62	86	274
	Maintenance	26	19	23	32	100
	Total	98	73	85	118	374

Fig. 19. Chart showing counts at the left of set expense standards, for Volume and for three types of orders, separated into four product groups.

Then your next step is to combine elemental costs within each department. Add together those time costs you can logically group. The purpose is to reduce the number of calculations required to build budgets and related controls.

Variable Ranges

Another factor determines the groupings you should use. This is the ease of identification of corresponding volumes of output in production and in sales. More about this phase in our next chapter.

At this stage of analysis, your selection of groupings depends upon two limitations you want to meet. These are

1. Separation of different types of business done into groups you want to watch
2. Subdivision of groups to hold the range of deviation of actual costs from averages within tolerable limits

Obviously, you need not adhere to either of these specifications indefinitely or universally. You should change groupings from time to time in order to meet current conditions.

Department Constant

Yet, at any one time, you must select groupings to start or to maintain your controls. In this process, you will try to clearly distinguish between overhead costs created by Sales Orders and those resulting from Volume.

As you analyze, you may decide that you have a third class—business, company, or institutional. Be careful. This part of cost can be swollen by mental laziness like any "miscellaneous" account. The closer you can place an overhead expense to its cause, the better will be the acceptance of your control. Said more emphatically, the less you will "spread with a shovel."

The constant costs that do remain after searching scrutiny must get into your totals. They are

1. Added directly when building budgets for expense control.
2. Prorated properly for establishing standard costs and price quotations.

Price Factor

Before moving to the volume part of control, I want to point out a vital detail. It grows out of sales efforts. Some of these may result in profit leaks. "That is another subject," you may say.

It is. But the sales order costs you have been studying in this chapter result from sales efforts, current or past. Consequently, your success in the control of overhead costs depends in part upon how sales efforts are directed.

In turn, direction of sales efforts should be guided by profit or loss results. Either may occur because of price or cost. That brings you two choices of actions.

1. Reduce the number of unprofitable orders.
2. Reduce the costs of order processing.

Both phases of overhead cost control hinge on knowledge of order costs before prices are quoted.

Route Cost

To get facts, you should go one step further in your study of order costs. You should assemble the costs of your several types of order paths. An example is shown in Fig. 20. The cost ranges

Steps in Stock Order Process	Order Cost		
	Type 1	*Type 2*	*Type 3*
Interpret order........	$ 5.00–$ 9.00	$ 9.50–$15.50	$16.00–$28.00
Check credit..........	1.00– 1.50	2.00– 3.00	3.50– 5.00
Type order...........	.50– .90	.95– 1.55	1.60– 2.80
Put in Inventory......	1.20– 2.00	2.10– 3.60	3.70– 6.30
Take from Inventory...	.75– 1.30	1.40– 2.20	2.30– 4.00
Pack................	1.40– 2.40	2.50– 4.30	4.40– 7.60
Deliver..............	3.00– 5.20	5.30– 9.00	9.10– 16.00
Type invoice.........	.25– .40	.45– .75	.80– 1.30
Post Accounts Receivable..............	.15– .25	.30– .45	.50– .85
Collect..............	.25– .40	.45– .75	.80– 1.30
Total Costs.......	$13.50–$23.35	$24.95–$41.10	$42.70–$73.15

FIG. 20. Examples of ranges in costs of processing orders filled from stock as drawn from Fig. 12.

were simply picked from the columns of Fig. 18 that were designated by the circled numbers. These were set down alongside the overhead operations shown in Fig. 12 as being required with an order shipped from stock. The totals range from a 65 to a 73 per cent spread. This variation in per cent results from rounding the change points to five or zero.

Constant Per Cent

In making such assemblies, knowing about one detail can save you a lot of worry. To visualize this, note first the wide range of amounts in Fig. 20. Under Type 1, the spread is from $.15 to $9.00. Yet each function's cost range is about 74 per cent and so is the total. That's because I used numbers read from the 10 per cent card on Fig. 18. The algebra is seen when using the first three sets of costs under Type 1.

$$\$5.00 \times 1.74 + \$1.00 \times 1.74 + \$.50 \times 1.74$$
$$= (\$5.00 + \$1.00 + \$.50) \times 1.74 = \text{approx. } \$9.00 + \$1.50 + \$.90$$

The $.19 difference is due to rounding.

What this method permits is the selection of cost ranges for individual functions that meet your overall tolerable error. Then when you combine, the same range will exist or be lessened in your total costs of order paths. Your spread will be reduced when any of your operation costs like Check credit, Type order, or Type invoice are fairly constant for all three types of orders.

With these path costs, you reach the end of this fork in the road to control. You now have available times or dollars that should be used

1. To build budgets for overhead expenses that are determined from the types and amounts of work to be done
2. To use in preparing quotations on orders that differ from the general type
3. To assign more correctly to product costs in order to determine in what directions to more profitably apply sales efforts

4. To critically analyze methods of operation in search of overhead cost reductions

Now let's turn to the other road. This one demands the separation of volume of output into convenient groups. How to get these will be outlined in the chapter that follows.

CHAPTER 5

Establish Volume Measures

Measurements made internally of work done by overhead functions can lead to "leaf-raking." Managers of overhead departments can make good showings by creating or taking on more activities. Quantities, counts, services can all be increased with our present forms of undefined dollar budgets.

Of more concern are the efforts made in some places to spend all the budgets allow, whether usefully or not. The silly excuse given for such practices is to avoid having budgets cut for the future. This is one reason why you and I pay such high taxes. We are expected to sustain wasteful bureaucracies in Washington. Such childishness stems, in part, from the ordinary form of budget.

Better System

If such methods of control were satisfactory, you would have laid aside this book before you got this far. It follows that you are looking for better ways. Keep in mind, however, that any new form of control is just another mechanism. Systems do not control costs. Granting that, it seems obvious that a better system should help toward better control.

One better system might be more easily seen if we turned back the clock. In the "good ole days," we gathered job costs. The purposes were two. One was to find out whether money was made or lost on orders. The other was to get data for estimating future sales prices. The measures were wrong because they included "everything but the kitchen sink." Also, the overhead applied was an erroneous average. Then, too, the costs were sometimes reported months after the work was done. Thus, control amounted to little more than, "Please don't do it again."

The notion had merit just the same. Each order could be measured separately. This is the goal we seek. But there are certain modifications. To explain, I can think of no good reason for getting individual costs of many orders that are alike. Further, you want to know what is happening to costs long before orders are completed.

Work Groups

Both advantages can be obtained. All you have to do is to apply the job order cost idea to groups. Some groupings were described in our previous chapter. There, the discussion centered around errors in arithmetic.

After my next comment, you may conclude that I approached the solution backwards. Maybe I did. I'll explain why and let you decide. I began with groupings determined from maximum tolerable error. My purpose was to get the fewest number of sales classifications. Said differently, I prefer the least costly control system I can get that will give me the degree of accuracy I specify. Groupings that met this specification were described and illustrated in Chap. 4. Their determination was based solely on arithmetic.

Maybe, some of these groups cannot be used for practical reasons. One limitation may be your inability to identify certain of your sales orders as they go through your plant. Another, more important reason may be desire to keep separate for critical observations some types of business.

Production Details

In any event, the next step is to reduce the errors of volume measurement by gathering together into classes volumes that are similar. To do this, you must make the connection between work done in the shop and work it causes in the office. All the basic details you need are already available. In the average shop, people make parts by operations. Consequently, you can collect control figures by

Operations	Sub-assemblies	Product lines
Parts	Products	Total output

You need these measures of output for overhead cost control. In essence, getting production output is the same first step you now take. There may be important differences, however. One is that you should use standard times instead of labor dollars to gauge output.

If you do not have standard times, you should create them. Use "guesstimates" if you have to. You must get some numbers for setting up standard costs at one time or another.

Constant Yardstick

Here, the reason is that you need constancy in your yardstick. You won't achieve this with either actual times or with actual dollars. Actual times conceal variations explained in Chap. 2 plus those of efficiency. Actual dollars include all these and, in addition, the variable of wage rate.

At this stage, you might like to review the comments made in Chap. 2. The point is that the variables in any measure of output cause inverse variations in your cost rates.

Sales Output

That brings us to another consideration. It is that you should use the same measures of goods sold that you use for manufactured output. For this reason, you should arrange the measures created in the shop so they can be utilized in gauging sales.

As measures of output made or sold, I use standard minutes. I call these "units" for brevity. I use "units" because most operations are done in minutes. Standard hours are satisfactory gauges if your operations are long ones.

Production Groups

Thus, we get to the question, "Can you apply the groups developed by arithmetic?" The problem is to relate these with the work done in the shop, and later sold. If this were easy to do, I suspect it would already be part of your control plan.

The chore is not too difficult. Otherwise, we would not have obtained job costs in so many plants. Had we related the overhead costs more closely to those jobs that created them, we would have gotten most of the way toward our goal.

The vehicle used in getting job costs was an identifying order number. It was recorded on the work tickets in the shop. When those numbers were recorded correctly, the costs got into the right piles in the Accounting Department. The same idea applies to the sorting you want for overhead cost control.

There are two major differences you are interested in. These are

1. To collect the time standard equivalents of the work made or sold during the period being measured. With job costing, the collection was made primarily (*a*) for charging sales and (*b*) in total for the job.
2. To gather time standard equivalents of work made and sold into groups of typical orders. Again using job costing to illustrate, this difference shifts the detail of collecting separate costs for each order over to that of grouping costs of orders by types.

Order Code

To initiate the flow of production reports you desire, all you need is a set of identifying numbers. They might take a form like that shown on Fig. 21.

The chart is designed to bring out three elements. Most important is the specific naming of order types. This is suggested by the column headings. The more descriptive these are of your typical order classes, the easier will be the application of your numbering plan.

Second is the use of a system of numbers that makes them self-indicating. For instance, if the first number is 3, it always means Bolts. This method has one chief advantage. It is that many people in a shop work on one or only a few products.

Thus, very shortly, such numbers will be memorized. Another gain, although minor, is the opposite. People will more easily detect errors in recording identifying numbers.

	Order	Regular Product	Special Product	Spare Part	Stock Item
Product		1	2	3	4
Nails..........	1	11	12	....	14
Screws.........	2	21	22	....	24
Bolts..........	3	31	32	33	34
Nuts..........	4	*41	....	43	44

FIG. 21. Chart showing code numbers made up to identify work done in the shop and later sold. It differs from the groups shown on Fig. 19.

Third is standardization. This element of design is portrayed by omitting numbers from three spaces. The omissions indicate either of the following:

1. There are no such classes of orders.
2. Some error has been made if such numbers appear.

In different words, these second numbers in my chart show the standard routings through your overhead departments.

Code Design

Of course, you realize this method has a by-product advantage. Code numbers like these make it easier to gather data from punched cards. To illustrate, you can readily collect all 3 (Bolt) orders into a single group. Similarly, you can sort into one pile all 2 (Special) orders.

To gain these advantages, you may have to back-track. You may be forced to modify some of the groupings determined by arithmetic. Generally, this means creating a few more than the minimum number of order groups.

The necessity will occur only if you cannot readily connect an overhead order process with its subsequent shop work. If you run into this problem, use your ingenuity. Try to invent new names that will allow you to retain a small number of order groups.

Assign Numbers

Code numbers you settle upon may be assigned to orders in several ways. Suppose, for instance, you make some or all of your products for stock. In this case, your code numbers could be used instead of the garden-variety production order numbers. If you insist upon production order numbers, then code numbers can be added to them. Again, you could devise a code number plan similar to that shown in Fig. 21 which would create production order numbers incorporating code numbers.

A like method can be followed with sales orders. I would assign code numbers when the orders are written up by Sales Department interpreters. This is a necessary step for orders to be filled from stock.

But this procedure has its uses with spare part and special orders that go to the shop eventually. It provides identifications of the

1. Several order paths you have established
2. Proper classes of counts of work done by your overhead functions along the way
3. Changes in procedures that will occur in order processing as time passes
4. Path numbers of the work done in the shop to complete the order

Work Record

With some code numbers devised, you can make the initial identification. This starts when code numbers are recorded on shop time tickets as production is turned out. Figure 22 shows a suggested design. It has three columns with blank headings. The number of such columns depends upon the daily frequency of different codes of work performed by one person.

These columns provide a simple sorting device. It is used as follows. The clerk extending the time ticket writes the code number of the first job at the top of the first column (41 in Fig. 22). Then she multiplies Quantity Finished by Production Standard Time and records the answer underneath. If the next job has a different code, she writes that in the heading of the second column. This is suggested by 44 in Fig. 22.

DAILY TIME TICKET								Date *Oct. 7, 1963*					
Sheet No _1_ of _1_ sheets				Dept. *54*		Name *John Smith*					No *2416*		
Order No.	Part No.	R C	Operation	Quant. Fin.	Standard		Measured					Minutes		
					Prod.	Exp.	*41*	*44*	Setup	Exp.	PIN	Wait	DW
41	*137215*	D	*Drill*	200	1.5	.09	300		12	18			
			Wait Bp.									15	
44	*210107*	D	*Drill*	80	2.5			200	28				
			Grind drill								10		
41	*196223*	E	*Drill & Tap*	5	4.0		20						
			Totals				320	200					
				Hours			PIN 10		Wait 15		Exp. 18		Prod. 520
				8			DW		On Std. 455		Total Meas. 578		Prem. $4.31

FIG. 22. Shop time ticket showing three columns provided with blank headings for receiving code numbers of work done.

When like code numbers occur later, outputs in standard time are recorded in corresponding columns. In this way, repetitive types of production may be collected together in totals. This step is indicated by the 320 total of the 41 code.

Volume Totals

Totals can be accumulated in several ways. One of the easiest is for the comptometer operator to leaf through a department's tickets and add all of one code. The total can be recorded on some form like Fig. 23. The amounts shown there are examples only, carried over from Fig. 22.

Similarly, the column headings were left blank. The form is flexible this way. Columns used are only those for code numbers that are worked on. In time, patterns will be revealed that may suggest improved form designs.

Carrying on, the total for each day is added. This is checked against the total usually accumulated for a department's sheets. Then if each day's totals are correct, those for the week should be right. These can be recorded on a form similar to Fig. 23,

WEEK ENDING *October 12, 1963*									DEPT. *54*
DAY	*41*	*44*							TOTAL
MONDAY	*320*	*200*							*520*
TUESDAY									
WEDNESDAY									
THURSDAY									
FRIDAY									
TOTALS									

FIG. 23. Form made to collect by code numbers the totals of standard times produced in the shop.

only longer. The left column may be used for shop department numbers. However done, the totals for each code number are obtained.

Volume Work

The code totals in standard time units represent the salable work done in the shop during the period. The grand total of these is what many accountants now use to compute overhead rates or ratios.

But, as previously stressed, this way of figuring assumes that each unit of labor requires the same overhead effort. That is not the case. More than that, it assumes that overhead work is directly related to production. That is not true either.

In our previous chapter, we found that only a portion of overhead work was related to volume. Probably, this work will differ in any one department with respect to your several products or sales order.

Therefore, it is important to find these differences. Try to determine the amounts of function time or cost given to each type of coded production. Your overhead standards for volume might look something like those shown in Fig. 24.

Product	Factor	Regular Product	Special Product	Spare Part	Stock Item
	Code	31	32	33	34
Bolts	Minutes Dollars	20 1.00	30 1.50	26 1.30	16 .80

Fig. 24. Work standards of Production Control caused by volume per thousand standard minutes of direct.

Such standards are multiplied by the code totals developed in this chapter. This is a sound way to measure the overhead effort caused by volume.

Two Records

Before leaving this subject, two more details should be explained. The first concerns order counts. Sales orders are a major cause of overhead work as described in our previous chapter. It is necessary, then, to count these somewhere in the process.

I mention again this matter of count for two reasons. First is that the Volume we have been discussing in this chapter is essentially started by the same piece of paper that causes the overhead setup costs. Of course, the shop work was done at a prior time in the case of a stock order unless the product was bought outside.

Second is that you need counts of overhead operations in order to measure work. This is the more important reason. More work is done by many overhead functions to process orders than to take care of their resulting volumes.

If this were shop work, counts would be recorded for every operation. This method may be necessary in the offices. It's a good way to start. After a while, you will know what the range in work volume is between peaks and valleys.

Then it gets to the question of time interval. If you take a count at one point, how far off are you in using that to measure output at other points? Test this error particularly for low and high days in the week. Check it also for seasonal changes. These tests should tell you where to take the counts to hold errors within tolerable limits.

The other detail has to do with sales measures. In time, the volumes discussed in this chapter go out as sales. Some may be shipped within days of production. Spare parts may be examples.

Regardless, what you need is a measure of the cost to sell the work done in the shop. This is the output we have collected by codes in this chapter. If all this output were shipped the next day, we'd have the necessary measure. But it isn't.

Actually, you will have several degrees of time lag. For instance, stock orders may be shipped within 24 hours. At the other extreme, you may have assemblies that take months to deliver. By studying these degrees like the time lapses of order counts just described, you can choose methods.

You can use code totals of those types of work that are shipped shortly after production. You can use total standard times for those products that take long times in the plant.

Separately, you should maintain an inventory accounting of standard times in and out. This is needed to check the correctness of outputs taken from two or more sources as just suggested. Incidentally, this check might help prevent some of the dollar inventory shortages I hear about.

With our volume measures and order counts, we can begin to gain control. Our next step is to tie these to our overhead expenses.

CHAPTER 6

Measure Function Output

"What tolerance shall we use?" That is the question we have to answer in setting dimensions for making parts in the shop. The same question was discussed in Chaps. 4 and 5 with respect to measures of overhead work.

Ranges of errors should be limited in establishing sales order groupings and corresponding output volumes. When these problems are solved, any one set of your overhead standards might resemble those shown in Fig. 25. These were made up for Production Control. They will be used in examples that follow.

Product	Factors	Regular Product	Special Product	Spare Part	Stock Item
	Code	31	32	33	34
	Volume	20 min $1.00	30 min $1.50	26 min $1.30	16 min $ .80
Bolts	Order	140 min $7.00	280 min $14.00	200 min $10.00	100 min $5.00
	Constant	5,000 min $250.00	5,000 min $250.00	4,000 min $200.00	2,000 min $100.00

Fig. 25. Time or cost standards should be determined for each type of overhead work created by sales orders and output volumes that differ from others beyond a tolerable error.

Time Lag

With such standards, you are almost ready to put together the parts of your control measure. The result you seek is portrayed in the 3D expense curve sketched in Fig. 26. To build up your measure, you need the three sets of figures explained in our earlier chapters. These are

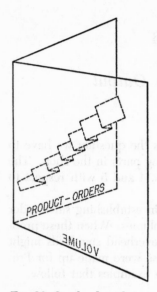

1. Volumes of production and sales with their corresponding time or cost standards
2. Counts of orders processed with their related time or cost standards
3. Constant costs of functions not included in either standards

But these figures have date stamps on them. That's why I wrote "almost ready" in the previous paragraph. Hence, your next step is to consider time relations. Major lags may occur between the times when work is counted and work is or was done. And there may be three of them, all different.

FIG. 26. Overhead work is a combination of efforts created by sales orders, output volume, and functional management.

1. Sales order work may be done days, weeks, or months before or after the shop creates the overhead work related to Volume.
2. Sales order work may be done in part before and in remainder after the Volume work is generated.
3. Constant work of a supervisory or administrative type may be given to planning, preventive, or corrective efforts that are wholly out of time phase with current operations.

These time lags cannot be overcome by any simple means. You must reckon with them, however. To emphasize, let me illustrate with profit sharing. This form of incentive is no good for the average individual. Its amounts are far too remote from his constructive actions for him to see any connection.

For like reason, the common form of budget is often way off base. Expenses are measured against volumes that combine different time relations to the current overhead work done.

Thus, to improve your control, you must reduce the major errors in time lag. One way is to gauge performances by running averages. A better adjustment is to compare volume of one period with expense of another. To make an example, suppose 3 weeks is fairly equal to your major time lag. On this basis, you can compare the cost of overhead work done in the first week with volume turned out in the fourth.

A third way is to take off the volumes of shop work involved in the orders before they go to the shop. These amounts should be available in any company that has sound production scheduling.

Precise Measures

You may use one measure for certain functions and another for closely related work. Don't hesitate to use two or more different gauges. You may take the order count from one period and the volume measure from another. Again, your decision relates to tolerable error. For instance, consider relative proportions. What per cent of a function's work is caused by orders? What portion is created by volume? The relative sizes of these two major portions suggest your likely degrees of error.

The point is, you want timely control. You need to be warned that some parts of overhead work load are increasing or falling off. For this reason, you should utilize the most precise measures of overhead work you can readily build up. Until you do, your control decisions can be wrong. Further, the departmental managers will discredit the performance reports that your decisions are based upon.

Work Output

Having determined your correct multipliers, you are in a position to build up departmental performance figures. You could compute these daily, assuming you get reports from the shop like those shown in Fig. 22. Daily reports of shop production are available in most shops I know about.

Then, overhead work done by a function can be computed much the same as for a shop time card. It would equal

1. Volumes by kinds × Related standards
2. Counts of orders × Types standards + Constants

The result should resemble the portion of Production Control work done on Bolts as shown in Fig. 27.

Product	Factor	Regular Product	Special Product	Spare Part	Stock Item
Bolts	Volume	1,600 32,000 min $1,600	350 10,500 min $525	230 5,980 min $299	120 1,920 min $96
	Orders	93 13,020 min $651	123 34,440 min $1,722	50 10,000 min $500	161 16,100 min $805
	Constant	5,000 min $250	5,000 min $250	4,000 min $200	2,000 min $100
	Total	50,020 min $2,501	49,940 min $2,497	19,980 min $999	20,020 min $1,001

Fig. 27. Figures in the upper left-hand corner are counts, while those in the center are Production Control minutes of work, with corresponding dollars in the lower right.

With such "standards" you can compute a department's rate of accomplishment in either of two ways. One is on the basis like budgets have customarily been set. This is illogical, however, as was pointed out in Chap. 4. "Unrealistic budget restrictions can cause and encourage dishonesty," warns William H.

McCarthy, Manager, Internal Audit, Lever Bros. Co.[1] I'm not much concerned about the kind of dishonesty this auditor finds. The more expensive type occurs with what I call wrong attitude. You may prefer descriptions like selfishness, self-preservation, or conformity. Evidence of the real problem is seen in the periodic attempts to overcome lack of control by "slashing indirect payrolls."

"Why do they cut our department?" is the question in the minds of staff managers. They think they have been doing fairly good jobs. They have kept their expenses close to their budgets. The answer is, "They and the big boss have been measuring performances with faulty yardsticks."

Better Budgets

What you need are budgets that are ". . . geared closely to the quantity and quality of work that can reasonably be demanded from the resources made available," William McCarthy went on to say. Such realistic budgets you can build up when

1. You know what work is required for each unit of volume of your several products.
2. You know the counts and work standards for the several types of orders processed.
3. You know how much the constant costs are of your overhead functions.

Better budgets will help you to reduce and control costs. In addition, they will save you many costly arguments and painful ulcers because they will more exactly fix accountability for results.

Of more concern here is that you can correct your budgets to keep abreast of changing conditions. You will make two basic changes in overhead work as you progress in cost control. One will come from shifts you make in product mix. This will hap-

[1] The Manager's Letter, American Management Association, January 20, 1963.

pen as you learn from more correct product costs where profits are made or lost.

The other change in overhead work will occur because of improvements you make in work details. These will be in two directions. One will be in cutting out losses and details you can't afford. The other will be in adding to overhead where it will make money for you.

Whether these effects move together or in opposite directions is beside the point. What I want to stress is the need for budgets that will more correctly measure work required.

Overhead work differs greatly among lines of products. It is much more for one type of sales order as contrasted with another for each of your products. For these reasons, your budgets should change with shifts in your product mix. Only when they are closely related to work required will managers believe in their budgets. This attitude is a necessary forerunner to getting managers to work for the company instead of for themselves.

Loss Analysis

In building better budgets, you can overcome another weakness in cost control. This is to develop more direct connection between realistic budgets and correct product costs. Both budgets and product costs should be directed toward accomplishing the profit-making objectives of the company.

The other of two ways to measure performance is a more sensitive and revealing control than the ordinary budget. It is obtained when you divide only the measure of production, (a) Volume, into the totals of (b) Expenses. Such a control relates overhead cost to salable output. To this approach you may say, "That's just the same old overhead rates we've been using." In the final analysis, it is. It should be, simply because that is the way business operates.

There is a major difference, however. You can tell from the control proposed where changes occur that cause fluctuations in your overhead costs. To show the fundamental principles, let's look at the fraction

$$\frac{\text{Labor} + \text{Overhead}}{\text{Pieces} \times \text{Standard}}$$

where "Labor" is the cost of standard time of only salable Pieces × Standards.

Let me demonstrate by using the amounts shown in Fig. 27 as though they were totals for Production Control. These will be treated in two ways.

First is that shown in Fig. 28. Figure 28a gives the arithmetic

Product	Salable Output		Production Control		
	M Units	*Per Cent*	*Payroll*	*Per M*	*Standard*
Regular......	1,600	69.6	$2,501	$1.56	$1.09
Special......	350	15.2	2,497	7.14	1.09
Spare........	230	10.0	999	4.33	.43
Stock........	120	5.2	1,001	8.34	.43
Total........	2,300	100	6,998	....	3.04

a. Basis for standard costs per 1,000 Units (standard minutes) wherein standards are weighted as per cents of Volume times Production Control order cost per thousand.

		Per Cent			Cost per M Units				
		V	*O*		*Regular*	*Special*	*Spare*	*Stock*	*Total*
Period	*Volume*	70	22	*Payroll*	1.09	1.09	.43	.43	3.04
May ...	2,500	71	20	7,450	1.02	1.10	.42	.44	2.98

b. Control sheet showing relations between actual costs and standard costs.

Fig. 28. Cost controls should be set up that measure overhead function costs in terms of salable output from the company.

used to build up the Standard Cost per 1,000 standard minutes (Units) of shop output. The standard costs in the last column are the proportions of each type of order work related to the whole Production Control function. The standards are obtained by multiplying the per cent that each kind of volume (Units) is of the total by the individual costs per thousand.

You may prefer to look at these figures in another way. The $1.56 for Regular is equal to $2,501 of Production Control divided by 1,600 minutes of shop work—both $1.56 and 1,600 being in terms of thousands.[1]

Cost Rate

With standard costs like these, you can build up cost controls by the method shown in Fig. 28*b*. The figures under Cost per M Units are cost rates. This form of control is based on the underlying fundamental of cost as we think of it. Stated in a few words,

   Cost equals Quantity times Rate.

In numbers, we might have a $40 cost resulting from several unlike combinations such as

                8 hours × $ 5.00 rate
                5 hours × $ 8.00 rate
                4 hours × $10.00 rate

Using the $5.00 rate as a function cost, assume we had four sets of period figures like

Period	Volume	Overhead	Rate
1	10	$ 50	$5.00
2	20	100	5.00
3	15	75	5.00
4	18	108	6.00

[1] Per hour of work in the shop, $1.56 amounts to $.094 of Production Control. Similarly, Specials cost $.43, Spares cost $.26 and Stock orders cost $.50 per hour of shop output.

Three of these tell us that, despite changes in volume and in overhead, our cost rate remains in control. The fourth period cost is out of line. This could be the result of an error. The volume could be under-credited or the overhead could be overcharged. Such errors are apt to be caught. Often, you can detect offsetting errors that exist in some other group.

The logical interpretations of the higher rate in the fourth period are

1. People were waiting for work.
2. Operations have been added.
3. Wage increases were given.
4. Personnel has been enlarged.

Other factors could cause the increase in rate. And the rise might come from a combination of factors.

Thermometer Readings

The basic principle I want to stress is that the rate is like a thermometer reading. It tells you what is happening. If you can look at it anytime you want to, you can act to maintain better control.

To make another point, our initial three $40 costs might have been grouped differently. We could have had one set of totals like

17 hours $120   Rate $7.05

Such an average rate would force you to excuse variations in actual cost rates in our example between $5.00 minimum and $10.00 maximum. Here is the basic reason why groupings should be kept within limits of tolerable error as emphasized in previous chapters.

With this understanding, take a look at Fig. 29. This is the second treatment mentioned earlier—another form of Fig. 28. The difference lies in the separate reporting of the overhead department constant cost. This control sheet conforms somewhat to the current approach called "direct costing."

The point is that the cost rates shown here indicate what

Product	Salable Output		Production Control		
	M Units	Per Cent	Payroll	Per M	Standard
Regular......	1,600	69.6	2,251	1.41	.98
Special......	350	15.2	2,247	6.42	.97
Spare........	230	10.0	799	3.48	.35
Stock........	120	5.2	901	6.67	.39
Constant....	....	....	800	....	.35
Total........	2,300	100	6,998	....	3.04

a. Details of standard cost buildup when overhead constant is separated from variables.

Pe-riod	Vol-ume	Per Cent		Pay-roll	Cost per M Units					
		V	O		Con-stant	Regu-lar	Spe-cial	Spare	Stock	Total
		70	22		.35	.98	.97	.35	.39	3.04
May	2,500	71	20	7,450	.32	.92	1.00	.34	.40	2.98

b. Control sheet that reports the effect of volume on the constant cost separated from its influence on variable expense.

Fig. 29. Controls may be designed to reflect the "direct cost" principle.

happened during May. Volume and payroll increased above the normals used in setting the standards recorded at the tops of the columns. But a number of other changes took place that can be interpreted from the figures.

Per cent V—volume on the Regular orders increased more than it did on the other three.

Per cent *O*—number of Regular increased less than did the other three types.

V is the per cent that Volume turned out on Regular orders is of Total Volume. *O* is a similar per cent computed from order counts.

Constant—cost per thousand declined because volume increased.

Regular—cost rate declined as a result of bigger orders.

Special—cost increased because either there were more orders in proportion or they were more costly to schedule.

Spare—cost declined because either there were fewer orders or they were less expensive.

Stock—cost increased, probably, because there were more orders in proportion.

More Indicators

Some of the either-or interpretations just mentioned can be sorted out if you want more precise answers. Two ways are open. One is to look at the supporting details. The explanations can be attached as a note to the report.

The other way has two alternative choices. First is to use additional columns of cost per 1,000 Units. Second, and easier, is to expand the per cent columns. All you need is one indicator for each pair of effects that are mixed.

Before we move on, let me point out a couple of variations that may interest you. One is that effective controls like those in Figs. 28 and 29 can be reported in time. You can have costs represented as minutes of Production Control per 1,000 minutes of salable output.

Another variation, and a good one when you are determined to cut costs, is to get more frequent reports. You could have them daily. All the facts are available when you build reports by the methods outlined previously.

About this frequency you may say, "Daily performance figures will vary too much. We should smooth out the fluctuations by using weekly or monthly figures." That's your choice. Just remember, however, that the usual reason for fluctuation is buried waiting time—lack of work. This is a reducible overhead cost. Therefore, I would not hide it in averages.

Product P & L

The better control just outlined should be carried further. You should relate your overhead costs to sales income—the money you collect for your overhead efforts.

	Total	Nails	Screws	Bolts	Nuts
Sales Income..............	$ 3,500	$1,400	$ 825	$ 560	$ 715
Material.................	$ 1,000	$ 600	$ 100	$ 120	$ 180
Labor...................	625	149	230	86	160
Indirect Labor...........	55	11	28	10	6
Setups..................	60	12	30	12	6
Supervision..............	30	7	11	4	8
Tool maintenance.........	30	9	6	4	11
Tool cost................	40	16	12	6	6
Power, Oper., Sup.........	65	19	15	11	20
Maint. Bldg. & Equip......	35	12	6	4	13
Personnel...............	20	5	7	3	5
Payroll.................	30	7	11	4	8
Production control........	25	5	8	7	5
Timestudy standards......	20	4	7	6	3
Engineering..............	85	17	33	25	10
Purchasing..............	40	12	18	6	4
Cost accounting..........	30	10	12	5	3
Deprec., Tax, Ins.........	215	65	60	49	41
Freight–Shipping.........	225	103	30	27	65
Sales invoicing..........	20	4	10	3	3
Sales expense...........	380	190	50	50	90
Administrative..........	110	43	26	18	23
Total conversion........	$ 2,140	$ 700	$ 610	$ 340	$ 490
Total cost..............	3,140	1,300	710	460	670
Profit–Loss.............	360	100	115	100	45
Per cent P or L.........	10.3	7.2	14.0	17.9	63
Minutes................	17,850	4,400	6,500	2,300	4,650

Fig. 30. Report of product sales and profits showing differing rates of return. All figures in thousands.

One such comparison is shown in Fig. 30. This differs from most P & L statements in three ways. The first is that it shows Sales Expense as a cost instead of a deduction from Gross Profit. Second is that it reveals the costs and profits of the four products sold. Interestingly, all four show profits. But don't be fooled. These totals conceal losses the same as do the averages I've been squawking about repeatedly. I'll bring these out later.

	Bolts	Regular	Special	Spare	Stock
Sales Income...............	$ 560	$ 390	$ 84	$ 30	$ 56
Material...................	$ 120	$ 84	$ 18	$ 12	$ 6
Labor.....................	86	60	12	9	5
Indirect Labor..............	10	4	3	2	1
Setups....................	12	4	4	2	2
Supervision................	4	2	1	1	0
Tool Maintenance..........	4	2	1	1	0
Tool Cost.................	6	2	2	2	0
Power, Oper., Sup...........	11	7	2	1	1
Maint. Bldg. & Equip.......	4	2	1	0	1
Personnel.................	3	1	1	0	1
Payroll...................	3	1	1	0	1
Production Control.........	7	2	2	3	1
Timestudy Standards........	6	1	2	2	1
Engineering................	25	5	10	6	4
Purchasing................	6	1	2	2	1
Cost Accounting...........	5	1	2	1	1
Deprec., Tax, Ins..........	49	34	7	3	5
Freight–Shipping...........	27	13	8	3	3
Sales Invoices..............	3	1	1	1	0
Sales Expense..............	50	10	20	10	10
Administrative.............	18	4	7	4	3
Total Conversion.......	$ 340	$ 157	$ 89	$ 53	$ 41
Total Cost.............	460	241	107	65	47
Profit–Loss.............	100	149	−23	−35	9
Per Cent P or L........	17.9	37.2	−27.4	−117	16.1
Minutes.................	2,300	1,600	350	230	120

Fig. 31. Report of sales of bolts only by types of orders. All figures in thousands.

Third is that it reports the costs of overhead expenses in detail. This is done here only because it relates to examples that follow.

Bolt Orders

The P & L statement we just looked at is a summary. It is made up by adding together a multitude of small amounts. It differs from the usual statement, however, in the way the amounts were grouped. They were built up from the order groups we have been laboring to get for several chapters.

An example of supporting details is portrayed in Fig. 31. The zeros are a form of "centsless" accounting. The expenses assigned did not amount to a thousand dollars. This example was given

	Total	Nails	Screws	Bolts	Nuts
Units (minutes).........	17,850	4,400	6,500	2,300	4,650
Labor..................	$35.05	$33.86	$35.38	$37.39	$34.41
Indirect Labor..........	3.08	2.50	4.31	4.35	1.29
Setups.................	3.36	2.73	4.62	5.22	1.29
Supervision............	1.68	1.59	1.69	1.74	1.72
Tool Maintenance......	1.68	2.05	.92	1.74	2.36
Tool Cost..............	2.24	3.63	1.85	2.61	1.29
Power, Oper., Sup.......	3.64	4.32	2.31	4.78	4.30
Maint. Bldg. & Equip. ..	1.96	2.72	.92	1.74	2.80
Personnel..............	1.12	1.14	1.08	1.30	1.07
Payroll................	1.68	1.59	1.69	1.74	1.72
Production Control.....	1.40	1.14	1.23	3.04	1.07
Timestudy Standards....	1.12	.91	1.08	2.61	.65
Engineering............	4.76	3.87	5.08	10.87	2.15
Purchasing.............	2.24	2.73	2.77	2.61	.88
Cost Accounting........	1.68	2.27	1.85	2.17	.65
Deprec., Tax, Ins.......	12.04	14.78	9.23	21.32	8.82
Freight–Shipping.......	12.60	23.40	4.61	11.74	13.96
Sales Invoicing.........	1.12	.91	1.54	1.30	.65
Sales Expense..........	21.28	43.18	7.69	21.74	19.35
Administrative.........	6.16	9.77	4.00	7.82	4.95
Total Conversion...	$119.89	$159.09	$93.85	$147.83	$105.38

Fig. 32. Cost rates developed by dividing standard minutes (Units) of production sold into the dollar costs of conversion tabulated on Fig. 30.

deliberately to show that the seemingly most profitable business contains losses. This is as you would expect. Small orders are usually filled at a loss.

Overall Guide

That brings us to the final control sheet I want to explain. It is similar to Figs. 28 and 29. The difference lies in the averaging necessary to reduce the expense of reports. This one, shown as Fig. 32, is a cost per 1,000 Units report of the four products, together with the composite average for the company.

While this is the final control sheet, it is actually the beginning point of the cost reductions you should seek. For instance, we found by the analysis reported as Fig. 31 that $58,000 were lost on Specials and Spares. Did these losses occur because

Prices were too low, or
Costs were too high?

We can't answer these questions by looking at the usual types of reports. But on Fig. 32 we can see some places where we might begin to dig. To illustrate, compare the cost rates for Bolts with the averages for the company. Those that stand out are

	Company	Bolts	Per Cent High
Indirect Labor..............	$ 3.08	$ 4.35	41
Setups....................	3.36	5.22	55
Production Control.........	1.40	3.04	117
Timestudy Standards.......	1.12	2.61	132
Engineering...............	4.76	10.87	128
Deprec., Tax, Ins..........	12.04	21.32	77

Are these higher costs for Bolts due solely to the nature of that portion of the business? Or are they the results of costly habits —unnecessary refinements, or ordinary carelessness? Probably both.

Even so, such comparisons are nothing more than starting points. They are of little more value than the commonly made comparisons of this month's results with the same month's last year. Both tend to take for granted that the bases are correct. We know that is not true of average overhead costs. Generally, they are higher than they should be.

To sort out the several causes of high overhead costs, you have to search more deeply. You must critically examine the operations that make up those costs. You should test everyone with the question, "Can we afford this expense?" That is the process we will go into in succeeding chapters. Remember, however, that as you move ahead, you can tell whether or not you are getting results. Whatever gains you make will clearly show on the cost control sheets you have set up to utilize the measuring principles explained in this chapter.

CHAPTER 7

Timestudy Indirect Work

"Choose your rut carefully. You'll be in it for the next 100 miles." That sign, once posted on the Alcan Highway, aptly describes how some managers get themselves into profit squeezes.

Average Company

The overhead cost control "ruts" they use are based upon "What we did last year" or maybe "Our industry pattern." Their practices are to cut the tops off of high costs. That is the method suggested by controls like those developed in our previous chapter.

Such controls could help you to go broke. You could be gauging your efforts by expenses that occur where

Sales forecasts are not practical.
Engineering specifications are incomplete.
Production control exists in name only.
Wage incentives are not worth the trouble.
Sales commissions are paid on volume.

Continuing in this vein, you could become very efficient doing work that should be eliminated. Unfortunately, practice does not make perfect. Some people practice doing the wrong things for 40 years. A farfetched example is the oft-repeated jest, "We make the best buggy whips in the country."

73

More People

Today, the need for better overhead control is growing. Business operations in the "space age" are becoming more complex. The new problems are underlined by Ernest Dale as follows.

"Control efforts, which are generally haphazard (management by exception), become more difficult as the area of control increases and the master's eye is no longer omnipresent. Planning, interpretation, paper work, and direction become more involved; more mistakes are made." [1]

All the mechanisms we are bringing into our plants to raise productivity require more indirect people. More than that, the improvement factor of 3 per cent we read about is created largely by increasing overhead costs. These advances are taking place in manufacturing. There, the savings can be calculated. But we hear very little about corresponding gains being made in overhead operations. Thus, the average productivity of employees in companies or organizations is going down.

Present Habits

The decline will get worse as more people exchange blue for white collars. Some companies have already passed the 50-50 mark. As the shift continues, America's standard of living will decline unless we improve the productivity of indirect operations. This is not likely to happen so long as we use controls built around our present habits. Such controls are very apt to permit continuation of those habits. The treachery of this process is seen repeatedly where managers think that meeting budgets typifies good performances.

This belief is a human one. It has been created by training. With similar experiences, hundreds of times workmen, foremen, and vice-presidents have honestly argued with me that, "No one can make 20 pieces an hour." What they should have said was, "No one *has* made 20 pieces."

[1] Dale, Ernest, "The Great Organizers," p. 146, McGraw-Hill Book Company, Inc., New York, 1960.

In the same way staff managers think with their *own* experiences. They assume that what has been done correctly measures what can be done. Consequently, budgets commonly used in industry include various amounts of excess costs. The amounts are illustrated by the darkened areas on Fig. 33. Those marked with the letter *E* represent extra or wasted work. Those marked *M* indicate savings to be made by improved methods. The large block on top labeled *P* shows the proportion of overhead costs

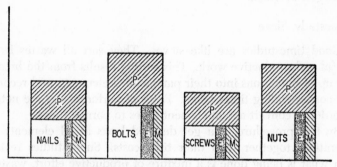

Fig. 33. The labeled rectangles represent correct and minimum product overhead costs. All the darkened areas indicate potential cost reductions.

that can be recovered when people turn out the "fair day's work" determined by good timestudy.

"Chronic Costs"

All of these excess costs are what Joe Juran might call "chronic costs." They continue primarily because of our present habits. To change habits, the best "conditioned reflex therapy" [1] I know is timestudy.

This is the second-degree analysis of overhead mentioned in Chap. 4. It requires additions to overhead. Probably, you know of many other ways to spend your money that will help to make major cost reductions. Each method will have its cost to get the returns you want. In weighing these, ask yourself this question,

[1] Salter, Andrew, "Conditioned Reflex Therapy," Creative Age Press, Inc., New York, 1949.

"Is there any dollar I can spend that will give me as high a rate of return as that produced by timestudy?" In comparison, most improvements you can make will give you more production and/or lower costs. Besides these two, timestudy incentives will also increase earnings when people respond. Timestudy incentives are the only "management tool" I know of that will help you achieve all three results—greater production, lower costs, and higher earnings. These come about for a reason that many managers overlook.

Timestudy Sieve

Good timestudies are like sieves. They sort all wastes from useful and productive work. This sorting results from the breaking up of operations into their parts, called elements, and recording corresponding times taken. Rates of performances are noted in order to convert actual element times to normal times.

By this procedure, you get detailed looks at all elements of operations together with their time costs. Such studies reveal that what is being done is a mixture of productive effort, wasted work, and waiting time.

Good timestudies will reveal that work done by white-collar employees is affected by the same kinds and degrees of management as are found in the shop. Similarly, work divides itself into productive and non-productive groups. For example, the secretary who types a letter three times to get a good one has turned out one that is productive and two that are rework. Maybe her boss can't dictate correctly. Perhaps he changes his mind repeatedly. For whatever reason, the cost in this case is three times—the overhead is 200 per cent to be carried by the usable letter. Some indications of the amount of such costs are suggested by the following per cents of total time.

	Unmeasured	*Incentive*	*Reductions*
Coasting	15	2	13
Waiting	10	3	7
Expense	25	6	19

These percentages are conservative. They are results achieved in manufacturing when operations are changed from "day work" to incentive. Returns from measuring indirect should be greater. One reason is what I call lack of "engineering." Let me explain and, at the same time, outline the next step.

Develop Specifications

Work standards in the shop have proven to be thoroughly practical for several reasons. Four of these relate to our subject. These are

1. We have developed "blueprints" of the work to be done.
2. We have established some definitions of quality of work required.
3. We have counts of how often work is to be done given to us by our customers.
4. We have been forced to adjust to shifts in product mixes demanded by our customers.

Probably, we developed "blueprints" for our mechanics in production because we found it next to impossible to get interchangeable parts made without them. In contrast, such vital controls are not provided by the ordinary types of budgets. Their greatest fault is that they are monies allotted without any specifications whatever of the work to be done in return.

Specifications for overhead operations are few and far between. Because we have not done as much to "engineer" overhead work, we waste a lot of money in extra work, hunting time, trial and error, and deciding what to do and how.

Define Quality

Consequently also, we have an excessive amount of rework. It occurs primarily because specifications are incomplete, or incorrect, or from some combination of these faults. You see evidence of this in the shop every day. Your costs of scrap and rework go up when people misinterpret the "blueprints" and the foreman fails to check the work. He controls such losses only when he makes sure that his people understand and carry out instructions.

Lacking specifications for indirect work, you have rubber standards of quality. You can "get by" without quality specs for one obvious reason. There is no final inspection as rigid as that you have in assembly operations in the shop. Pieces of paper do not have to fit together, or be reamed or filed for assembly. Also, demands for specifications can be avoided because scrap and rework do not affect the paycheck of the employee.

As a result, you may have important amounts of overhead work that are done to play safe. People do more than is necessary to avoid criticism. Shop people regularly turn out better quality than is required "to be on the safe side." Isn't it fair to assume that their brothers, wives, and cousins working in overhead departments are about as conscientious or fearful? You may not think so. Before you can correctly decide, however, you must separate the failures due to lack of specifications from the errors and disinterests of your people.

How Often

Another cause of high overhead cost is in the failure to specify how often work is to be done. For example, a trucker may move material several times an hour or once a day. An expediter may "jack up" the foreman twice a day or once a week. A clerk may get out reports of cost leaks daily or once a month. A messenger may deliver mail once an hour or twice a day. A salesman may report his calls daily or weekly. Each of these frequencies has its cost. What shall overhead cost be? You have to decide "how often." Thus, to get control of overhead costs, you must decide what is to be done, when, and how often. This is the crux of the process we call *scientific management*. The principle was stated by Frederick Taylor this way.

> "The work which was all done in the past by the workman is divided into two great parts, and one of those parts is deliberately taken over by the management. . . ." [1]

[1] "Industrial Relations," Vol. 1, p. 776, Government Printing Office, 1916.

Set Standards

Having specified work and frequency, you should establish standards to measure the "fair day's work." This is done by adding together those elements of work necessary to complete operations at specified quality.[1]

You need some kind of work standards to control costs. Either you set standards or your people set their own. The difference is large. You can see it pictorially in Fig. 34. It amounts to about

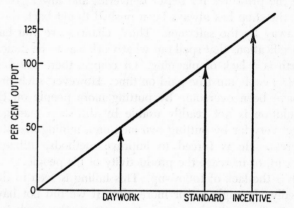

FIG. 34. Major increases in output can be gained by means of work measurement and sound incentives.

67 per cent excess costs when employees decide how much work to do. The 67 per cent is the difference between 100 per cent you pay for and 60 per cent experts say you get on "day work." In amount, this excess cost may be greater than your company makes as profit.

The oft-quoted 60 per cent has been determined from shop operations. Such past performances are readily measured when work standards are installed. But shop productivities on "day work" are apt to be better than those in overhead operations because of the continuing customer pressures for production and

[1] Carroll, Phil, "Timestudy for Cost Control," 3d ed., Chap. 20, McGraw-Hill Book Company, Inc., New York, 1954.

delivery. Consequently, you should not be surprised to find actual performances of indirect people to be lower. There may be several reasons.

Incomplete Managing

First is that you do not have customers screaming for paper-work deliveries to help push out production. Second is that your staff managers have not made the repeated analyses of their methods such as shop managers have had to make so as to relieve the pressures for better deliveries and lower costs. As I find it, the shop has always been pushed to get back the profits given away by the salesmen. Third, chances are you have not had specifications that spell out what work was to be done.

Fourth is a lack of planning. Of course, there are deadlines to meet. People must be paid on time. However, such problems may have been overcome by putting more people on the job. This solution is not readily usable by the shop manager. He can't get very far by putting two men on a milling machine or a drill press. He is forced to improve methods, utilize better equipment, or increase the productivity of his people.

Fifth is the lack of follow-up. This failing is seen in the shop repeatedly. It might occur more often if we did not have customers to "keep the heat on." In contrast, the work in many overhead departments that does not get done today may be finished tomorrow.

Measure Indirect

Such cost leaks should be reduced. "Continuous cost reduction is as necessary in a plant today as is, say, supervision," says Robert Rice.

"You can't live without it. And competitive cost cutting is now reaching into the indirect functions. If work measurement is a really good tool for cutting costs, its application to indirect work is sure to come. In fact, that's where substantial rewards are likely to be." [1]

[1] "The Truth about Wage Incentives and Work Measurement Today," *Factory,* April, 1959.

Utilize Incentives

After you have set standards for the work to be done, your next problem is to get it finished on time. In this direction, you need some kind of incentive.

None I know of can equal that of inspiration. Even so, William Reilly once said, "Only 10 per cent of those who succeed do so through inspiration." One reason may lie in the answer to this question,

"How much of the leader's inspiration will bring about the desired actions from people who are shielded from him by several layers of interposing supervisors?"

There is no system you can substitute for good management. But managers make decisions that have to be carried out to be of value. How do you get the necessary action? My experience is you have more likelihood of success when you utilize wage incentives. Financial rewards for accomplishment are positive. They are more effective than the negative incentives of force and fear. As Crawford Greenewalt puts it, "Of all the motivations to which the human mechanism responds . . . none has proved so powerful as that of financial gain." [1]

Wage incentives provide the best means I know for getting people to turn out a "fair day's work." This is an important consideration. The chief reason is that your people think they have been working diligently. Besides, you have been assuming their production was satisfactory.

Money Symbol

To overcome these types of inertia, added take-home pay can be a big help. And that costs are reduced is shown by 96 per cent of the reports from 249 plants in answer to the *Factory* survey just cited. Other important advantages were gained also as tabulated in Fig. 35, question 14. The reported outstanding dis-

[1] Greenewalt, Crawford H., "The Uncommon Man," p. 37, McGraw-Hill Book Company, Inc., New York, 1959.

14. In general, what are the results of wage incentives in your plant?

Reports from 249 Plants

Reduced costs..........	96%	Raised labor costs......	4%
Improved morale.......	77%	Increased grievances....	44%
Helped supervisors......	95%	Burdened supervisors...	10%
Improved quality.......	35%	Lowered quality........	20%

1. What categories of employees are covered by work measurement?

Reports from 302 Plants

Direct.................	99%	Maintenance..........	13%
Receiving and shipping..	36%	Tool and die service....	11%
Inspection.............	35%	Clerical, shop..........	5%
Materials handling......	33%	Clerical, general........	4%
Housekeeping..........	14%	Engineers..............	1%

FIG. 35. Findings from a survey entitled "The Truth about Wage Incentives and Work Measurement Today," published in *Factory*, April, 1959.

advantage, namely, "increased grievances," I have tried to explain in another book. While there are many causes, my findings are that the major one is "money." Money is the symbol of success in the minds of many people. More money is the opportunity provided by wage incentives. Thus, my analysis is that ". . . grievances are *caused* by roadblocks in our paths toward getting ahead" as commonly gauged by dollar amounts.[1] Note also Fig. 35, question 1, shows that a substantial proportion of 302 companies are already measuring some types of indirect work.

Continuing with cost reduction, another article reports annual savings of $1,170,188 in ten overhead functions.[2] These dollar savings are impressive. Percentagewise, however, they appear to me as being much less than should be achieved by sound time-study.

The opposite was true in a plant in Tennessee. Incentives were installed with major reductions in personnel. The unusual factor

[1] Carroll, Phil, "Better Wage Incentives," p. 1, McGraw-Hill Book Company, Inc., New York, 1957.

[2] "Workers Help Set Own Standards," *Factory*, p. 62, December, 1962.

in this case was that the employees voted "no union" on the fourth attempt to organize the plant.

No Experience

At the suggestion of incentives, your reaction may be something like, "They won't work with overhead people." That is the view taken by many. For instance, academicians write as though incentives will disappear when we are fully automated. Ignorantly, they start with erroneous assumptions and reason to fallacious conclusions. They assume that incentives are applicable only to shop operations because, in the main, most managers have restricted their use to production work. But they overlook the important fact that incentives apply to people regardless of the type of work they do. In addition, they may not know that most of overhead cost is people cost.

Some managers have not seen this fundamental even when unions have demanded wage increases for indirect people. They have granted wage sops. This is money paid out in lieu of timestudy and, as a rule, is more expensive. Such wage sops commonly run from 10 to 25 per cent.[1] Any such amount is greater than the cost of timestudy personnel, if the figures reported in incentive surveys can be relied upon. What is bad management also, in my opinion, is that proper job evaluation is destroyed. Two wage curves are created by this type of tinkering.

Avoid Ratios

Remedies used by other managers are simple ratio plans. These are cooked up to pay indirect people some per cent of the premiums earned by those they serve. Such devices are wrong for at least four reasons.

1. The ratio of indirect to direct varies with volume. The relatively large constant in indirect makes the "allowance" tight at low and loose at high volume.

[1] Carroll, Phil, "Better Wage Incentives," p. 89, McGraw-Hill Book Company, Inc., New York, 1957.

2. The unknown work content of the indirect leaves only an arbitrary way to adjust the ratio for method changes in either direct or indirect work.
3. A ratio plan covers a group of people, and so there are no measures of individual skill and ability. You may be stuck with seniority.
4. The ratio is based on past or existing relations of indirect to direct that have in them the wasted time and work already discussed.

The trouble with too many managers is that they are "practical." They should be reminded of Disraeli's definition, "The practical man is one who practices the mistakes of his predecessor." They should realize, as Ralph Davis puts it, that "There is no such thing as practical experience in doing something that has never been done before." [1] This phase of the subject is best summarized by a story I stole from Bernard Haldane. He writes,

"Back in 1943 a bomber pilot trained in sunny California got his plane and crew as far as Iceland where the weather is more variable at hundred-yard intervals. The next morning he managed to taxi his plane through a blizzard, but when he got to the runway for his take-off to England, he had to call the control tower with the information that he couldn't see halfway down the runway.

'That's all right, you're cleared for take-off,' assured the voice from the tower. 'When you get half-way down the runway, you'll see the other half.'" [2]

Extra Work

Let me try to help you see the other half of incentive utilization. Work standards with incentives provide measurements that are necessary to gain real overhead cost control. To make this more clear, note how Webster defines measure. He says, "Meas-

[1] Davis, Ralph C., "A Philosophy of Management," p. 1, *The Journal of Insurance,* November, 1958.

[2] Haldane, Bernard, "How to Make a Habit of Success," p. 91, Prentice-Hall, Inc., Englewood Cliffs, N.J., 1960.

ure (is the) act or process of ascertaining the extent, dimensions, quantity, degree, capacity, or the like, of a thing." His definition tells us that we must have some sort of measure in order to apply the principle of "management by exception." We must know what correct performance is before we can tell whether or not there is a difference. To explain, suppose you decide to have the office desks dusted twice a week. Then work standards would be set accordingly. The janitor's performance would be measured by those standards. The janitor's boss would be held responsible for getting a "fair day's work for a fair day's pay." In this way, you have attained one important degree of control.

But there is another that is more vital. For instance, suppose the common tendency exists in your plant of some manager to request more dusting. Maybe he wants his desk dusted every day. If the janitor takes on this extra chore because he likes the fellow, his performance will drop. Now, the janitor is on the spot. If, in turn, the janitor gets his boss to have the work standard raised to cover the extra dusting, then the boss man is on the carpet. The extra dusting shows up as a variance—unless or until the budget is increased.

This is the kind of help you get from the people who are measured. They are taught exactly what work is allowed for in their standards. These are set for prescribed methods and conditions. It is obvious, then, that they know when exceptions occur —when extra work is required.

People Help

They will call attention to unfavorable conditions unless their supervisors have already warned them of their existence. Their earnings will drop unless they are compensated for extra work. For this reason, standard time allowances should be made to cover added work.

Under such circumstances, the majority of timestudy men set what they call "temporary rates." "Temporary" means that in time, the conditions will or should be corrected. But the value of "management by exception" is lost. The exceptions are buried in the total allowed times.

The exceptions may be caught by the accountant if he uses standard costs. The differences would show as variances. It is easier, better, and more correct to make the separations at the start. The exceptions, variances, extra work required should be set apart as separate standards. By this method, everyone knows that extra cost is being created at the time it is happening. Besides, and this is very important, the extra work is not productive. It is not increased production. It is simply higher cost.

Delay Time

Similarly, good standards have another control advantage. They do not include wait time. Yet, you and I know it is not possible to operate without having delays. These may occur regularly because of peaks and valleys in work loads. Also, delays occur during every work day.

Asking people to record delays does not give you correct answers. People will not point their fingers at their bosses, as a rule. However, conditions are different when you have incentives. Each minute is worth between three and four cents to the employee. This is too much to give up without squawking. The usual result is that waiting time is exposed and paid for. From this forced choice application, you derive three valuable elements of cost control.

1. People call attention to exceptions that increase cost and hold up production.
2. Allowances made separately for extra work and wait time show amounts and locations of "management errors."
3. Standards set separately for any and all added operations clearly show where overhead costs are going up.

Cost Choices

In this way, cost leaks get dollar signs. Until they are pointed out, your managers cannot correct these losses. Nor can they correctly weigh the costs to improve conditions until after they know how much is involved.

When they take actions, costs go down and productivity increases. When they put off or rule out corrective steps, people become dissatisfied. Note carefully, therefore, that an incentive plan is not a cure-all. It is nothing more than a monument to someone's ingenuity like pretty Kardex Cards that are punched later with IBM holes and eventually run off on endless forms *until progressive actions give it life.* These must come primarily from management. As Henry L. Gantt says, "The setting of a proper task for workmen necessarily sets a task for and imposes obligations upon the management." [1]

An incentive plan works when people want it to work. "Want" has to be more than wishful hoping. The people who want the extra pay have to know what they're supposed to do. Then they must do it correctly and often enough to earn satisfactory premiums. Most people will—when their supervisors reduce and control irregular conditions and delays. Unless supervisors really manage their functions, people lose interest in their work. Costs remain high or increase. Turnover grows.

What is worse, people see that their bosses are not managing. They know that control of abnormal conditions and wait time is part of their manager's job. They look to him to reduce or remove interferences of all kinds that block their performances, and, in turn, their wage increases and promotions.

Getting Ahead

Most people are trying to get ahead. Despite their uses of wrong measures of getting ahead, quantity and quality of output do carry considerable weight. To that end, you make dual gains when you reduce roadblocks to productivity. And timestudy is the best method we have invented for sorting out these "management errors" that hold up production.

Drives to get ahead provide an inherent control advantage. In brief, people on incentive strive to make the same amount of money every day or week. This amount is "geared to the mortgages (installment payments) that have to be met," as I analyze

[1] Gantt, H. L., "Work, Wages, and Profits," p. 143, McGraw-Hill Book Company, Inc., New York, 1913.

this urge. Accordingly, unit labor costs are stable under a well-managed incentive plan.

Knowing what costs will be is a valuable asset in all types of predicting. It is especially helpful in a progressive company. Frequent changes can be made with assurance. Probable costs of new products and new methods can be predetermined. Not only are your future costs more correctly "guesstimated," but also, they are more certain to be realized when the work standards used in your predictions become the work standards applied subsequently under incentives.

Applied Skill

Related to the advantages cited is another that many managers pass up. This opportunity has two forms—present and future.

In the present, performances on incentive help to indicate people who are misplaced, both employees and managers. Granted, performances measure only applied skill and ability. They do not reveal capabilities. But without such measures, you can be stuck with only seniority to go by in making decisions about capability. That can be both dangerous and costly.

For instance, probably you saw these or like direction pointers in the news. "We believe we are only an inch away from the guaranteed annual wage and we are going to make the last inch next time," says Walter Reuther.[1]

"The year 1961 was selected as a base . . . as production costs per item decrease, worker pay checks will get larger . . . . The agreement provides for retraining employees who lose their jobs because of automation,"

reports Kaiser Steel.[2]

"The court says this loss ($592 million a year on railroads) was in wages for unneeded employees, pay for time not worked, and in compensation 'that was not commensurate with the value of the services rendered.' "[3]

[1] *Business Week*, p. 124, November 25, 1961.
[2] *Newark Evening News*, December 18, 1962.
[3] *Newark Evening News*, December 1, 1962.

Round Pegs

Sure, we talk about proper selection and placement. Perhaps, some day we will get more round pegs in round jobs. As we improve, we will release somewhat the brakes that hold back productivity. But in the meantime, as Edward Schleh writes, ". . . frequently poor workers are not discovered until after they have been on the job 5, 10, or 15 years."[1] As Earl Wilson states it, "Quite a few people are already working a four-day week. Trouble is, it takes 'em five or six days to do it."[2] Not many are discovered, however, like the fellow who told his physician, "I can't pay my bill, doc. I slowed down just like you told me to . . . and lost my job."

In summary of these dangers, note what Alexander Heron wrote, with my interpretations in parentheses.

"What can be done to injure sales by raising the cost (wage rates) of the day's work too high can be done just as promptly by making the value (productivity) of the day's work too low."[3]

Future Prevention

What has happened in the past is difficult enough to correct. Unfortunately, some managers seem not to be aware of the additions being made every day. They continue to hire people to fill openings.

It is after this mistake that the future advantage of incentive mentioned earlier can be helpful. In theory, new people are trained for their jobs. Time limits are long or nonexistent. Consequently, major losses occur because of

1. Taking too long to "break in" new or transferred people
2. Relying on trial and error to sort out the successful trainees, letting inexperienced employees catch on as best they can

[1] Schleh, Edward C., "Management by Results," p. 87, McGraw-Hill Book Company, Inc., New York, 1961.

[2] *Reader's Digest*, August, 1958.

[3] Heron, Alexander R., "No Sale, No Job," p. 85, Harper & Row, Publishers, Incorporated, New York, 1954.

Most of these high learning costs could be cut with very little extra effort. Supervisors could develop the relatively few learning curves they need. Their patterns would resemble that shown in Fig. 36.

Taking a chart for each new employee, the supervisor can plot his or her incentive performance each day from the start. If it follows the representative curve, chances are the new person will succeed.

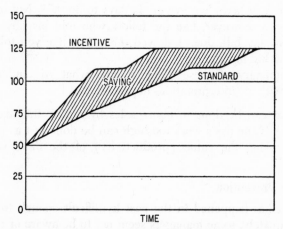

Fig. 36. Saving in the chart is of at least three kinds (*a*) wages from start to 100 per cent, (*b*) fringe costs throughout, and (*c*) equipment and space costs throughout.

If performance falls below the curve, something is haywire. One conclusion is that the employee is not suited to the work. Another is that the supervisor or his delegate has not done the proper job of teaching. Either way, this is a device you can use to reduce learning costs. These may increase markedly as seniority rights, formal or informal, are broadened.

Seniority Rights

To emphasize, consider a recent arbitration case that hinged upon this question, "How long is a company obligated to train a senior man who bumped into a job he had never performed?" Then recall the items in recent newspapers.

1. The "labor pool" created by Kaiser Industries to hold people made surplus by automation
2. The long New York printer's strike over job security threatened by automated typesetting machines
3. The drawn-out battle in railroading about pay for work not performed

Add to these Walter Reuther's plan quoted as being,

"Each company would establish a policy under which qualified production workers would be given preference over persons not employed by the company in filling white collar vacancies." [1]

The overhead cost questions in transfers as well as new hires are, "When and will the employee qualify?" Out of these come other costs like those of, "Let's give him another chance," or "Transfer him to Dept. 36." How many trials, perhaps grievances, even arbitrations, does it take to determine qualifying? And what are the definitions of degree, breadth, and performance that are applied to measure qualifying?

Learning curves derived from work standards are one of the many benefits accruing from timestudy. Their primary value is preventive. They help to reduce the frustrations and gripes of people who get into jobs they are not suited for. In so doing, learning curves nudge supervisors into doing their work of training more thoroughly. Both by-products reduce overhead costs.

Six Gains

In summary, there are six basic gains from timestudy that can be used in your efforts to control overhead costs. These are

[1] "What Will Walter Reuther's Office Plan Mean to You?" *Modern Office*, June, 1962.

1. To get the facts about time spent so as to sort the wasted effort and wait time from the productive work.
2. To study elements of work as a means for specifying what is to be done and how often.
3. To set work standards for the best available methods and to get people to use them. You know about the native who was "not farming half as good as he knows how now."
4. To get people to work diligently and to point out when unfavorable conditions occur. You remember the fellow who said he wasn't afraid of work. He could lie down right beside it and go to sleep.
5. To gain control of work to be done by showing as variances all extras that may be added by either failures in management or current desires.
6. To utilize incentives to increase earnings and to reduce costs of learning new jobs and continuing them.

With work standards established, you have the means for controlling costs of your existing methods. The next step is to use these standards to help determine what systems and parts you should eliminate because they do not give you a fair return on your money.

CHAPTER 8

Determine Your Return

Control can be very much like the power steering on your car. Its almost effortless adjusting is so enjoyable it could let you travel a long way down the wrong road. You could find yourself in a place you didn't want to be.

Standard Costs

Some managers are there now. One reason is that they have been following road maps that were marked incorrectly. They have been guided by road signs we call standard costs. They have compared standard costs with prices to see if profit margins were satisfactory. Such comparisons are misleading for two important reasons. These are

1. Standard costs are usually computed with averages that fail to reflect marked differences in the actual overhead costs of the several diversified products.
2. Standard costs are based upon average quantities that, in effect, assume costs per unit of product to be the same regardless of the quantity made or sold.

Both errors can be reduced when you use work standards, as outlined in our previous chapter, to get better cost facts.

Product Costs

Having indirect operation standards, you can learn how your overhead costs are caused. For example, you will not charge overhead to products you make that belongs on those items you buy. Such findings will enable you to correctly charge overhead costs to products or processes as you now charge direct labor and material to part numbers.

In so doing, you can correct the errors in product costs being ground out with allocated overheads. This is of tremendous importance. See Fig. 37*a*. The primary reason is that it will aid in

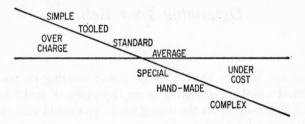

a. In using average overheads, too much expense is applied to regular production and too little to the unusual.

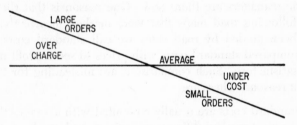

b. Average overheads fail to assign proper costs according to types and sizes of orders.

FIG. 37. Correct product costs are not obtained when overhead costs are "spread with a shovel."

directing the efforts of the company toward more profitable sales. Also, as pointed out in Chap. 6, it will enforce the search for system luxuries you can no longer afford.

Finally, it will help you to gain values instead of errors if you elect to use computers. These electronic marvels will give you lots of answers in a helluva hurry. But these will be misleading if your questions are based on the kinds of erroneous costs most companies are getting. For instance, I smile to myself when I read such items as, the Jones company ". . . put one of its own $125,000 computers to work to guard company costs."[1] I picture a guard who is blind and equipped with a water pistol.

All a computer can do in cost control is answer "Yes" or "No" to questions. Thus, you won't get very far by spending $125,000 for a computer until after you can ask the right questions. Most of these regarding where to point the efforts of your people get back to comparisons of price with cost. The difference—profit—is off by whatever error there is in the cost. It's silly, I think, to try to get where you want to be by looking at road signs that mislead. Therefore, you should make maximum use of work standards to assign overhead costs to the products that cause them.

Order Quantities

In addition, you should make full use of these same operation costs to learn how much quantity affects profit. Actually, there are an infinite number of product costs instead of a relatively few standard costs. The number is caused by the division of the several different constant order costs by the wide range of order quantities. Therefore, business decisions based solely on standard costs are probably wrong.

What you should obtain are cost adders related to quantities. These are the extra expenses that will occur when quantities are less than those used in calculating standard costs. These are shown graphically by Fig. 37b. These adders will come out of profits if not paid for by your customers. How you work with these extra costs is your decision. All I am trying to make clear is that those decisions will be profitable more often when you have better cost facts to guide you.

Now, don't let my comments about standard costs upset you. I'm not agin' standard costs. Quite the opposite, I urge their development and use. Here, however, we are talking about controlling overhead costs as they affect profits. Or the other way around, you want to plug profit leaks that result from excessive overhead costs.

[1] *Time*, p. 76, February 1, 1963.

What System

You need more profit in order to keep up to date. You must get the money to develop new products, to buy better equipment, and to improve managerial skills. For these and other reasons you think of, you should go deeply into the third degree of overhead cost control mentioned in Chap. 6. This degree requires a major break with the past. It goes beyond (1) cutting the tops off high costs and (2) improving productivity and reducing wastes in existing systems.

Here, you want to put the systems themselves through the "third degree." You want to look at them from two viewpoints. These are

1. Can you afford the "systems" you have?
2. Are you getting fair returns on monies you spend?

These questions may appear to be the same, at first glance. They are different, however, and I will try to explain why in this chapter.

Losing Sales

The first question—"What can you afford?"—has many answers. An important one is in losses from sales income. To look at some of these from the cost side, I made a summary of results shown in Fig. 31. These are tabulated in Fig. 38. The figures show that losses occurred on 20 per cent of the sales volume. This per cent is about what I have found in a number of such company studies.

	Sales	*Profit*
Regular...............	$390,000	$ 149,000
Stock.................	56,000	9,000
	$446,000	$ 158,000
Special...............	$ 84,000	$−23,000
Spare.................	30,000	−35,000
	$114,000	$ −58,000
Totals................	$560,000	$ 100,000

Fig. 38. Even the most profitable portion of your business may have in it some profit leaks.

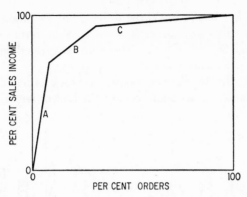

Fɪɢ. 39. This example of Pareto's Law clearly shows that you do not have one realistic cost of order processing such as is implied in the calculation of a standard cost.

Chances are there is some direct connection between these losses and the maldistribution of your orders. To see this more clearly note the curve on Fig. 39. This picture of Pareto's Law is the "*ABC* Inventory Analysis" reported in *Factory*, July, 1951.

We can change this into money and show why faulty sales decisions can result from standard cost thinking. Suppose we have $10,000 of system cost in $100,000 sales. Then the distributions would be as follows:

	Sales	*ABC* Order Costs	Standard Costs	Losses
A	$ 75,000	$ 800	$ 7,500	$ 0
B	20,000	2,500	2,000	500
C	5,000	6,700	500	6,200
	$100,000	$10,000	$10,000	$6,700

While the losing volume in this example is 25 per cent, it is because we are using the *ABC* divisions chosen by the author of the article.

Order Break-even

The cause may be more readily seen in Fig. 40. This shows three conditions with equal product costs per unit. Added above these in darker blocks are three different order processing costs. These were discussed in earlier chapters in terms like Stock, Regular, and Special orders. These are suggested in graphical form by the *a*, *b*, and *c* curves.

Note that the break-even point for Stock orders is between quantities indicated as 2 and 3. For Product orders, this point is

a. Example of total costs when order process is low as for an item from stock.

b. Curve suggesting total costs when a Regular order goes through a normal process.

c. Graph depicting total costs when a Special order requires extra overhead work.

Fig. 40. The break-even point on an order changes with the extent of cost required to process the order.

around 4 and for Specials it is about 8 pieces, dozens, or thousands. The break-even point is perhaps most easily connected with profit by using an equation. Its make-up is this.

$$\text{Quantity} \times \text{Price/pc} = \text{Order Cost} + \text{Quantity} \times \text{Cost/pc}$$

$$\text{Quantity} = \frac{\text{Order Cost}}{\text{Price} - \text{Cost}}$$

$$\text{Quantity} = \frac{\text{Order Cost}}{\text{Profit}}$$

Obviously, the break-even point on an order shifts with both the order process cost and the profit. To show these two factors in numbers, Fig. 41 was worked out. Its answers are in whole dollars. But you can easily apply them to your business by moving decimal points.

Order Process Costs	Dollar Profit per Piece								
	1	2	3	4	5	6	7	8	9
5	5	3	2	2	1	1	1	1	1
10	10	5	4	3	2	2	2	2	1
15	15	8	5	4	3	3	2	2	2
20	20	10	7	5	4	4	3	3	3
25	25	13	8	6	5	4	4	3	3
30	30	15	10	8	6	5	5	4	4
35	35	18	12	9	7	6	5	4	4
40	40	20	14	10	8	7	7	5	5
45	45	23	15	11	9	7	8	6	5
50	50	25	17	13	10	9	9	7	6

FIG. 41. Figures in the chart are order quantities needed to break even on a sales order.

Reduce Work

You can see by the chart that "something has to give." That may not be in the direction of bigger orders. Your customers may not want larger quantities. Also, probably, they would balk at increasing your profit by paying higher prices. That leaves the alternative of turning the spot-light on your overhead system.

The result you seek can be visualized by looking at Fig. 42. Suppose the *a* curve represents the present cost of your system. Then assume that you cut out enough paper shuffling to achieve the cost shown in the *c* curve. The diagrams indicate two ways to make this improvement. One is to stop spending selling expenses in going after some types of orders. The other is to cut the costs of order processing.

a. High break-even point caused mainly by salesman's expense.

b. Break-even point lowered when selling cost is eliminated.

c. Lower break-even point achieved when order processing costs are cut.

FIG. 42. You cannot afford some of your "systems" unless order quantities are above break-even points.

Figure 43 presents the facts in numbers. It charts the dollars of overhead in sales incomes remaining after paying for labor and material and providing 20 per cent profit. You can see that there isn't much left in many cases. For that reason, probably, you

Per Cent Labor and Material	Sales Dollars on the Order									
	5	10	15	20	25	30	35	40	45	50
10	4	7	11	14	18	21	25	28	32	35
20	3	6	9	12	15	18	21	24	27	30
30	3	5	8	10	13	15	18	20	23	25
40	2	4	6	8	10	12	14	16	18	20
50	2	3	5	6	8	9	11	12	14	15
60	1	2	3	4	5	6	7	8	9	10
70	0	1	2	2	3	3	4	4	5	5
80	0	0	0	0	0	0	0	0	0	0

FIG. 43. Amounts in the body of the chart are dollars of total overhead available after deducting labor, material, and 20 per cent profit.

can't afford some of the systems you now use. So ask yourself the question posed by Dr. Biot, "Are we drowning in complexity?"

Extra Costs

An excellent approach to overhead cost reduction is stated by Theodore Levitt in one sentence. He writes, "The governing rule in industry should be that something is good only if it pays." [1] The more incisive method for breaking away from habits is given to us by Lawrence Miles. He writes, ". . . no cost should be included in the product without adding a function causing it to perform or causing it to sell." [2]

His method allows for very little overhead, if we interpret his prescription strictly. Even so, we might agree that costs like engineering, purchasing, inspection, and supervision do cause products to perform. Too, that overhead expenses such as selling, advertising, production control, and timestudy can cause them to sell. Just the same, the basic principle of value analysis is to start with the simplest conceivable design that will perform the desired function.

Grocery Store

As a starter, compare your system with the one you go through when you walk into a store to buy something. There, you may find only three steps.

1. You ask for what you want.
2. The storekeeper hands it to you.
3. You give him the money to pay for it.

You may add two more because you hand him a $10 bill and he must give you change. If you present some form of credit card, then different steps are introduced.

At another store, the clerk writes out a sales slip. She places

---

[1] Levitt, Theodore, "The Dangers of Social Responsibility," *Harvard Business Review*, September–October, 1958.

[2] Miles, Lawrence D., "Techniques of Value Analysis and Engineering," p. 12, McGraw-Hill Book Company, Inc., New York, 1961.

this in a cash register so that the amount "rung up" may be stamped on your slip. Then, she gives you a copy together with your purchase and change.

Even fewer operations are required when you buy something at the supermarket. Your work consists of walking in, choosing the items you want, and paying the cashier. His work consists of adding the prices of your choices, making change, and packaging your purchases so you can carry them to your car.

I know you aren't running a grocery store. But the basic function of your business is the same. This simple example is brought in only to emphasize by contrast the multiplicity of systems we have piled on top of the basic act of exchanging goods for money.

Least System

Do you really need all the system you now have? Why not look at your system from the "value analysis" point of view. You might begin with the question, "What is the least system we must have?" One answer is, "Make the customer a present of any order less than X dollars. It's cheaper."

Everybody rebels at this notion I often advance. Chances are you do too. Therefore, the minimum system you may be willing to accept is (1) to tell your customer how much he owes you and (2) to deposit his check when received.

To this least system, most companies add costs to gain reliability. The first step may be to check the customer's credit. Then, if the order is shipped, it is insured. Inventory is debited. Next, the amount owed by Brown & Company is recorded on Accounts Receivable. Perhaps a statement is sent at the end of the month. When a check comes in, the amount is credited to Brown & Company's account. Often, the sales are reported by territory, customer, and salesman. Finally, to further increase what may be a loss, sales commissions are calculated, credited, and paid.

To reduce costs in such systems, you have to make what I call a "choice of disadvantages." You must choose between cost alternatives. To illustrate with one set of choices, you may do either of the following:

1. Increase losses in "bad debts" due to failure to pay.
2. Increase costs above a minimum to get insurance.

In arithmetic, assume you have $10,000 in small order sales. Suppose you decide not to record these on Accounts Receivable. As a result, let's say your "bad debts" go up 50 per cent—from 2 to 3 per cent. Your loss would be $100. That's choice No. 1.

To be weighed against this loss is the money you spend to keep track of the customers who owe you for goods shipped. Suppose it costs you $200 to post and credit accounts for 1,000 orders of $10 average amount. This is choice No. 2.

The difference of $100 is the price of insurance I'm calling reliability. You may prefer "security"—the cost of feeling safe. But whatever terms we use to describe the extra costs, they can and should be trimmed. They are profit leaks in this complex we call overhead. They are "chronic costs" that many managers permit because they lack cost facts. They continue to spend lots of money on systems that are more elaborate than essential.

Thus, one way to reduce overhead costs is to find out what systems you can afford. Determine what are the least mechanisms you require to satisfactorily perform the necessary functions. This is the opposite approach from cutting off the tops. It is one of adding to the least system demanded. It is the surest way of breaking through time-honored habits.

Manage Costs

Further impetus will be given to your system pruning when you look at overhead costs as Marshall Evans does. He calls them "managed costs." They are the costs remaining after setting aside, say 20 per cent for profit, and then subtracting "product costs and committed costs." [1]

Product costs consist chiefly of material, labor, and related indirect. These are difficult to reduce, if the work is done efficiently, until major changes are made in designs or cheaper materials are substituted. Committed costs include depreciation,

[1] Evans, Marshall, "Profit Planning," *Harvard Business Review*, p. 45, July–August, 1959.

taxes, insurance, and other expenses that are quite fixed by existing conditions.

Managed costs are mostly people costs. You can have few people or many according to what you want done. Wants, as I see them, fall into three degrees. I describe these as Necessary, Optional, and Luxury. You might like some other descriptions better. But if you will define as necessary only such work as paying bills, writing paychecks, reporting to Uncle Sam, and the like, many overhead operations will be left over. These you should study critically.

Trivial Many

In your first go-around, let me suggest three quick ways to find gold. The first one is to carefully study the "trivial many" small orders shown as the *C* line on Fig. 39. Have someone sort these to get groups of like sales dollar amounts. Then with some available amounts of expense you determine, similar to those recorded on Fig. 43, you can get a "fix" on how much has to go— what you must manage to do without.

Your basic problem here will be the result of what I call "carrying standardization too far." To illustrate, many companies use the same systems for small orders that were devised for large orders. In part, this practice goes on because we like uniform procedures. Also, don't forget, the wastefulness continues because of our standard cost habit of thinking.

You don't use standard methods in the shop. You can't afford to. In planning production, you try to decide before you install or change methods whether or not an improvement will pay off. You know you can spend very little for tools when quantities are small. Actually, you have degrees of tooling ranging from little to much according to your quantity multipliers.

Carrying this type of analysis into office work, I ask, "Why only one system?"[1] The question is just as correct in overhead operations as in production. Three answers, at least, are indicated by the maldistribution revealed in Fig. 39. Whether you

[1] Carroll, Phil, "Profit Control: How to Plug Profit Leaks," p. 59, McGraw-Hill Book Company, Inc., New York, 1962.

should have three or some other number of systems is not important. The managing of costs requires you to "cut the cloth" to suit the fit.

Tree Trunk

The necessary change in system to adapt to small orders leads to the second place you should take a quick look at. This may be visualized if you think of your sales order system as the trunk of a tree.[1] From this trunk grow all of your branches or "sub-systems."

The trunk of your system will differ from that of other companies. An AMA survey reported overhead function cost differences as much as several hundred per cent. One explanation is degree of complexity. Another is, "It just grew." A third is that methods vary. For example, one company may prepare six copies of an invoice while another makes only four. Besides differences in quantity, there are unlike methods of production. One company may use snap-out forms while another uses inserted carbons. You can think of several other methods of producing invoices. Each has its individual cost. As you look at any one of these methods, you can see that the cost is created in two ways. One is what you do, as illustrated by the number of copies—six or four. The other is how you do it, here suggested by the two ways of using carbon paper.

Both can be improved upon. Your progress will be greater if you will think only of costs. Don't look over your neighbor's shoulder to see what methods he uses. He may have the wrong answers.

Study the tree trunk of your system. Any steps you eliminate will reduce costs and, probably, shorten your order process cycle. In addition, the part you cut out may also kill the branch system growing from it.

Empire-building

The third place to look for quick results is where empires are built up. Some over-extension may even have been encouraged,

[1] Carroll, Phil, "Profit Control: How to Plug Profit Leaks," p. 70, McGraw-Hill Book Company, Inc., New York, 1962.

as in Washington and in other bureaucratic endeavors, by basing manager salaries in part upon the number of people supervised. The tendency to add people occurs in many technical departments. Certain types of staff managers seek more and still more refinement in their specialized fields of interest. They diligently turn out varied arrangements of the same data and multi-copy reports that approach handbook thickness. Then, more people are required to sustain what Edward Schleh calls "A great flurry of activity." Too, as Henry L. Gantt points out, "Many a man in authority wants a system that will force everybody else to do his duty, but will allow him to do as he pleases." [1]

Some portion of the "empire" problem is caused by drives made to cut costs. These usually slash indiscriminately some per cent like 15 from all overhead departments. In these cutting operations, staff managers are often allowed to choose what types of work they will continue. Therefore, you must dig deeper.

Beyond such extra costs are the wastes of auxiliary devices. I call these patches. Some managers add patches to systems hoping these will make the systems work better. One example is the RUSH RUSH tag placed on the RUSH order. Many such additions are tacked on to bolster existing systems. We seem unaware of the fact that systems are designed to help people. They are not substitutes. They do not work automatically. Thus, you want to look critically to see if remedies have been applied that raise your costs without achieving results.

Finally, examine the extensions to your existing systems and reports. Sometimes these are urged upon managers by salesmen. They point out the unused capacities of data-processing equipment already bought or rented. The sales pitch goes something like, "It won't cost you anything. You are paying for equipment you are not utilizing to its fullest." Similarly, lots of extra work is done because, "we have the people to handle it." All such extras are nice to have if someone can use them with profit to the company. That brings us to the second way of viewing your overhead costs.

[1] Gantt, H. L., "Work, Wages, and Profits," p. 163, McGraw-Hill Book Company, Inc., New York, 1913.

What Return

To be really practical, you should weigh overhead costs against returns. You ought to ask yourself the question, "Am I getting fair returns on the monies I'm spending?"

You could assume that you get a 20 per cent return on each part of costs if you made 20 per cent on a sale. Conversely, you could say that you lost 20 per cent on each portion of cost if you lost 20 per cent on a sale. But you know that both suppositions are wrong. Both are illustrated by the "average" stated under Mathemagicians in *Reader's Digest*.

"Consider a group of 10 girls: nine of them virgins, one pregnant. On the 'average,' each of the nine virgins is 10 per cent pregnant, while the girl who's about to have the baby is 90 per cent a virgin." [1]

Your return on costs is even more confused. Unfortunately, you can't prove where profit or loss occurs. But you can get some answers for cost control by looking at rate of return. You should try to find out what each overhead expense contributes to profit making.

Your job—the manager's job—is to spend money (investment) to make money (profit). Similarly, many functions of your company spend money to earn money. For staff departments, Edward Schleh suggests that the "earn" should be double.[2] You pick a number. In theory, every dollar you spend in your business should earn a fair return. Each of those dollars would earn about 3½ per cent if you left it in the bank. But when you risk losing it by spending that dollar in business, it should earn more.

Consider, also, that the dollars you spend are different as Louis Newman explains. He uses as examples the decision to buy a storm window for $300 that will save $50 a year in fuel bills and a 10-cent evening paper that will give you pleasure and information. Then he shows that

[1] *Reader's Digest*, July, 1943.
[2] Schleh, Edward C., "Make Your Staff Pay Its Way," *Harvard Business Review*, p. 119, March–April, 1957.

". . . the simple 10-cent decision resulted in a net *loss* of cash to the household that amounted to $312 in ten years. And the apparent $300 loss of cash for storm windows resulted in a net *gain* of cash of $200 in ten years."

He outlines his basic premise as

". . . it is necessary to introduce two new elements into our expenditures decisions: (*a*) the setting of a *fixed time period* for evaluation of all financial decisions, and (*b*) an estimate in *dollars* of the *risk* being taken in each such decision."[1]

Earn Enough

The point is that all money used in your company should be returned "with profit" if it is wisely spent. Take an example like adding three people to Production Control. How much are they supposed to contribute toward the success of the company for how long a time? If you will predict that, you can measure what was accomplished later on. Where such expenses are compared with returns before they are spent, you have two measures. One is a way of gauging managerial ability. The other, more vital one is to improve your rate of return by selecting the most profitable of the many projects suggested each day. In this way, you can allot the available funds to those functions whose projects will contribute the most toward profit making.

That's what you do when you approve requests for tooling in the shop. You consider whether to buy or to make tools. You may approve a full set of tools for each operation or you may believe it necessary to restrict tool expense to bare essentials. Sometimes you have no choice because quality specifications force you to use tools of some kind.

Diminishing Returns

At the same time, you recognize that there are several degrees of tooling within any one choice. You can make up a "baling wire" fixture that will enable you to "get by." Each de-

[1] Newman, Louis E., and Brunell, Sidney, "Different Dollars," p. 74, *Harvard Business Review*, July–August, 1962.

gree added beyond the minimum has a lower rate of return on the money invested.

You try to find out before you spend the money whether or not it will be returned in some period of time. Many managers want their money back within a year. This reasoning is typified by the several break-even lines drawn on Fig. 44. This diagram

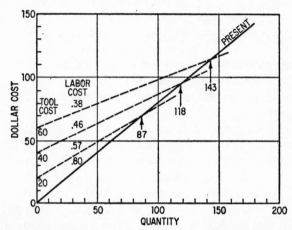

Fig. 44. Each different method improvement has its break-even point—the number of repetitions of an improved method that are required to pay off the money invested in making the change.

shows three degrees of tooling. Changing the diagram to numbers, the following table was worked out on the basis of 200 pieces and present labor cost of 80 cents each.

Tool	Investment	Cost of Each	Saving	Rate of Return
$20	$20 (20− 0)	57¢	$46 ($.80−$.57)200	2.3 (46/20)
$40	$20 (40−20)	46¢	$22 ($.57−$.46)200	1.1 (22/20)
$60	$20 (60−40)	38¢	$16 ($.46−$.38)200	.8 (16/20)

In the right-hand column are the rates of return. The first $20 spent earns more than a two-for-one return. The second $20 spent is just about a break-even. The third $20 was not returned through additional savings. This simple example is my way of emphasizing the Law of Diminishing Returns.

Element Analysis

This type of analysis we use in deciding about spending money for tools and equipment should be applied to all other forms of overhead expense. It is easier, I know, to determine the pay-off for methods improvement. Many companies use similar arithmetic to determine the values of suggestions. The computations seem easier because we have numbers like dollars of tool costs, savings in labor cost, and quantities of pieces produced last year. But all such figures are estimates. I say "estimates" because all three figures have to do with the future.

Part of your problem is solved when you get "labor costs" from work standards set as recommended in Chap. 7. The more difficult job is to put dollar values on the returns you expect from your overhead operations. But you should start.

Unless you do, you won't ever get to the stage of "decision making by computer" we read about. Computers can't solve equations that are half-completed. They can't conjure up dollar signs for the values of intangibles like customer good-will, employee morale, and market losses. You have to establish such values. Until you do, pushing the starter button will not lead to the much heralded answers to management problems.

Begin with the question Peter Drucker raises.

"How do we distinguish creative overhead, which cuts down total effort required, from parasitical overhead, which only adds to costs?" [1]

That question will be hard to answer if you look at overhead functions as entities. However, each department carries on many operations. Some of these can be readily evaluated. Others you will have to "guesstimate."

[1] Drucker, Peter F., "The Practice of Management," p. 73, Harper & Row, Publishers, Incorporated, New York, 1954.

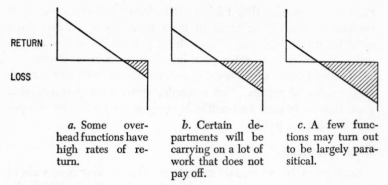

a. Some overhead functions have high rates of return.

b. Certain departments will be carrying on a lot of work that does not pay off.

c. A few functions may turn out to be largely parasitical.

FIG. 45. You should determine what parts of every overhead expense pay their ways.

Result Producing

The analysis you should make is no different basically from determining the rates of profit you earn on your several products. Ratings of elements of work in any department will show some to be highly profitable. Others will be losing items just as are some of your sales. A picture for three overhead departments arranged in declining order of contribution might look like Fig. 45.

If the results of such studies were shown in the form of a bar graph, they might look like Fig. 46. The first bar at the left is

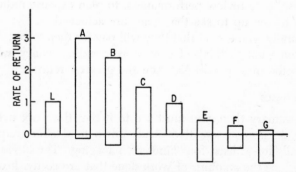

FIG. 46. The first bar representing direct labor suggests one-for-one return. In comparison, some overhead departments have higher returns, others lower, and many include expenses that are losing items.

marked *L*, meaning direct labor. It is drawn to indicate an even exchange. You might think of it as representing "a fair day's work for a fair day's pay." You almost get one-for-one when you utilize a modern incentive plan based on sound timestudy.

In comparison, some overhead departments will show much larger rates of return. For example, many managers say that good timestudy men and methods analysts return 300 or 400 per cent on salaries paid.

Raise Overhead

Such gains, however, add more to overhead. This comes about because good timestudies reveal profit leaks. These sorting devices show profitable reasons for developing better specifications, better supervision, better methods, better tools, and better planning. Take a simple example. Suppose it now costs you $1,000 a week for waiting time in the shop. Can you cut $800 of this loss by spending $500, $600, or even $800 in better production control? What is the break-even point?

Sure, the proper answer to that question implies an increase in another kind of overhead. That is one phase of managerial control. Often, you spend money as overhead expense in order to save money in other parts of cost. Every "tool" you adopt to help manage better adds to your overhead costs. Budgets are another example. You spend money to get them set up, to report results, to review performances, to plan expense reductions, and to follow up to see that goals are achieved.

Naturally, you expect that they will pay for themselves. Therefore, you want to think of control as spending money where it will do the most good—give you the greatest return.

Four Phases

In summary then, you must see to it that the work overhead people do is more creative—"cuts down total effort required." This calls for at least four kinds of managing. The obvious one is to reduce the amounts of work done that are costly, luxurious, unnecessary refinements. Every such loss you retain must be offset by creative effort elsewhere to break even.

The second is to set cost reduction goals for staff men. Require them to both determine and cut their own costs per operation. True operation costs are the chief unknown in most overhead departments. These and many other facts, such as losses in poor methods and wasted work, are best obtained through good timestudy.

The third is to require your staff people to help departments outside their own to achieve cost savings. The phrase "outside their own" was used purposely. I want to stress the fact that staff men can do many things to help each other as well as to serve the "line." In some plants, this will mean knocking a few heads together to break down jurisdictional walls. The basic problem to be solved is to get people to work for the success of your company instead of feathering their own nests.

The fourth kind of managing is the primary one. It is the same as that of carrying on the enterprise—to make money. This demands some forms of measuring returns on the money you spend for overhead services. With these gauges, you will decide to increase the budgets of those staff departments whose costs per operation make them highly "creative."

Keeping these four phases in mind, you may unearth some helpful suggestions in the chapters that follow.

CHAPTER 9

Develop Your Goals

Managers have to decide where a company is to go and at what pace. This part of managing is currently called circular, in that (1) facts are gathered, (2) decisions made, (3) actions taken, (4) results reported, (5) new decisions made, and the process is repeated.

Obviously, managing is much more complex than my simplified description spells out. For instance, the vital factor of timing was glossed over. How much time elapses between each two of these steps? Time comes into play also in a more important way. How far ahead or behind the competitive parade is your company now operating?

Managing is complicated further with respect to profit showing. Is the present rate of return satisfactory? Apparently not, or you wouldn't be concerned with "overhead cost control."

More Profit

Improving profits is a worthy, and I think necessary, goal. Many signs point toward requirements for still more taxes to pay for benefits being given to increasing numbers of people. Too, economists seem to say that we need more profits to spend for capital improvements so as to increase our national growth. Besides, profits are low.

For whatever reason, your primary goal may be to raise profits. To do so requires planning. This calls for something better than following common practice if you expect to achieve your objective. The average manager thinks that more volume will automatically result in more profit. Oftentimes, this will happen. And I use the word "happen" deliberately. I mean that the profit results more from good luck than good management.

The degree of profit improvement depends upon what product mix is sold. To illustrate, *Business Week* recently reported that one company added $1,000,000 to sales and only $20,000 to profits. Some of the reasons why have been pointed out in previous chapters.

NUTS / BOLTS	1,000 800	1,200 1,000	1,400 1,200	1,400	800	1,000	1,200 1,400	NAILS	200 400 600 800 SCREWS
200	220	197	168	145	119	93	70	45 18 4	34 56 108
200 BOLTS	164	141	112	89	63	37	14	11 38 60	90 122 164
400	125	112	LOSS		34	8	15	40 67 89	119 141 193
200	108	85	56	33	7	19	42	67 94 116	146 168 220
400	79	56	27	4	22	48	71	96 123 146	175 197 249
600 200	51	28	1	24	50	76	99	124 151 173	203 225 277
400	23	0	29	52	78	104	127	152 179 201	231 253 305
600	(7)	30	59	82	108	134	157	182 209 231	261 283 335
800 400	35	58	87	110	136	162	185	210 237 259	289 311 363
600	63	86	115	138	164	190	213	238 265 287	317 339 393
800	93	116	145	168	194	220	243	268 295 317	347 369 421
600	118	141	170	193	219	245	268	293 320 PROFIT	394 446
800	149	172	201	224	250	276	299	324 351 373	403 425 477
800	200	223	252	275	301	327	350	375 402 424	454 476 528

Fig. 47. Thousands of dollars in the chart represent losses or profits resulting from sales of four products.

Here we can portray in numbers some other examples drawn from Fig. 47. First note how much range in loss or profit for a given volume may exist in a company. Then on Fig. 48*a* are shown five different mixes of products sold for $2,400,000 with losses and profits ranging from $—51,000 to $+50,000.

Taking the middle position, let's go after "more volume" and increase sales by $400,000—about 17 per cent. The additional sales might be made uniformly throughout the line if all conditions were equal. What is more apt to happen is that some products will be easier to sell than others. Thus, the added volume is shown in each of two products in Fig. 48*b*. The profit increase

SALES	P OR L	NUTS	BOLTS	SCREWS	NAILS
2,400	-51	1,000	200	200	1,000
2,400	-23	800	400	200	1,000
2,400	7	600	600	200	1,000
2,400	24	400	600	400	1,000
2,400	50	400	600	600	800

a. Profit for a given volume of sales varies greatly depending upon the product mix.

SALES	PROFIT	NUTS	BOLTS	SCREWS	NAILS
2,400	7	600	600	200	1,000
2,800	115	(800)	600	200	(1,200)
2,800	134	600	600	(400)	(1,200)
2,800	149	(800)	(800)	200	1,000
2,800	168	600	(800)	(400)	1,000

b. More sales volume creates differing amounts of profit or loss according to what product sales are increased.

Fig. 48. Product mix of goods sold is a controlling factor in the resulting net profit or loss.

differs, as you would expect, according to which two products are bought. These are facts you already know.

Sales Plans

What may not be apparent, however, is that you cannot get real control of overhead costs when products are sold willy-nilly. Maybe, I should say, "when salesmen act only as order takers." Therefore, you need to forecast the sales that are to be made in order to establish the overhead costs that are to be incurred.

This preplanning has to be in more detail than might be assumed. To emphasize, the chart on Fig. 47 and the examples drawn from it are built upon uniform rates like standard costs. They are calculated as though each added dollar of sales of a given product will bring in a known profit.

That ain't so. This fact was illustrated by Figs. 38 and 39 in our previous chapter. To oversimplify, if the $400,000 increase in sales we just obtained were all in small orders, our net results might be a loss instead of an improved profit. That would be unfortunate.

However, I am trying to stress the relation between the types of sales made and the overhead costs they cause. In different words, an increase in proportion of small to total number of orders will usually cause relatively higher rates of overhead. Similarly, an increase in per cent of "Specials" may create more overhead in proportion. Thus, to get a base to work from in controlling overhead, you need to know what will be sold, when, and in what quantities.

1. *What* determines the rates of overhead because some products and types of orders cause much higher costs than others.
2. *When* affects the pressure costs of peak and valley work loads and shortness of delivery.
3. *Quantity* influences the counts of setup costs of all kinds that are created by sales and production orders.

Sales Incentives

Now you and I know that forecasting isn't selling. And it may take a lot of doing to bring these two into phase. It may call for a whole new design of sales incentive plan. As one element, it will require the modification of sales volume as a dominant factor. If, for instance, you turned a commission plan 180 degrees to one based on profitability, chances are it would wash out credits for small orders and some specials.

In this connection, pricing becomes an important factor. To handle this properly, you must know and consider the order setup costs explained in Chap. 4. The difference between the probable actual order cost and the average included in your standard cost will come out of profit to the extent it does not get into your price.

Life Cycle

From the viewpoint of correct pricing, you may conclude to discontinue making or selling certain products. Your decision may be in either of two parts. Perhaps, you can realize a satisfactory profit if you stock an item and let customers order it. In this compromise, you should save sales, advertising, and related expenses.

In contrast, you may drop a product completely. Your reason may stem from either of two general conditions. One is that the profitable life of the product has approached its end. The other is that the item is replacing sales of a more profitable product.

Such decisions bear on the control of overhead costs. You recognize that products have life cycles like people do. There may even be some connection between the two. You and I know, for example, that newly installed managers often start off by changing existing practices. Many of these revisions can result in the purchasing of different products. Beyond this, we know that these managers, and most other people, change their regards for things as they progress from babyhood to old age.

Getting away from the philosophical, dynamic organizations are developing new products or variations every year. If the new ones compete to any considerable extent with existing products in the line, sales are divided between them. Overhead order costs are roughly doubled. Despite this, overall profits may go up for the time being. But just as new products or items are born every year, so will some die, in the profit-making sense.

Many managers do not recognize the dead items. The main reason, I think, is because the garden-variety cost system does not reveal the symptoms of decease. Another may be the habit of hanging on to the known. This putting off of the inevitable and letting profit leaks increase might be curtailed if we believe with Peter Drucker. He says,

"The moment a company introduces a new product is the moment it should put its own technological resources into obsoleting it." [1]

[1] "AME Beats the Drum for Innovation," *Business Week*, p. 88, June 22, 1963.

That type of drive for keeping up or ahead of the parade still leaves the problem of arranging the burials. One solution may be found in the method followed by a Controller I know. Each year he hands the big boss a list of products with his request that so many be cut off.

Establish Budgets

After you have decided what is to be sold, you can correctly establish expense budgets that correspond. Tools for doing so were suggested in Chap. 6.

There, I tried to show that overhead work was not directly proportional to volume. Some functions apply much of their efforts to processing orders. A further lack of relation to volume occurs because some orders (products) require a great deal more work than others. These differences were illustrated by rough standards in time or money. Such components are necessary to build budgets that represent the work load to be carried.

Similarly built budgets will fairly measure what is to be done, provided. . . . Now we come to another fork in the road. One way goes along with methods and habits continuing much as they are. The other, much rougher road leads through a series of changes. In general terms, these are

1. Shorten your customer time cycle so as to increase rate of return on investment.
   a. Realign overhead duties to minimize duplications and interferences.
   b. Eliminate and side-track operations to expedite process flow.
2. Reduce unprofitable portions of overhead methods and systems now in use.
3. Create measures of results in order to determine and develop capable managers.

Any or all of these may markedly alter the standards, and hence the budgets computed from them, for certain overhead functions. Some will be reduced. Others will be increased. And both movements may be altered considerably by what you do in the way of timestudy and work measurement, with or withou incentives.

Better Managing

You realize that item 3 is the key to success. As you know budgets do not control costs. Control that is done is carried or by your managers. Their efforts may be entirely satisfactory un der present stabilized conditions—when products are designed sales forecasts are working, methods are established, work meas ures are installed, and so on.

However, when you choose the rough road of change, profi improvement, cost reduction, overhead cost *control*, you ma learn that certain of your managers limp very badly. A few ma have to be carried, for a while. Some will not survive the jour ney. Even so, you shouldn't expect to make a major "brea through" in overhead costs without casualties.

Your chief concern is with the development of managers wh can successfully run the more dynamic functions. They will hav to make change after change as you work through successiv stages toward your goal. More than that, they must generat ideas that will lead to profitable innovations. While we gran that "two heads are better than one," you should expect eac functional manager to be the expert in his own field.

Unprofitable Methods

One part of your approach was suggested by item 2—reduc the unprofitable portions of methods and systems. This start with knowledge of existing costs and forecast demands. Fron these, you can get a number of pictures like Fig. 49. These ar ways of studying what system you can afford as indicated b Fig. 43.

On the diagram is a line labeled "Income." It denotes hov much your customer is paying you for overhead. This rate o income will differ, of course, with each product and its price.

The horizontal lines typify your system costs. The solid, to line suggests one present method cost. The *b, c,* and *d* line indicate costs you can get after removing some frills.

Looked at another way, the *d* method cost is one you must get down to for customer orders of quantity *d*. This relation is gauged from 20 per cent profit on overhead contribution. Similarly, the other order quantities were located on the baseline. Naturally, my 20 per cent profit was picked out of a hat. You

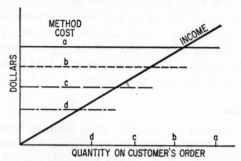

Fig. 49. Each method cost has a break-even point with the money paid by the customer for overhead system.

may select a bigger rate of return. Probably you will, if material is a major portion of your sales dollar.

Control Goals

Such break-even analyses are necessary. You should face the either-or choices. Either certain products and orders are sold at low or minus profits. In this choice, the overhead costs must be allowed in budgets. Or products and orders are discontinued or costs are cut.

I favor cost reduction. Overhead costs are too high. We have not controlled them to anything like the degree we have managed shop costs. In addition, we improve our standard of living only when our dollar will buy more. And neither of these reasons is intended to countermand my plea for burying the dying products.

To get the cost reduction you require, and also sort out your real managers, you should set specific cost reduction goals. These should be piecemeal with time limits. Remember, this rough road of change is long, narrow, and treacherous.

One of the chief difficulties lies in the never-ending argument between Sales and Manufacturing. Regardless of rules and incentive plans, the true salesman will try to serve his customers. Consequently, there will always be the irregular condition—the extra staff and shop work to be done that are not included in the budgets. Yet, many companies can greatly reduce the wastes in this "gray area." One way has been mentioned—get away from dollar volume measures of Sales performance. During this redirection of sales efforts, you cannot expect your overhead budgets to be precise. Nor can you rightly hold overhead managers accountable for costs beyond their control.

Income Limits

The goals you can set—and the steps between here and there —are suggested by the principle underlying Fig. 49. The idea is to reduce overhead costs enough below those paid for by the customer to leave profits for the work done.

In essence, pay for overhead work is received with each customer's check. Theoretically, the amount is that applied in the overhead rate used in computing the cost. Here is a starting point.

Why not credit each overhead manager with his share of the income? Then deduct profit or add loss, as in reality you do for your several products. The nets are budget goals to be achieved at some stated future time. What a maelstrom of arguments this would stir up.

Nevertheless, you can't escape the limits of income received, and make profits. With profits low and overhead high, control is necessary. Thus, living within our incomes with savings (profits) is a logical approach to overhead cost control. Besides, it is bound to induce more managers to take seriously the "company objectives."

Jurisdictional Disputes

At the same time, it will create two more hazards in this rough road. These will be disputes about (1) quality and timeliness of services rendered and (2) who's supposed to do what work.

These arguments go on now. Unfortunately, they diminish only through higher overhead costs. This was my reason for listing item 2 earlier—realignment of overhead duties.

Bickering results from many causes. This is understandable when we realize that the average company just grew. Overhead departments were built up as needs developed. Work was rearranged and loosely prescribed. Then to increase the unknowns, we have slashed expenses between efforts to control them by ratios.

Disregarding the ambitious empire-builder, we have trained managers to get by as best they can. We have insisted that they overcome difficulties passed on to them because time did not permit retracing steps. To make the grade, they have set up systems, records, and assistants to help. Much of these are "duplicated" costs.

All such problems will not be solved no matter what methods you devise. There will always be the rush to beat the competitor. But you can reduce the extra costs that habits have made chronic. Attempts in this direction have been made for years, in some plants. Charges for extra work caused by an outside department have been computed and reported. This procedure has four basic weaknesses.

1. The department charged learns about the cost too late to do anything corrective.
2. The department making the charge relieves itself of all responsibility.
3. The costs of cross-charging and related discussions come out of profits.
4. The system has no sharp teeth that will aid in gaining the ends sought.

Two levers that would make such a system work more effectively have been described. One was realistic budgets based upon work required. The other was measurement of a department's cost against income received from customers for its contribution.

Define Duties

Both of these are essential, I believe, for sound overhead cost control. Further, even though they can put teeth in a cross-charging penalty plan, I do not recommend its use. To my way of thinking it is only remedial.

To effect a cure, you ought to rearrange and realign your overhead operations. This can be done completely only after you go behind your organization chart and define duties in detail.

For example, it is not enough to say, "Engineering is responsible for engineering," I have found as much as 25 per cent extra labor cost in the shop that was caused by "failure to specify." Maybe the engineers were not given sufficient time. Maybe they worked ineffectively. Maybe they never learned what actual conditions exist in the shop. Anyway you twist it, some part of that 25 per cent came out of profit.

You can recall cases of failures to complete work in nearly every department. Similarly, we are reminded of related problems in articles describing periodic reviews. The boss can't understand why the budding manager did this and didn't do that. We call these "failures to communicate."

Part of the problem lies in failure to analyze and then prescribe in writing all the duties. This is only the start. Next is gaining understanding of the words. Then follow revisions, discussions, and further revisions. Keep in mind all the attempts at contract clarification and still we have occasional arbitrations to interpret meanings.

The necessity for work specifications is depicted in Fig. 50. This is a simplification of a multitude of circular processes mentioned at the outset of this chapter. To portray just a few would have made the diagram confusing. For example, there are paths like

Design—Customer, Engineer, Sell, Manufacture

Promise—Customer, Sell, Production Control, Purchase, Manufacture

Procure—Purchase, Engineer, Production Control, Manufacture

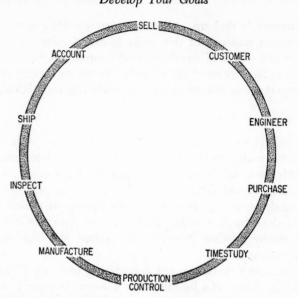

FIG. 50. A greatly simplified picture of interrelations among functions of a company.

Make—Manufacture, Timestudy, Engineer, Production Control

To further complicate these and the many other circles within circles is the overlay of Industrial Relations actions.

Time Cycle

Who is supposed to do what, when, and to which degree? The "what" portion has been discussed. Yet this part is not satisfactorily answered without establishing time definitions. For instance, frequently in my job-shop experiences shop men have said, "We get the time that's left after Engineering makes up its mind." [1] Maybe Engineering did take too much time. In any event, the important consideration is the complete customer cycle depicted in Fig. 50. It roughly represents the time your com-

[1] Carroll, Phil, "Profit Control: How to Plug Profit Leaks," p. 156, McGraw-Hill Book Company, Inc., New York, 1962.

pany's money is tied up. All these money costs are overhead. Our common measure of this cycle is called turnover. Hence, an important phase of overhead cost control lies in shortening this time cycle. Its corollary of better customer service may be more important in raising profits and reducing complaints.

Better Sorting

Your efforts to reduce your customer cycle will probably require some realignment of duties. This may create contradictions with the usual forms of organization. For instance, we say, "Accounting should do accounting." I agree, in principle. But in this analysis, we are concerned with timing. If timing is late for work done by accounting, that phase of the cycle should be carried on by another function. Of course, the cost must be about the same or less.

In mentioning costs, I'm not considering ordinary differences in methods. These can be taught to whoever is capable of performing the task. Nor am I thinking of wage rates. Like work should pay like wages wherever done.

I'm thinking of the 1,000,006 major, medium, and minor chores that have to be done in completing your customer cycle suggested by Fig. 50. Who should carry out which details that will result in

1. The lowest cost of the work done, at
2. The most expeditious time cycle with
3. The least amount of bickering and
4. The minimum cost of duplication

Such are the kinds of specifications you should have in mind while realigning the duties of your overhead departments. As you study these operations, keep one eye focused on the tomorrow that Auren Uris predicts.

"Many (middle management) jobs will be merged out of existence. Entirely new ones will continue to spring up, as did value analysts, materials managers, industrial psychologists, systems specialists, and full-time planners."

He also accents the urgency for reckoning your rate of return (Chap. 8) since

> "Foreign companies have only one-half or one-third as many managers as we do in a similar type of company. When competition becomes truly international—as it will when the Common Market hits its stride—our front office fat will become intolerable." [1]

[1] Uris, Auren, "The Future of Middle Management," *Factory*, p. 66, July, 1963.

CHAPTER 10

Interpret Recorded Figures

"How are we doin'?", progressive managers are continually asking. That's why we have scorekeeping functions we call Accounting. The work they do is much like that of the navigator on a plane. His job is to help the pilot get where he is supposed to be, on time.

There's a big difference, however, between the pilot's job and that of the manager's. The pilot is told where his plane is to be flown. In most instances, its destination is known beforehand and printed on time-tables. In contrast, the manager has to decide where his company is going. His "flight" is further complicated by having to steer several planes simultaneously. Some are to be flown over uncharted territories. All are pointed toward higher payloads even though capacities, costs, and customers differ.

Gas Remaining

One hazard in the manager's flying was pointed out by a recent headline—"Pilot lands with five minutes of gas to spare." The gas remaining was little enough margin of safety. The Pacific is very deep and uncomfortably wet off Hawaii. The near-miss was brought about by several factors. Bad weather prompted the pilot to change his course. Some of his decisions may have been wrong. Perhaps his instruments were in error. But the plane, its crew, and passengers were saved to fly again.

This close-call has parallels quite like those the manager operates with currently. The gas he has left is about 5 per cent.

128

His decisions are a mixture of right and wrong ones. His instruments are faulty. And he, his helpers, and his customers are continuing their efforts to get some place.

Better Instruments

In this course, better indicators are essential to more successful managing. Facts are required so the manager can sort those decisions that were correct from the poor and bad ones. All of the hundreds made every day can't be right.

Usually, he is shooting from the hip at a complex of moving targets. And too much time passes before he finds out how close his shots come to hitting bull's-eyes. His efforts to manage are described by some critics as "putting out fires" and "flying by the seat of his pants."

Considering the indicators he now has to guide him, I'm surprised to see the average manager do as well as his score shows. As Sash Spencer observes,

"When a new man moves into the president's spot, companies will paint the office and change the sign on the door, the organization chart, and the telephone directory. But they almost never re-examine the information with which the president is supposed to run his operation, and most of the time the new president will uncomplainingly accept the existing information as it is." [1]

Even so some critics may be thinking that the manager is to blame for not getting the better instruments he feels he needs. This presents another circular problem that should be analyzed further. On the one hand we say, "The manager is responsible for running the company." With this charge goes the obligation to request and get whatever information he needs to guide its progress.

On the other, we say, "The professional manager is not expected to be expert in all the functions he supervises." Hence,

[1] Nicholson, Scott, "The Crisis in Corporate Control," *Dun's Review and Modern Industry*, July, 1963.

he should not be criticized if he cannot phrase his questions in applicable technical jargon.

To make this problem more acute, the top man is often selected from the Sales side of the company. This is the best choice among men having one-sided experiences, as I view it.

Trends change, however. Some recently elected presidents have been chosen from the accounting profession. This is one solution to the problem. It may be the best in those situations. For the average company, however, there are better ways.

Develop Controllers

To begin with, the typical accountant is too conservative. His basic nature prompts him to avoid gambles. In contrast, we think of the head-man as one who takes risks, tries new ideas, ventures into untried fields. Or at least he will readily approve likely innovations.

That's how I get to my prescription for industrial success. It is "a starry-eyed president and a bilious controller." These opposing personalities seem to develop enough practical new products and methods to keep a company growing.

If this is a sound concept, then we should go the other way to make controllers of our accountants. This is a distinction without a difference, according to Mr. Webster. But in using the term controller, I'm carrying forward the definition of control as "exercise a directing influence over."

Or as G. Charter Harrison cites the start of his change in viewpoint. He quotes his new employer as saying,

> "I have hired you, Harrison, as controller of this company for one reason only, namely to use figures so that I can make more money." [1]

In other words, go beyond the static, periodic, accounting, auditing of still pictures to the dynamic, continuing, analytical, presenting of moving pictures.

[1] Harrison, G. Charter, "The Dead Hand of John Gough," published by the author, p. 4, Madison, Wis., 1941.

New Role

The change that seems to be called for is perhaps best suggested by the title "New Role for the Financial Man." In this article, Ernest Breech writes, ". . . many companies confuse a large volume of paper work and reports . . . with good financial control."

He goes on to explain that the control system ". . . is always focusing attention on company objectives and on how plans and performance compare with goals."[1]

In the main, financial reviews direct attention to revenues, profits, costs, cash position, and return on invested capital. These are informative and interesting distillates that bring out the financial facts of performance.

The need to make reviews "interesting" was emphasized by David Chappius. He suggests the application of advertising skills. He pointed out that

"A good advertisement does exactly what a responsibility report should do: It gets *attention*, arouses *interest* in what it has to say, and invites *action*."[2]

Control Interest

The initiation of such reports must come from the managers. They must formulate the questions before controllers are expected to answer them. And as Ernest Breech says, "The more incisive the question the more meaningful will be the answer." This is an important clue to the success of a control or any "system." It is underscored by John Garrity in explaining the big gap between leading and average results achieved with computers. He reports,

"In every lead company, executive management devotes time to the computer systems program in proportion to its cost and potential and in relation to the executives' other responsibilities."[3]

[1] *Think*, p. 3, April, 1963.
[2] Keys to Action—Getting Reports, *Management News*, January, 1962.
[3] Garrity, John T., "Top Management and Computer Profits," p. 10, *Harvard Business Review*, July–August, 1963.

Thus, we can't blame accountants too much for comparing this month with last, this month with the same period last year, and year to date. According to Sylvester Weaver,

> "We all still think of information being available in the traditional forms. No doubt it was hard not to think in terms of stone tablets after papyrus was first available. And no doubt it was hard not to think of monks copying after movable type became available." [1]

Accountants are just as human as other people. They try to give the boss what he asks for and appears to be interested in. Yet, a true professional will often bring in at least two answers —one to the question asked and one to the question that should have been asked. Too, if we understand correctly the team or task force method of solving problems, he will contribute all he knows in his specialized field toward their solutions. Such groups are put together in our space age primarily because no one man knows enough about all the complex elements to reach a workable solution by himself.

Main Difference

The only real difference I see between these two kinds of problems—creating satellites that will orbit and developing control systems that will guide management—is one of interest. We have to design the rocket or component and submit a competitive bid in order to get the business. Granted, you have to get the order before there is any need for cost control. Still, "all you get out of working is exercise" if you do not make the profit you anticipated. In this, the management of overhead costs can be an important factor.

It seems obvious, therefore, that managers must set the goals as explained in Chap. 9 and determine what rates of return are acceptable as stressed in Chap. 8. Then the Controller can make forward-looking reviews. Concurrently, he should be expected to put in his "two-bits worth." He should point out answers to

---

[1] Weaver, Sylvester L., Jr., "The Managerial Function and the Communications Revolution," *Proceedings of the CIOS*, Vol. XIII, 1963.

pertinent unasked questions. He should analyze results, attempt to point out probable causes of shortcomings, and reduce his reviews to understandable essentials.

Triple Function

The foregoing is consistent with expectations of other functions in an organization. Engineering, Purchasing, Manufacturing, and Selling, to name a few, are supposed to keep the boss man informed about their operations. These experts teach the

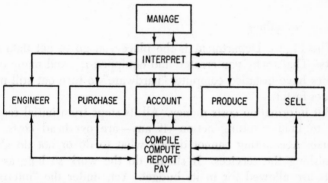

FIG. 51. Diagram showing types of work done by Accounting for other functions with added Interpret responsibility.

president and other managers the phases they need to know about their several specialized functions.

Right here seems to be the crux of the problem. Managers have learned about accounting from specialists who do *accounting*. In addition, probably, they have looked to accounting as with other prime functions to carry on their duties expeditiously. In part, this may explain why many Accounting Departments simply grind out figures and set them down in orderly forms called financial reports.

If, in essence, these are the conditions, then improvement is necessary. To achieve the "new role," a function should be added to Accounting. It might be called "Interpret," as indicated on Fig. 51. It belongs with Accounting as the better of two choices. Mr. President has neither the time nor the skill. He must acquire it as engineers have done for designing space-age products and maintenance men for nursing automated equipment.

Such skills are further demanded when we recall that Accounting puts dollar signs on many proposals and all tangible outcomes. In this respect, they measure what managers execute. This brings in a second, already existing, and now a third, function of Accounting. Examples are suggested by the lowest box on Fig. 51 containing labels of compile, compute, report, and pay. This work of "producing figures" needs "interpretations" also.

Doing Something

The Figure Department is the place you go to get data and costs. That's why you created and equipped it. And many companies have installed computer "hardware" to turn out still more figures faster.

But information costs money. All its steps from initial recording to final resulting action—if any—are overhead costs. Of course, Accounting cannot decide what to do or not do about furnishing the services. It should do the work so long as the costs are allowed for in its budget. Yet, under the "interpret" function, the Controller should be expected to call attention to wasted efforts.

For example, Lawrence Appley points out,

". . . officers of corporations . . . ask for far more reports than they have reasonable need for—just so they will know the answers when the boss asks a question. This is multiplied in volume as you go down through the ranks . . . . As a result, the same information is being prepared by accounting and other departments in many different ways."

And here is his vital comment.

"Many department heads, plant superintendents, and division heads are busier gathering information than they are doing something about it." [1]

[1] Appley, Lawrence A., "A Different Approach," *Management News,* January, 1962.

Bosses will ask questions. Subordinates will try to answer them. This is the forerunner to all manager decision making.

But . . .

When bosses are given answers to questions—both asked and anticipated—by skilled analysts, there should be less need for protective duplications.

When bosses are shown the costs, and rates of return (when obtainable) of information furnished, they may elect to spend part of the money in more profitable ways.

When bosses are concerned with profit performances, they are more apt to work on causes than to search for "scapegoats."

Delegate Work

Thus, the kinds of questions determine to a large extent the kinds of information Accounting is asked to turn out. What attitudes are behind the questions, however, is the important influence. To see this, go back a short space to Lawrence Appley's pointed note—"busier gathering information."

One drive involved here may result from "delegation." This is suggested by Don Schoeller in his talk, "Learn to Manage Yourself First." His basic reason is, "Time spent efficiently on A items could be 19 times as valuable as time spent on C items." [1] The computation of his multiplier 19 is not apparent. Yet the import is much like that indicated by the ABC per cent values shown on Fig. 39.

Don explains that

"When anxiety and stress occur we tend to neglect important items and . . . (take) 'flight to the familiar.' We literally bury ourselves in detail."

Relearning will help. But delegation can do little more than cut the wage cost of C details. Shouldn't we go further and reduce the quantity?

Changing the boss's emphasis to profit performance should help. A bigger difference would come, however, from holding his managers accountable. Of course, he dare not allow the

[1] *Proceedings of the AIIE Conference,* p. 131, May, 1962.

short-sighted ones to play tricks. Both he and they should avoid making current gains that will under-mine the company's future. Still, when the boss asks questions about tomorrow instead of yesterday, there should be

1. Far fewer questions related to details of operation
2. Much higher percentages of questions directed toward developing managers who "make things happen" (Odiorne), or "do something about" (Appley) them

Accounting Prescription

Mixed in with this mass of detail may be another attitude to be squared away. Some accountants exercise more domination than others. Their reasons grow from their responsibilities as guardians of the company "bank." Some "pass the buck" by saying, "Our Auditors require this."

I'll bet a cigar it wasn't one of this type that advocated the procedure noted in the newspaper on February 15, 1963 (Fig. 52). I've heard too much quibbling about controls of nickels and dimes. Consequently, my conclusion is that some top-man made this decision. Anyhow, my added point is that some accounting detail can be eliminated only by edict.

Kaiser Mails Blank Checks

NEW YORK, Feb. 15 (AP)—Kaiser Aluminum and Chemical is handing out signed blank checks—and saving money.

Previously, when the company bought some-

This is done on all orders of $1,000 or less, a category that embraces 92 per cent of all its orders.

We have cut electrical and paperwork oper-

Fig. 52. Newspaper announcement of a startling method of cutting Accounting costs.

Juran Universal

Taking a broad view of these many details, you should keep in mind the "universal" Joe Juran gives us. He says,

"The vital few must be identified if a program of improvement, of planning, of control is to succeed. The trivial many must be identified if there is to be any balance between the cost of planning and control vs. the value of planning and control." [1]

His perceptive phrasing of Pareto's Law gives any alert controller an excellent sorting device. He is specified because he is in charge of the "counting house." All transactions relating to money, and many others, go through his department.

Chief Sorter

In this position, he becomes "chief sorter" of data. He should look at every transaction with a jaundiced eye. He should maintain an attitude like that expressed by an expert in Arthur Anderson & Company. His comment was,

"To assume . . . that all costs are either useful, or even interesting, is a great mistake. To assume that all data as to production are necessary and need transferring is just as great a mistake. Some pieces of information are not worth recording." [2]

Little worth may be found in the *C* items stressed in Chap. 8. These are the costs, records, and transfers that may amount to 67 per cent of the total. Yet they are "worth" only 5 per cent of the money involved. By putting dollar signs on these conditions, the "chief sorter" can help to make major savings in both managerial time and clerical costs.

[1] Juran, J. M., "Universals in Management Planning and Controlling," p. 3, American Management Association, New York, 1954.

[2] "Keeping Closer Tabs on Costs," *Business Week*, p. 80, December 9, 1961.

Shadows Cast

To vividly portray these possibilities, Fig. 53 was drawn. It shows proportions, costs, and potentials. The volumes of work represent proportional costs of detail effort. They also suggest potential savings of manager time and clerical cost. In contrast,

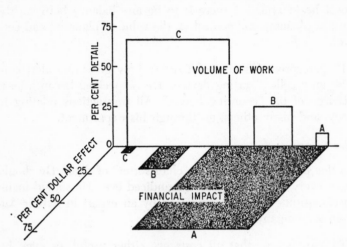

FIG. 53. An adaptation of Fig. 39 designed to show that most of the clerical work done is with items that altogether equal a small fraction of the total money.

their effects upon decision making, report accuracy, and business outcome more nearly resemble the "shadows cast."

Dollar Types

In utilizing these measures to balance costs versus values of information, both managers and controllers should remember another factor. For lack of a better name, let's use "dollar reality." My point is that we should distinguish between an external and an internal dollar. An external dollar changes hands. To illustrate, it comes in from a customer or is paid out to a supplier. If, as noted from the Kaiser Aluminum headline, you can treat real dollars in amounts of a thousand with blank checks, what about bookkeeping dollars?

These internal dollars, right now, are often erroneously applied. Dollars are put in direct labor instead of overhead, charged to maintenance Job *A* when they belong on Job *B*, or applied to Cost Center *X* rather than Cost Center *Y*.

These bookkeeping dollars are considered less seriously in other ways. Let me cite two examples. First, some companies use standard costs for years without revision. Second, most companies count all the pieces they can find once a year to figure out how much inventory they actually have.

And you know about the mad scrambles that ensue trying to reconcile inventory differences. Some of these are caused by errors. People make mistakes. This is true even with 100 per cent inspection (sampling)—in the shop and in the office. So you do not get accuracy even when you try for it. Witness the check for $1,000,125 initiated by a computer and sent to a lady who had $125 coming.

Cut Losses

All these viewpoints were put together in this chapter for several reasons. Primarily, they determine the degree that overhead costs are to be managed. Data costs will remain high if everybody can have all the data and reports they think they need.

This leads to the second reason. Managers and Accountants will continue to think they need most of the information they have been getting. Part of this attitude will be overcome when the Head-man turns the spot-light on performance in achieving projected goals. Another part will be altered when the Controller interprets the relations between costs and values of information. Such reports should lead to cost reductions in nearly every phase of company operation. The underlying principle is that, probably, *whatever is done to cause or to process C items is adding to losses.*

Behind this is the third reason. The Controller in particular and many managers also will not readily accept the fact that one dollar is not like another. Many have been trained for years, as one example, to believe that more volume means more profit. They will have to be shown repeatedly that some dollars are worth very little.

Finally, this collection seemed like a good way to reduce repetition. Many of these ideas apply to the several departments that are to be discussed in subsequent chapters.

PART TWO

How Staff Functions Can Help
Cut Overhead Costs

People costs are the large part of overhead expense in many companies. The work people do can be made to contribute more toward profit making when costly habits are changed and wasted efforts are reduced.

CHAPTER 11

Cut Accounting Costs

"Accounting gets into every department," said President Brown, with a bit of irritation in his voice. Maybe he spoke this way because his experiences were those of president of a subsidiary. His comment reflects, however, the attitudes displayed by many department managers in wholly independent companies.

Such reactions could become more prevalent and intense when the controller takes on his "new role." Aggravations can be stirred up by his efforts to carry on the two responsibilities assigned to him in our previous chapter—interpret performance causes and sort out many trivial wastes.

Outweigh Opposition

Some of these negative, or at least tolerant, managerial attitudes can be lessened only by the Head-man. Bickering will diminish to the degree that he presses for gaining the profit improvements indicated by the cost control system. His leadership will tend to outweigh opposition to new ideas. This will direct energies wasted in blaming Accounting into strivings to make good.

The remaining gripes will have to be overcome by the accountants. In this process, they have the best persuader available. They have numbers—costs. The trick is to use them correctly.

Accountants should avoid taking on the hurt attitude so often displayed. They talk as though the excess costs were coming out of their pockets. Rather, they should remember that they only write down the costs. The managers responsible make costs whatever they are.

With this frame of mind, they can emphasize the service nature of their work. They should explain that their functions are to collect, compute, interpret, and report. They can state that they are ready and willing to furnish all data requested up to the limits of their budgets. Then they ought to go on to show what the information costs. In effect, they should hand the manager a bill for services rendered.

Outside Services

This charging idea should be strictly informal. Yet it is a necessity of fact finding. Its prime purpose is to induce the "buyer" of information to seriously consider its worth. Secondarily, the cost incurred becomes part of a total expense of work done for outsiders.

However large this amount may be, it is only partially controllable by Accounting. For this reason, service expense should be kept apart from primary accounting. Services rendered ought to be considered as another budget when reviews are made. This separation has two advantages.

1. Accountants will hesitate less in getting out the data because the cost isn't coming out of "their" expense allotment.
2. Management will have a means for exercising better control over "how often" information is turned out.

Cheaper Service

The mere process of "charging" should lead to cost reductions. It will start, most likely, with managers saying, "That's too much!!" Such comments have behind them three elements of cost that warrant study. First is the matter of specifications. Do the manager and the accountant clearly understand what information is wanted? This is important. Fundamentally, the accountant thinks in terms of precise monies. Instead, managers are more interested in quick answers. These can be approximate. If they were using my words, they would say, "Speed is more vital than accuracy."[1] This is because progressive managers are going to reduce costs, whatever they are. Their chief concerns are with how far they are along the road. Hence, better understandings of what is wanted and how it is to be used will tend to cut the costs of information.

The second element is another form of the preceding application of "sales engineering." It relates to degree or type. Degree has to do with extent of information. In this, every added detail increases the cost. And some items have far less informative value than others. Too, type has a bearing on usefulness. Here, the skilled accountant might see that the manager is "asking the wrong question." In still a different way, the accountant might explain that he already has data of another type that will be "close enough."

Touchy Element

The third element concerns method, in a broad sense. It includes how the work is done and how efficiently. Also it takes in the factor of time. Does the project require a special digging operation? Or can the information be collected currently? You can think of other variations that affect the ultimate cost.

This third factor is the touchy one. It lies underneath the resentment that comments like "That's too much" can arouse. The "too much" may carry an implied criticism of inefficiency, particularly when a production man says it to one of "those guys upstairs."

Bill Customers

The number of such barbs directed at overhead people can be reduced by raising their productivity to the level expected from manufacturing. And Accounting is a good place to start. Improvement here will help to offset the pressures created by the controller in his "new role."

In this direction, one of the first steps is to find out what accounting operations now cost. A good way to start is to make a

[1] Carroll, Phil, "Profit Control: How to Plug Profit Leaks," Chap. 16, McGraw-Hill Book Company, Inc., New York, 1962.

list of all regular operations performed. Then corresponding costs, values, and counts should be gathered.

From these figures, operation costs can be determined. These may be used in several ways. One is to give each "customer" a bill for the information he gets. With this should go a request for evaluation of its worth to him.

In the first round, perhaps the second and third, he may still want to buy it. Remember, however, that under the "new role" of controllership, the study doesn't end here. Several more steps should be taken. For example, in many cases it will be possible to prove from results accomplished whether or not the information paid off. In others, it may be necessary to pressure managers into placing values on intangible worths.

However done, these services should be weighed against their costs. All such costs come out of money that might otherwise have gone into profit. This holds true for all future services requested.

Four Rankings

Further analyses of operation costs may be made with a series of rankings. The first might be a list ranging from high to low dollar amounts. This is our usual approach. Big amounts suggest locations of large potential savings.

A second ranking from high to low should be made of operation costs. These are obtained by dividing counts into corresponding costs. The high ones may indicate poor methods or too much detail. Again, the high costs may conceal "gold mines" worth digging into.

A third ranking is of costs per dollar of value. These are computed by dividing cost amounts into total values. Value here means the amount shown on the transactions processed. High values may be indicative of worthwhile efforts. They may prove also that either little work is done with the large values or the methods used are better.

A fourth list should be made ranking counts. The high ones in this group may point out where much of the accounting effort is being expended.

Study Distributions

Studies of these rankings should point the directions toward further analyses. Perhaps the best method to use in this second stage is to plot counts and values (amounts). These are made in order to show distributions. See Fig. 54.

The curve on Fig. 54a is shaded to portray the 67 per cent of C items originally drawn on Fig. 39. The proportion shown here, however, is correct only with a normal distribution of occurrences. Such a curve would be brought out if you made it with tally marks like those on Fig. 54b.

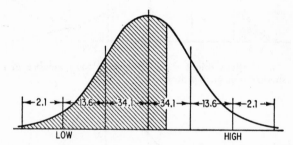

a. Bell curve of normal distribution showing the 67 per cent of C items shaded.

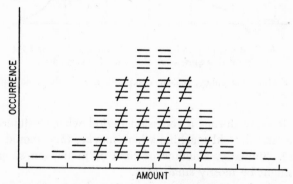

b. Normal distribution as it would look if made up of tally marks.

Fig. 54. Plottings of counts and values will show normal distributions when there are no distorting factors.

You will get curves of balanced distribution about an average, however, only when "nature takes its course." More likely, your curves may be distorted—one way or the other. For example, you might have an excess of small amounts as revealed by Fig. 55a. This could occur in any older company where, to illustrate, there were lots of orders for repair parts. Probably, it would

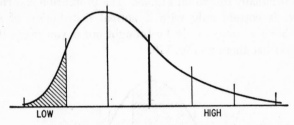

a. Plottings might show an extraordinary number of short runs or small orders.

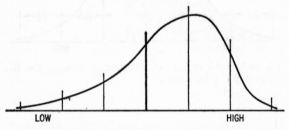

b. Plottings of purchases on Saturdays at supermarket might reveal that most were above weekly averages

Fig. 55. Factors like policy, season, competition, and advertising may distort occurrences.

show this skew during a recession period when customers decided to "fix" the old machine when, maybe, they should buy a new one. Similarly, amounts of time or money on shop time tickets might be mostly small ones.

You might not have any amounts less than a given figure as suggested by the shaded portion at the low end. For instance, my stationery supplier recently sent back an order. To this was stapled a form reading, "Sorry, orders amounting to less than

$3.01 not acceptable." Of course, the message was more politely phrased. But the order was rejected just the same.

Take another example. A similar cutoff could show up in a plot of wait time recordings on time tickets. This might happen for any one of several reasons.

1. Maybe the foremen frown on requests for waiting "check-outs" that are small.
2. Perhaps the timestudy man included some per cent for "un-avoidable delays" in work standards, thus ruling out short times.
3. Possibly the time clocks are graduated in tenths of hours with the consequence that the least delay is 0 or 6 minutes.

In contrast, your curve might have a hump on the high side like Fig. 55*b*. One cause is seasonal. This came out in a discussion about two peaks in a curve of production. Mr. P. C. Manager said, "School budgets are made up twice a year."

Again, a similar distortion in large amounts would occur when a company "builds inventory" as a hedge against a strike. Or when it notifies customers of a forthcoming price increase.

Control Sampling

Analyses of your rankings and plottings should enable you to skim off the cream. Some operations may be eliminated entirely. Others can be almost wholly saved. Major reductions can be effected by using the method now called "sampling."

In simple accounting terms this means regularly figuring or checking only a few per cent of the total. Or calculating or veri-fying all items of a kind every so often. Chances are you have been doing this for years under the name of "spot checking." But "sampling" goes on to consider degree of probable error.

The process is described in a paper entitled, "Application of Statistical Sampling to Accounting Procedures," by Robert Nelson. There he highlights several large savings.[1]

He defines statistical sampling as,

[1] *Proceedings of the SAM–ASME Management Engineering Conference,* April, 1962.

"A small part of anything for inspection and analysis (scientifically chosen so that the laws of probability operate to provide predictable precision) in order to give information about a total to a degree of exactness consistent with the precision requirements of a problem or with funds available to do the job."

No Funds

It appears to me that his last phrase should be left off. If the boss went all the way and made no "funds available," you could eliminate certain accounting operations. Actually, for a different reason, a successful and well-known company has no product costs.

Seriously, the sense of the definition is to at least make periodic audits. "Sampling" offers a sound way to find answers to the "how often?" question raised in Chap. 7. You must decide "how often" if you are to "manage costs" or to apply "value analysis" as discussed in Chap. 8.

What Error

The determinations you want to make might be viewed as representing two sides of many equations. On one side are answers to the question, "How much is an error? Or what are the chances of error? Or what are the consequences of this much error?" On the other side are the costs of avoiding those predictable errors.

To illustrate, Richard Neuschel reports the results of an analysis of vendor invoices. In this it was

". . . learned that 61 per cent of all invoices . . . were for less than $50 each, and in total accounted for less than 2 per cent of the dollar value of all invoices received."

In a sample of 7,500 invoices, errors were found amounting to $30.33 gain by the company.

"These facts led to a discontinuance of all checking of invoices under $50, which change—in turn—saved six clerical positions throughout the company and $32,000 annually."

Earlier, he underlines "saved clerical positions" this way.

"In a company that earns 5 per cent on its sales dollar, the elimination of just one $4,000-a-year clerical position contributes as much to net profits as sales orders totaling $80,000. But—and this, too, is often overlooked—the $80,000 worth of merchandise must be resold each year, whereas the saving in operating expense automatically repeats itself year after year." [1]

He might have gone on to say that $80,000 in added sales may require the hiring of one more clerk. Also, of course, there would be increases in selling expenses and other overhead costs.

Break Point

Going back a little you will recall that the $50 break point was at 61 per cent of the total of supplier invoices. Differently, the $1,000 "blank check" decision of Kaiser Aluminum cited in Chap. 10 took in 92 per cent.

Both cutoff points may be correct in their specific situations. Both possibilities were suggested by Figs. 55a and b. A method of arriving at your break point is shown graphically on Fig. 56. This occurs where

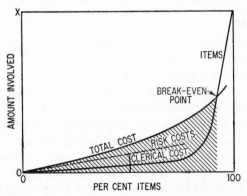

Fig. 56. The break point occurs where the total costs of protection equal the total amounts involved.

[1] Neuschel, Richard F., "Management by System," 2d ed., p. 76, McGraw-Hill Book Company, Inc., New York, 1960.

$$\text{Insurance Costs} \quad = \text{Predictable Losses}$$
$$\text{Clerical} + \text{Risk Costs} = \text{Predictable Losses}$$

This point will change with both time and economic conditions as discussed earlier. Therefore, you might choose to back off a ways for safety. But each per cent of the total items you pass up will cut into the overhead savings you can make. These are illustrated by the shaded portion under the curve of total cost on "insurance."

Wholesale Attack

These cases concerning vendor invoices are but two that involve "real dollars." There are others that should be studied for their potential savings. These overhead costs expended on the "trivial many" ought to be trimmed as much as managers will hold still for.

Similarly, consider another way to get fast results described by Peter Drucker. He writes,

> "I suggested that all reports be suspended simultaneously for two months and only those be allowed to return which managers still demanded after living without them. This cut reports and forms in the company by three quarters." [1]

Next Degree

Next, you should turn your attention to the operations performed with what I called bookkeeping dollars in Chap. 10. Many of these are even more susceptible to pruning. The term pruning is used to indicate a way to get lower costs of those operations you expect to continue—for a while.

You might call this method improvement. A prime example is the day-after-day conversion of time to money. Why? We say, "Time is money." Since this is true, why not save most of the conversion expense by recording and reporting time? And many reports would be more understandable to their users. For instance, labor lost in extra work and wait time.

[1] Drucker, Peter F., "The Practice of Management," p. 135, Harper & Row, Publishers, Incorporated, New York, 1954.

One company keeps its labor inventories of work in process and finished goods in Units (standard minutes). So internal accounting does not all have to be in dollars.

If dollars are required later, say for costing, then use an in-between method. To illustrate, let's take Maintenance. Many jobs are done every day. Most of these are charged to departments, cost centers, or machines. All costs can be collected in time for a period. This might be a week or a month depending upon when you define "How often." Then the total times can be converted to money.

Figure 57 illustrates. Here are the totals of time charges to departments for the period. Then the total hours (1,600) were

Hours	14	15	16	17	18	22	25	26	Dollars
1									

1,600	200	185	365	213	87	348	136	66	
Dollars	440	410	790	470	190	780	300	140	$3,520

FIG. 57. If time must be converted to money, do it in totals at the end of a period.

set over their dollar equivalent ($3,520) on a slide rule, and the departmental charges read off to the nearest ten. The error in proration was offset by changing the big charge.

An intermediate saving can be made. You can add all time charges to a department on a comptometer before posting or punching IBM cards.

Call Overhead

In ferreting out this type of saving, you may come across amounts too small to record. For example, elements of cost correctly defined as direct labor or material may be insignificant. Illustrations of labor costs are in tumbling, blanking, and slitting.

Such costs should be treated as overhead. One reason is that they are dropped, anyhow, when operation costs are totaled. They are separated from the significant figure by a zero or two. Thus, their cost gets in neither direct nor overhead.

Reason two is that all the recordings, wherever made, of operations, standards, and costs will be saved once the label of direct is removed. In one plant, this change on heat-treating eliminated 80 per cent of the IBM labor cost cards.

The effect may be understood more readily if explained in terms of reciprocals. Think of a part or an assembly as consisting of a series of operations. Either may have times similar to those following:

Operation Time, Minutes	Quantity per Hour	Cost at $.03 per Minute
10.00	6	.30
1.00	60	.03
.10	600	.003
.01	6000	.0003

Thus, any total is made up of sums of costs like those in the third column. These are reciprocals of productions per hour. Hence, the relatively fast operations should be studied critically to see whether their significances are worth recording. What per cent error will you make? What per cent is your error in labor cost, for instance, of the total part or assembly cost?

Added Task

The foregoing details, and many more that could have been mentioned, should be thoroughly worked over. All the uneconomical operations done, both for Accounting and for all others, should be eliminated or drastically cut. This will not only reduce overhead costs but will also make room for other, more constructive efforts.

The first of these added jobs should be the temporary extra work of making more precise assignments of overheads to products. This is the forerunner to getting product costs that reveal where profits are actually made or lost. "How to" explanations may be found in two other books.[1]

Afterwards, correct product costs can be maintained with much less than usual clerical effort. In addition, they tend to directly cut overhead costs in two ways. One is to cause reductions in sales of unprofitable items. The other is to induce searching studies of the disproportionate overhead costs found in the low-profit products.

Connected with this study is another added chore. This is in the finding of overhead order costs (Chap. 4). Out of this comes a third task—the building of budgets that measure work loads (Chap. 6). These will require more computations. Then a fifth addition may be the collecting and reporting of expenses by "responsibilities."

Timely Trends

The added work briefly described will provide control figures that Juran might include among those he calls the "vital few." Beyond getting them, however, are two other factors of using them that should be stressed. These are trend and time.

Trend is important in gauging progress—or lack of it. Neither tendency may be seen by comparing current results with two or more columns of figures. Rarely will product mixes and volumes be the same. Consequently, conclusions drawn from such comparisons may be wrong. Besides, degree of up or down cannot be determined by eye.

For such reasons, control figures are better shown in continuing curve or graphical forms. And the important detail is in the yardstick used. This should either take out the effects of change in product mix and volume or adjust for them. Only when the measures are correct can managers tell whether or not overhead costs are in control.

But control depends upon time. This is the meaning of that

[1] Carroll, Phil, "How to Control Production Costs," McGraw-Hill Book Company, Inc., New York, 1953, "Profit Control: How to Plug Profit Leaks," Chap. 15, McGraw-Hill Book Company, Inc., New York, 1962.

old phrase "after the horse is stolen." I try to emphasize the importance of time with the example of a leaking faucet. If you learn about it soon enough, you may stop the leak with a loss of only a teacupful. On the other hand, you may not find out there is a leak until a bathtub is filled.

Or you may prefer to look at the problem as Drucker points out. Managing is

". . . especially the ability to extricate one's self from the consequences of decisions that turn out, in spite of our best efforts, to be wrong."

Whether overhead should increase or decrease to meet company objectives, the change or lack of it should be reported promptly. Failure in this respect is a common mistake made by many Accounting Departments. Reporting 30 to 45 days after events take place is much too late. Even accountants won't wait that long to get scores. When World Series games are going on, they bring radios into their offices.

Electronic data processing isn't the answer. Yes, it will spew out information in a helluva hurry—after you push the button. The time lost that has to be overcome is in starting. Most managers now get their reports on schedule—30 days late. If these can be kept on schedule that far behind time, why can't they be on schedule much earlier? You must get the signals to act much sooner if you are to cut the losses now caused by control lag.

CHAPTER 12

Raise Timestudy Productivity

Frederick Taylor said,

> "Timestudy is the one element in scientific management beyond
> all others making possible the 'transfer of skill from manage-
> ment to men.'" [1]

His deduction may be interpreted in many ways. Actually it
is. You can see these if you look at the different varieties of work
carried on under the name of timestudy. Some might disappear
if we said the prime function of this department is to *study
time*. This is an important distinction when we are concerned
with the control of overhead costs.

"Rate Setting"

The difference shows up in any comparisons of timestudy
processes. The majority of so-called timestudy men appear to
believe that their basic function is to "set rates." Whereas, the
meaning of "study time" includes analysis as an interim step.

Some timestudy men will tell you that they do make analyses
of their studies. They do. Many insist upon changes in methods
and corrections of faulty conditions before they set their "rates."
The less informed may even refuse to take studies of operations
that are "not running right." Still others will work under the
ruling that foremen are responsible for setting up the operations.

[1] Copley, Frank Barclay, "Frederick W. Taylor," Vol. 1, p. 227, Harper
& Row, Publishers, Incorporated, New York, 1923.

And if foremen insist their methods are right, the timestudy men may proceed to set "rates" accordingly.

From this hodge-podge of "rate setting," we get distortions in our measures of direct labor–volume (Chap. 5). Thus, our controls of overhead and product costs are in error. Further, such "rates" include varying amounts of cost that actually are overhead —not direct labor.

Final Inspection

To this you may say, "That's detail." It's more than that, if you are really concerned with control of overhead costs. You can see why when you look behind this host of irregularities that occur whenever people work. The jobs they do might be likened to assemblies. The people are trying to put together their productions with the materials, machines, conditions, instructions, skills, and time limits they have. All these factors come together at the point where "the transfer of skill from management to men" takes place.

These "assemblies" are the operations that timestudy men observe. Their watch readings of element times are records of the effects. This is the key. Its usefulness depends upon the degree and kind of analyses timestudy men make of these effects in their efforts to determine causes. These may be more apparent if you will study the following briefest of examples of transfer.

Effects	*Causes*
Incorrect specifications	Engineering
Delay times	Production Control
Incomplete instructions	Supervisor
Faulty material	Purchasing
Inadequate skills	Personnel
New variation	Salesman
Poor equipment	Maintenance
Rush operation	Manager
Off-size dimensions	Inspection

These are but some of the causes. They are mentioned, however, first to make clearer the analogy of an assembly to the daily tasks people carry on. Second, to show wherein good timestudy can be made an important "tool" in getting control of overhead costs.

Remove Causes

Of course, the benefits to be gained largely depend upon how the boss interprets the function of timestudy. Also, obviously, they hinge upon the diagnostic skills of your timestudy men. Beyond these are other influences. For instance, if your timestudy men say to themselves, "We have to live with some of these 'management errors,'" (Chap. 2), they may be averaged into your work standards.

If instead, they look upon their occurrences as suggesting problems requiring solutions, you can get lower costs. Here again, is a touchy situation. Like accountants, timestudy men can be accused of sticking their noses into every department. Still, if they do so for the purpose of working on causes rather than criticizing people, many profit leaks can be plugged.

Paying Now

Similarly, if the feeder departments at fault will assume their full responsibilities, reoccurrences of these chronic costs will be minimized.

The managers of these departments may think or say, "We haven't got the manpower." This is a natural reaction. Nearly every department head feels like he is pushed to the limit.

Regardless, here we are trying to control overhead costs. One way to do this is to get all like expenses together. This means having Engineering, Purchasing, and the other feeder functions do all their work. Then parts of it will not be paid for in "wages" of people, equipment, floor space, and inventory tie-ups in waiting, hunting time, and extra work. This is part of the realignment of duties stressed in Chap. 9.

Maybe certain budgets will have to be increased. If so, the overhead will be where you can see it. Further, it will be under the control of experts who should be able to get the work done more efficiently. At the same time, they can take steps to prevent repetitions of like mistakes. In the main, however, the many savings that can be made should result in an overall reduction, assuming no major increase in volume.

Fewer Safaris

To bring to light the losses in these failures to "transfer" requires a better than common method of timestudy. The usual practice is too costly. This one-at-a-time special trip made to study an isolated operation I call a safari. Each one is undertaken as though there were no other duties to be performed. Of more pertinence here is that each of these "rates" is recorded and filed with a finality that suggests conditions will remain unchanged indefinitely.

Not only are such "rates" set in error, but also they are roughly seven times as costly as better standards set from data.[1] This refers only to the standard setting cost. In addition are all the other overhead expenses growing out of arguments, compromises, contract restrictions, grievances, and arbitrations. These occur much more frequently when the one-study–one-"rate" method is used, for several reasons. One is the chance for personality clashes between single employee and lone timestudy man. Another is the long-time practice of "informal negotiation" carried over from "piece rate setting." Third, and opposite to the standard data method recommended, there is no tie-in with all other standards for a type of work.

Low Coverage

What is worse from our control viewpoint is that too often jobs are "let go on day work." "Rate setters" say they can't get to them to make allowances for "management errors" that create extra work. They fail to realize that costs may be doubled through neglect. Frequently, these are looked on as short jobs not worth measuring. This is the common explanation given for failure to measure jobbing work.

[1] Carroll, Phil, "Better Wage Incentives," p. 38, McGraw-Hill Book Company, Inc., New York, 1957.

We should remember our second-grade arithmetic. If a job is to take 60 minutes on day work, it can be done in 30 minutes under work measurement, in about 24 minutes with incentive. The saving in cost is 30 minutes. If setting the 30-minute standard costs no more than 30 minutes, the effort was a break-even neglecting all the overhead savings. But why should it take 30 timestudy minutes to set a 30-minute work standard?

Because of such inept timestudy thinking and practices, many operations are not measured at all, particularly indirect. Thus, large amounts of overhead cost are buried in so-called labor cost. A diagram of this mixture might look like Fig. 58. In studying this, remember that the failures to "transfer skill" by the feeder departments may be greater percentagewise in overhead operations.

Productive	Overhead		
	Wait time	Extra work	Lower pace

Fig. 58. One day's time—direct or indirect—a mixture of productive and overhead.

The gains through higher productivity, depicted not to scale as "Lower pace," were discussed in Chap. 7. Remember, however, that with day work—direct or indirect, overhead expenses like space, equipment, taxes, insurance, and interest are about double. These may be substantial amounts.

In addition, there are all the other extra costs suggested earlier by the list of Effects and Causes. These cannot be separated, let alone located, diagnosed, or assigned from any known accounting records. Only skilled timestudy men can uncover and analyze most of these profit leaks. And many gold mines remain concealed because the prospectors never get to them. These you can open up at lower timestudy costs by insisting that the wholesale method of standard data replace the one-study–one-rate safari.

Price Quoted

Going further in this direction, timestudy men can make another profitable contribution to the control of overhead costs. This is in helping to overcome a "lack of communications" that the average timestudy man cannot see with his single-study blinders on.

Timing what one sees in the shop will ordinarily enable an alert observer to sort bad from good. However, the good, direct, or productive work often contains extra elements or whole added operations. These creep in as the work passes through the cycle shown on Fig. 50. "Down-the-line communications" about just exactly what was agreed to are often vague. The result is that many extra refinements are put on just to be safe. Others are tucked in by the salesman in his desire to render service.

Giving the customer more for his dollar is our only non-socialistic way of increasing our standard of living. I'm in favor of that principle. But here, we are discussing the amount of unknown, unplanned giving—the extras that are in the product but not in the price. Strictly speaking, the extra "direct" labor and its fringe benefits are overhead. Added to these are all the other overhead costs of both work and arguments that occur in back-tracking around the cycle.

No Increases

The cure is simple to state. I tell timestudy men, "From now on, every increase in standard time is indirect labor." This sets apart as plus variances the added work. It's the only way I know to inform managers that we are "giving away the plant."

To apply this rule is more difficult. To do so, timestudy men must be able to recognize the increases. These can be found only when you have standards and baselines to measure against.

Baselines can be set up when timestudy men use standard data for work measurement. This method not only enables them to increase coverage to about 98 per cent much more cheaply. It also provides a way to preset standards.

For example, standards can be established as the basis for the labor and overhead parts of price quotations. If such quotations were used with every sale made, you would have a universal base for finding the trimmings given away.

Find Repetition

Actually, there are many unfilled gaps in the pricing process. Few companies I know have all the "options" pinned down like the automobile manufacturers do.

That leads to another approach. This is also a second way to cut the overhead cost of timestudy—the first being to use standard data instead of "rate setting."

The second improvement comes from taking advantage of repetition. It is simply an extension of the principle underlying standard data. It utilizes the patterns that repeat in parts of operations, in operations, in parts, and in assemblies.

This means that standards can be built up for doing work under normal conditions. These are based upon using the best methods available in our present state of ignorance. These can be charted so that standards can be set much more quickly and cheaply. Even very complex operations can be put together by charting. Methods are explained in another book.[1]

Completed charts can be furnished to estimators, foremen, even operators. Thus, many people can recognize when variations from normal conditions occur in day-to-day operation. Thus, all allowances made for extras are apparent and should be reported separately.

Standard Method

This idea of utilizing repetition of patterns was carried further by John Burlick. In so doing, he made further reductions in standard setting costs. At the same time, he created another baseline for preventing as well as detecting differences. What he did was to standardize methods.

His development was in two parts. One was a book of outline sketches of parts without dimensions. Thus, all parts performing

[1] Carroll, Phil, "How to Chart Data," Chaps. 19–20, McGraw-Hill Book Company, Inc., New York, 1960.

similar functions were gathered together. Each was assigned a code number. The code number identified cards showing operations to be performed. These recordings were his second saving. It was twofold. First it avoided the costs of reinventing process methods one at a time. Second, it caught excesses that might have been included in "new" methods.

He went further. He recorded alongside each operation the standard when it was a constant. Otherwise, he noted a code number identifying the chart or general data from which the standard was to be set.

These suggested methods improvements in timestudy serve dual functions. They enable timestudy men to greatly increase their productivities. More importantly, they should be used to call attention to extra work done that was not paid for in prices quoted.

Posted Charts

In still other ways, timestudy men can save themselves work. For instance, many calculate pieces per hour equivalents of their standards. I would eliminate this step altogether. But if this has been a habit, then you should make up a chart covering the range. Put up copies of the chart where they may be seen by those interested in finding out how many they are supposed to make. This single charting will save the more costly one-at-a-time calculations thereafter.

Even more work can be saved with another type of chart. This is any that records specifications regularly copied onto operation sheets. Feeds and speeds are one example. All such information, if consistent, comes from recorded data. So why not copy the data onto one or more charts for general consultation? This is much less costly than to copy it in part on hundreds of thousands of operation sheets.

Still more work can be eliminated if we could point out where in more detail. But the foregoing ideas have enough savings in them to enable timestudy men to use the time gained to initiate some constructive efforts.

Help Engineering

For example, they can carry this pattern idea further to help engineering. This is brought in here because it can be used to reduce engineering, tooling, setup, scheduling, timestudy, accounting, and inventory costs. In addition, it leads toward eventual automation.

The point is that most plants have an accumulation of prior engineering variations. These just grew with time. Yet, in many instances, they continue to appear in the shop, probably without the knowledge of Engineering.

Consequently, timestudy men approaching 100 per cent coverage see all these differences. More than that, they have their time costs. Thus, the service they can perform is to call attention to the operation costs that might be reduced by standardization. You can make a start in this direction by taking the following steps:

1. Select some repeatedly run type of product.
2. Get identifying numbers of all parts of that type.
3. Collect all the corresponding operation sheets.
4. Sort sheets into groups that have like numbers and sequences of operations.
5. Make a big chart starting with the list of operations down the left found to be most common.
6. Record part numbers at the tops of columns and standards alongside their related operations.
7. Enter additional part numbers at the head of any column when operations and standards in that column are identical.
8. Add operations below the first listing whenever different operations occur. Otherwise, post standards on the lines of those already listed.
9. Continue across the chart until all parts, operations, and standards are recorded.

Such a chart will show engineers where similarities and differences exist. Also, it will point out the time costs of those variations. These can be translated into dollar amounts by using multipliers of forecast or past production quantities. Such figures represent money that Engineering could spend to gain more standardization in design.

Cost Education

You recognize that the fact-finding just described is really an Engineering chore. It is brought out here for two reasons. One was mentioned when I said, "Timestudy men see the differences." Thus, they can bring to Engineering's attention the higher costs of those parts that are active. In contrast, Engineering might have to tackle this study by considering all designs of a type—active and obsolete. Too, when done, they would turn to Timestudy for time standards.

The second reason is educational in nature. All such reports of time costs help to show Engineers how much their designs really cost. This has the long-range advantage of reducing costs that might otherwise be built into future designs.

One everyday example might make this potential saving more apparent. This concerns jig design. Some are less costly to load and unload than others. Differences of about 100 per cent are frequently found in timestudy.[1] These variations are not usually known by designers. Therefore, efforts made to reveal alternative costs to them can reduce future built-in costs.

Preventing Costs

When this type of preventive work is done constructively, big savings can result. These possibilities are known to everybody. We admit that it's cheaper to change mind on paper than in metal. Yet, few managers carry out these better methods they already know about.

Whether the extras show up on paper or in metal, alert time-study men still act as inspectors. They are even worse than accountants when it comes to guarding the company bank. Their added concern is about losses in productivity.

[1] Carroll, Phil, "How to Control Production Costs," p. 206, McGraw-Hill Book Company, Inc., New York, 1953.

Consequently, good timestudy men never cease to point out cost differences. And as explained earlier, these occasions are greatly multiplied when baseline measures are created by utilizing standard data. One example will serve to emphasize.

The instance comes from a proposal to make a newly designed product. All blueprints were turned over to Timestudy for setting estimated standards. Naturally, there were many questions and answers about proposed equipment, tooling, and methods exchanged between Engineering and Timestudy.

In time, the estimate was completed. The new design was put into production. Standards were set on the actual operations in the shop. Then the lid blew off. The total of the standard times required was double that originally estimated.

The dynamite that caused the explosion was the difference. Yet, some or most of the excess cost might still have been incurred had it not been for the baseline established by the original estimate.

Some part of the excess was caused by engineering optimism. Some part by manufacturing habit. Both tend to be corrected when good timestudy is used in the planning stage. Chronic, built-in costs can be reduced through better engineering knowledge of actual shop facilities. Shop habits can be improved by incorporating better methods in new designs.

Finally, foreknowledge of probable costs can alert top-management to take either of two courses if necessary. One is to abandon the project as unprofitable. The other is to say, "We have to get $30 out of the cost or we can't afford to make that product." This vital test is not obtainable from accountants. Only skilled Engineers, Value Analysts, and Timestudy Men can put together costs of production turned out by methods and designs that *should be used.*

CHAPTER 13

Control Sales Efforts[1]

"Nothing happens until somebody sells something." This lucid premise is the motto of Sales and Marketing Executives International.

Said another way, "Sales start and sustain the lives of our businesses." Without sales, none of us would have jobs. The customer is the one that gives us job security. His wants will ultimately be satisfied by us or someone else. But, since, as Peter Drucker says, "There is only one valid definition of business purpose: to create a customer," we must recognize that the markets for our products must be created through our actions.[2] Very often the customer is unaware that his desire for our product even existed until we sell him.

And selling is not limited to the efforts of your field representatives. Many times it has been said, "The salesman sells the first order, and the plant sells the rest." This is only partially true, of course, but repeat business comes only after the customer receives what he specified—quantity, quality, price, and delivery.

Create Customers

Thus, the purpose of your business is to retain old and to create new customers. But, you must do so profitably or your stockholders will take back their money and invest it elsewhere. Therefore, to be successful in achieving your purpose, you must

[1] This chapter was contributed by Phil Carroll, Jr.

[2] Drucker, Peter F., "The Practice of Management," p. 37, Harper & Row, Publishers, Incorporated, New York, 1954.

reduce and control the excess costs caused by your sales and related efforts.

Collectively, American industry spends enormous sums of money "creating customers"—much of it wastefully. To reduce your portion of these overhead wastes, you must help your sales organization sell more profits rather than more dollars. At the same time, they must fulfill their other obligations to your customers. They are the ones that send you your paychecks.

To my way of thinking, your company must be customer-oriented to be successful. But it should not be customer-dominated. We must be alert to the needs of the customer, and satisfy them. But, who controls the situation? Does the customer buy, or do we sell?

Historically, in the customer-dominated company, the salesmen sell the "easy products"—the ones in demand. Often they're easy to sell because they're real bargains. They are sold for less than cost. We may even offer 10 per cent "summer discounts." In these instances, the customer buys. The salesman doesn't sell. Why should he? We've preached sales dollar volume to him all his life. In addition, we've compounded the felony by paying him straight 3 per cent commissions on all sales—profitable, break-even, and losing. These incentives urge him to increase his volume. His best way is to let the customer have anything he wants. This might take the form of non-standard products, special discounts, or over-liberal terms. And, very often, unfortunately, the customer is unaware that he is getting anything special.

New Day

Now, a new day dawns. To survive, we must continue to be customer-oriented. But we must control the situation through our own actions. We will have to decide what we will sell and to whom we will sell it. We must build up a sales forecast with the help of the sales force that meets the profit goal set for the company. Through analysis, we will have to decide to reduce the number of items—to slough off those that are dragging us down. We may even redesign a few products, and increase the prices of some. Also, we must develop one or more new methods of getting and processing customers' orders so as to reduce our overhead costs and our profit leaks.

In other words, we have learned that we must have planned selling in order to reach our profit goal. Our goal can be attained only when

1. *Each product* in our "line" is sold at a profit. Immediately you object. You say there are items that you must carry to have a "complete line," whether they show a profit or not. Maybe so. I admit there is a place for the "loss leader." But, each time you sell it, make sure that it pulls with it enough sales of profitable items to more than offset the loss. Similarly, you will have development losses when you introduce new items.
2. *Each customer* returns a profit to you. Or, in the case of a new customer, has a definite profit potential at some specified future time. This does not mean that each order will be profitable. But, the total orders from each customer must contain a profit per cent approximating your profit goal.
3. *Each territory* or sales representative sells at a profit. Here again, we anticipate losses when we open up new markets. But, it's a planned loss, with a break-even time specified.

Sales Expense

With the objective of planned selling and predetermined profit goal in mind, let's take a look at the sales overhead we should incur in carrying out our plan.

For this purpose, an analysis of just the traditional sales expenses like commissions, travel, entertainment, advertising, and the like is inadequate. You must consider the overheads in all selling costs. You will have to sort through the entire organization to ferret out all the other costs that can be properly classified as sales expense.

The questions you must answer are of this kind. Who *caused* this expense? Who should we hold accountable? For example, sales people can increase "manufacturing expense," particularly setups and overtime, by their failures to forecast. By the same token, manufacturing can increase "sales expense," as shown in reports of "returns and allowances," through faulty production and late delivery.

Either way, *the job of the manager is to control* the costs that are caused by his actions. Hence, you must identify for him *all* the costs for which he can be held accountable.

Price Reductions

For instance, all sales dollars at the top of the P & L statement are often assumed to be of equal value. This is not true for two main reasons.

1. Many reductions in price are netted out in the billing. The same product may show in sales dollars at a number of different prices.
2. Various degrees of profit or loss exist among the several products. For such reasons, all deviations from your regular "list prices" should be picked up and reported by classifications. Then when you make your sales people aware of the magnitudes of these sales costs, they may discover more productive uses for the same or fewer dollars. For example, dollars spent for customer service, advertising, product improvement, and sales promotion are possible alternatives that can be made to bear more fruit than price reductions.

Products Profits

Again, your total sales are an accumulation of dollars received from your customers for the purchases of "your line." But, as Peter Drucker says,

". . . only a few products in a line produce practically all the sales and every penny of the profits while other items contribute only costs." [1]

Try listing every item your company sold in the past year. In a

[1] Drucker, Peter F., "Three Steps to Competitive Strength," *Nation's Business,* March, 1962.

column alongside, put the volume in sales dollars, and in the third column, the profit contribution. Then rearrange the list with the highest volume item on top and the lowest at the bottom. You should end up with something that looks like Fig. 59.

Item	Sales Volume	Profit Contribution
P2014	$1,650,000	$250,000
R4304	1,200,000	150,000
P3705	850,000	80,000
S1803	400,000	12,000
S1226	250,000	−5,000
R0441	200,000	−8,000
P2102	175,000	−9,500
P3630	150,000	−12,000
R2700	100,000	−15,000
S1505	25,000	−10,000

FIG. 59. A list of last year's sales in declining order of product dollar volume together with product profits.

You may find as management did at New England Confectionery Company (Necco) where

". . . analysis revealed that only 50 per cent of the products were accounting for 94 per cent of the sales and—more startling, 97 per cent of the gross profit." [1]

Then Necco went through a product line "house cleaning."

On the other hand,

"Chevrolet could build over 2,000,000 automobiles without duplications, so great is the variety of engines, body styles, and accessories available."

And yet, "Chevrolet actually makes a profit on a 20,000 annual production of the $5,000-plus, plastic-bodied Corvette." [2]

These seeming contradictions, to me, point to the same principle. That is, "specials" can dissipate the profits your company

[1] *Candy Industry and Confectioners Journal,* October 10, 1961.

[2] MacDonald, Donald, "The Bumper-to-Bumper Boom Years," *Think,* p. 7, July–August, 1963.

has earned on its regulars. But, if your sales people "must have those specials," and are willing to ask your customers for *fair prices,* your specials may contribute their share to your profit picture.

Many companies, such as Chevrolet, are dedicated to the idea of giving their customers one-stop places to shop. Thus, anyone who has bought a car recently knows that variations from standard models are amply covered by sufficient price dollars. So, it's really a question of costs.

The bottom items in your line can't help but cost relatively more than the top items. As a result, you must do one of three things:

1. Find a method of reducing costs on short runs.
2. Raise prices to cover added costs.
3. Cut the specials from the line.

Product Life

As you consider each of these three courses, remember that every product has a life. The trouble is most of us are unable or unwilling to say whether a product is "living" or "dying." To find

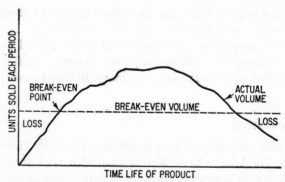

Fig. 60. You can plot the "life chart" of any of your products.

out, you can chart the life of any of your products by the over-simplified method illustrated by Fig. 60.

To make such charts, you must be able to roughly approximate the volume required to break even and the time when you should expect to see profit results. This goes back to estimates of probable sales made before deciding to "come out" with the new or revised product. With this, you couple the high overhead bill you ran up in R & D, Engineering, Tooling, Scrap, and Sales Promotion. This latter, along with your more "direct costs," must be recovered over some reasonable period of time.

Further, your new products will, generally, have a life expectancy similar to some other products in your line. This should help you predict the life span of the new item. So, if you will chart your expectations you will

1. Know enough not to introduce some new products because they don't stand a chance.
2. Know when to let a new product die a-borning (as Ford Motor Company did with their Edsel), because you could tell it wasn't going to make it.
3. Know which items to push because they offer your greatest profit potentials.
4. Know when to make an orderly retreat, or a rout, from the market place with a product that is dying.

Most sales organizations constantly long for new products. Yet, very few will attend the burials of obsolete products. But, don't fall into this trap. Don't be sentimental about a dead or dying item. The graveyard is full of companies whose products were no longer desired, and who refused to change in time to avoid bankruptcy.

Sales Forecasting

To survive and enjoy success, recall that Alexander Heron says, "No Sale, No Job." [1] Let's add to that, "No sales forecast, no goods when your customer orders them, hence no sales because of poor service." You say I'm exaggerating, and maybe so, but customers will drift, or leap, to the company that offers fair

---

[1] Heron, Alexander R., "No Sale, No Job," Harper & Row, Publishers, Incorporated, New York, 1954.

values on time. Why should a customer stay with us if we keep him waiting for the products he wanted yesterday?

"Given the chance to plan that a forecast affords, the shop can avoid a lot of costly 'Drop everything! Rush this!' It can save setups, scrap, overtime, stock chasing, telephone purchases, and high spot prices." [1]

These excess costs are really sales expense. You should label them as such. What is more important, your customer is the one that really suffers, because of delays in receiving his order, and, if he will let us get away with it, paying for our inefficiencies in higher prices.

If your sales people are like most, they constantly complain about manufacturing's inability to fill customer orders. At the same time, they "refuse" to forecast their sales. What they mean is, "We won't tell you what we will want or when we will want it —you guess, but don't be wrong."

How many companies do you know that forecast at the home office from past records? It should be done "in the field." The field man is in the best position to know

1. How your products are being received
2. How your customers are doing financially, their potentials, their loyalties to your products, and their degrees of aggressiveness
3. How strong your competition will be

I am not saying that we can accept a salesman's forecast without question. The very fact that he tells you ahead of time what he expects to sell, gives you the opportunity to predict the profitability of the product mix in his forecast. And, if your company is going to make its profit goal, he may have to adjust his sales emphasis. With forecasts made, he can do this before the "horse is out of the barn."

An added plus to having the salesman forecast is that he has something to say about establishing his quota. Not that I think

[1] Carroll, Phil, "Profit Control: How to Plug Profit Leaks," p. 27, McGraw-Hill Book Company, Inc., New York, 1962.

you should negotiate standards. Still, to get forecasts to function properly as controls, and to induce the Salesman to "put his job on the line," you will be "ten giant steps ahead" when he says, "Yes, I can sell this forecast."

For your forecast to be of much help, it should be made for at least a 12-month period, broken down into monthly forecasts. (Your production scheduling should take care of shorter periods.) With monthly forecasts, you can predict with reasonable accuracy how you're doing. Too, you can adjust your longer-range forecast according to what you learn from follow-up illustrated in Fig.

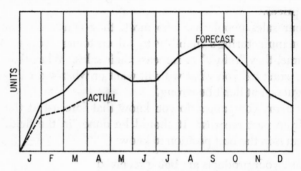

a. Month-by-month forecasts compared with actual sales.

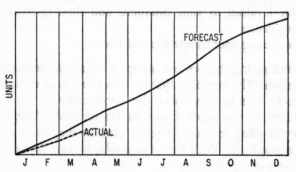

b. Accumulative forecasts compared with accrued sales.

Fɪɢ. 61. With a plan to follow, you can tell where you are and take the actions indicated.

61. Now you can begin to exercise control. You can ask, "Why is our actual running behind our forecast?" Is it our product? Our salesmanship? Whatever, you have an opportunity to do something about the difference before it's too late.

Returns and Allowances

Even with sound forecasting and alert follow-up, some of your products may be returned. This is visible proof that your sales have come unstuck. Your customer received the goods but would not keep them. Perhaps he would keep them, but only if you gave him an adjustment. These losses you know because you record them. But what about the customer that doesn't buy from you because of dissatisfaction in the past? Who is now earning the profit on his purchases?

Returns and allowances can be critical weather vanes to profit-minded managers. You can spot potential losses that may exceed the amounts recorded in R & A. When R & A goes up, sales go down. Hence, potential profits are lost.

Toward better control of overhead costs, then, let me suggest that you analyze returns and allowances by product, customer, and salesman. Then seek the answers to questions such as these.

1. Is the product properly engineered?
2. Is manufacturing guilty of faulty production?
3. Is quality control measuring the right quality characteristics?
4. Is the product properly stored, shipped, installed, and serviced?
5. Is the salesman over-selling or the customer over-buying?
6. Is the customer misusing or misapplying the product?
7. Is there some inherent weakness in the product?
8. Is the bulk of your R & A caused by a few of your products, customers, and salesmen?

Driving your answers to sound conclusions will net you a double-action reduction in losses. You will cut returns and allowances and increase sales.

Constant Expense

Next, you should study the constancy of certain sales costs. Industry is shot full of costs that are virtually the same per occurrence regardless of the volume involved. The engineering cost is the same on a low volume item as it is on a high one. The automatic screw machine setup costs the same for a 100-piece run as it does for a 10,000-piece order. Sales expense is no different. The cost is the same to edit, bill, post, and collect a $50 customer order as for a $5,000 order. And, the cost of pushing the paper through the shop is the same.

This characteristic is particularly true of manpower costs in the field. This is very likely your largest element of sales expense. It is made up of salaries, commissions, travel, entertainment, automobile expense, and fringe benefits for your own man, and brokerage fees for your agents.

Field manpower costs run 25 per cent of sales in one company I'm familiar with. Yours may be only 4 per cent. No matter, both figures are averages. As such they tell us little of our real cost. Analysis will reveal that the cost is nearly constant per salesman's call, regardless of the size of the order he obtains. With a cost per call of say, $5, your real manpower cost is 20 per cent on a $25 order. It is only 1 per cent on a $500 order. This is what prompts Gerard Brooks, U.S. Rubber's Director of Marketing, to say, "The average salesman in the U.S. in any industry spends over 55 per cent of his time on less than 10 per cent of his business." [1]

Let's check that statement with a little arithmetic. Assume we pay our salesman $20,000 a year and his volume is $500,000. Ninety per cent of his volume would be $450,000 gained with 45 per cent of his time, or $9,000. The manpower cost on this portion of sales is 2 per cent ($9,000/$450,000). This looks like profitable business.

On the other hand, our salesman spends 55 per cent of his time, costing $11,000, to sell 10 per cent, $50,000 of his business. On

[1] Brooks, Gerard, "The Big, Big Headaches Ahead?," p. 72, *Sales Management*, November 10, 1960.

this portion, the manpower overhead cost is 22 per cent ($11,-000/$50,000). No wonder so many companies are going broke.

What Gerard Brooks's statement doesn't spell out is that 90 per cent of our business comes from less than 50 per cent of our customers. Add up all these ideas and we can come to only one conclusion—we can't use the same system that we apply on volume accounts.

If we know we're going to lose money processing a customer's order, why do we add to that loss by sending a salesman out to get it? And then, let him "wine and dine" the customer? Why not get a battery of sweet-talking telephone order girls, outfit them with customer card files showing background information, and let them gather the business from the low volume customers? Long-distance phone rates are low compared with putting $50-a-day men behind steering wheels of expensive cars.

If we make this shift, our field men have 55 per cent of their time available. One choice is to reduce our sales force. But, we would be better off profitwise, if salesmen will turn their attentions to increasing the volumes and profitabilities of their large accounts. Better yet, salesmen can work to land those large accounts we're not selling that are in every salesman's territory. Our aim must be to increase the effectiveness of our sales force. We can't do that until we sort out the differences in products and customers and then develop ways of handling each group profitably.

Direct Overhead

Most of our "hidden" sales costs can be controlled with sound sales forecasting and product line analysis. But, hanging loose in most companies that I'm familiar with is the large amount of field sales expense. Hence, until we find ways of measuring the effectiveness of our salesmen, and develop sound incentive for rewarding *effective effort* we won't make any real headway in attaining our profit goal.

Basically, we know what we want them to sell, and who we want them to sell it to. But, we can't control their every move. We wouldn't want to if we could. Besides, we would need a sales manager for every man in the field if we attempted to control his actions rigidly. What we must do is develop his ability to *manage*. Since he is virtually alone in the field anyhow, why not put him in "business for himself"? Then we can measure his individual effectiveness.

His first important change will be in his habit of reasoning. Too many sales people think in terms of sales dollars only. But if your company is like most, Product A, for example, has a 10 per cent profit, whereas Product B has a 3 per cent loss. Hence, to get your sales organization to be more productive, you must make it aware of these differences in profitability, and encourage it to increase profits through selective selling. To be effective, a sale must produce a profit. Otherwise, the company and/or the salesman cannot continue. This does not mean that every single item of every order must produce a profit. It does mean that the aggregate sales to every single customer should be profitable. Neither the salesman nor the company should expect the profitable customer to do without service. Nor should he pay higher prices in order to sustain your losing accounts.

Therefore, a sound sales incentive plan should be based on selling profits. The selling profit is earned whenever items are sold at prices greater than the cost of producing plus the cost of selling. Cost of producing, in this sense, includes all costs expended on the product up to and including factory warehousing. Cost of selling includes all costs expended in consummating the sale. These costs are delivery, service, discounts, selling salaries, commissions, fees, advertising, promotional allowances, traveling, and other expenses incurred by sales personnel.

One such incentive plan that has been used successfully is based on a monthly profit and loss statement for each territory. All sales made within the territory are credited to the territory manager, at the gross amount of the invoices. The goods are billed to him at the "cost of producing." He can determine the gross profit of each order since *his* copy shows sale price, cost of each item, and extensions of both.

All expenses incurred in his territory are charged to him. Thus, the difference between the sales credited and the expenses charged is the territory manager's profit for the month. His profit is then increased or decreased by the amount of under- or over-absorbed "fixed" overhead the company realized because the territory manager under- or over-sold his portion of the sales forecast. This incentive method helps you insure that your salesmen will sell the company's planned output. An illustration of the plan is shown in Fig. 62.

TERRITORY 14

Profit and Loss Statement
Month ending April 30, 1964

Gross Sales..		$87,342
Less cost of goods sold...................................		67,066
Gross Profit...		$20,276
Less gross profit on returned goods.......................		114
		$20,162

Expenses:		
Territory manager's draw...........................	$1,500	
Brokerage fees.....................................	383	
Detail man's salary and travel......................	672	
Service salary and travel...........................	714	
Installation charges................................	226	
Freight to warehouse...............................	605	
Warehouse charge..................................	147	
Freight out—common carrier........................	2,194	
Freight out—company trucks........................	1,983	
Freight allowances.................................	242	
Allowances..	819	
Quantity discounts.................................	576	
Price adjustments..................................	63	
Advertising..	121	
Sales promotion....................................	76	
Display material...................................	102	
Samples...	147	
Bad debts incurred.................................	40	
Cash discount.....................................	1,489	12,099
Territory manager's net profit.............................		$ 8,063
Plus profit earned for exceeding the sales forecast...............		416
Total profit for the month.................................		$ 8,479

Fig. 62. An incentive plan that puts the salesman in business for himself helps to insure achievement of your company profit goals.

A plan such as this, that enables the territory manager to increase his earnings by sharing in the profits earned through his own efforts, satisfies company objectives to

1. Emphasize the sale of profitable items.
2. Sell the sales forecast. Hence—attain your profit goal.
3. Encourage regular, rather than spasmodic sales effort.
4. Sell what you have—inventory, products, and plant capacity.

Specific Objectives

Further, you can superimpose upon this framework added incentives to accomplish specific goals. You can utilize bonuses to induce such "creative" efforts as getting new customers and pushing new products.

A plan similar to this is an important aid to the reduction and control of your day-to-day selling overhead expenses. When designed properly, it helps also to control the many other internal overhead costs that result from sales orders and salesmen's demands for service. With added incentives, it can assist in reducing and controlling those several overhead costs related to plant capacity and "product line" complexity.

CHAPTER 14

Revise Engineering Specifications

"The normal inclination of most engineers is to design to the best product performance. Many times even the best is not good enough, but also many times the customer may not expect or desire a high performance. He may desire a longer life, a lower repair bill, less maintenance problems, or a lower price,"

writes W. A. Kinnaman.[1]

The essence of his article is to reduce customer complaints and repair costs so you won't go broke under a warranty plan. This is timely advice. Many companies are already giving guarantees. Chrysler offers 5 years of trouble-free driving. Maybe warranties will become as common as S & H trading stamps.

Customer Needs

In any event, Mr. Kinnaman's statement points toward several kinds of overhead cost arising in and stemming from Engineering. Of course, repairs are wholly overhead. And they are very much more costly when performed in the field. *Fortune* reports,

". . . the cost of putting to rights one improperly installed engine part is 2¢ in the factory (Chrysler); outside, in a completed car, its replacement under warranty leaves the company $100 out of pocket." [2]

[1] "Product Design and Warranties," *Mechanical Engineering*, December, 1962.

[2] Smith, Richard Austin, "Detroit Is Flying by the Seat of Its Pants," *Fortune*, p. 82, January, 1961.

The foregoing is an example of just one cause of the large overhead expense we call customer complaints. Apparently, the part was all right. It was improperly installed. We can't tell, however, whether or not the customer was satisfied after the repair was made. Certainly, his confidence in the reliability of his car dropped a notch or two. Still, the service man may have done no more than sooth a man's irritation—who actually wished he had bought a different car or, perhaps, a motorboat. If the latter is the case, then more complaints will follow.

Naturally, there are many degrees in this merry-go-round. Some seeds of complaint are planted when a salesman persuades a customer against his wishes. Generally, salesmen or sales engineers try to learn the customer's needs and supply products that will fit.

Whose Design

Right here is one weak link in the line of communications illustrated by Fig. 50, Chap. 9. What does the customer need? Will the product delivered meet his requirements? Does the price quoted actually pay for the product he wants or the one furnished?

Another weak spot is suggested by the opening quote. Was the product designed to meet customer needs? One answer to that question may lie in your answer to the next one, "How many special orders are caused by customer efforts to adapt your designs to their needs?" This leads to a third. "Are designs initiated from within or from outside?" Do you design products and then try to sell them? This procedure tends toward lower engineering and higher selling and complaint costs. Or do you find out what potential customers desire and then design your products to suit? This way tends to increase engineering and reduce selling costs.

A middle ground is recommended by Edward Schleh. He puts it this way,

"A research engineer may feel that a product should be designed in a particular way . . . . Although the product will be difficult to sell the way he designs it, he is inclined to fight any suggestion of change . . . . If, however, he is made accountable . . . for the sales realized in the first years of production . . . , he is much more apt to be in harmony with the sales department." [1]

Much of this "creative pride" washes out in companies where everything is made to customer order. But most companies turn out mixtures of standards and specials. Likewise, a great many make long-lasting assemblies that require spare parts.

Replacement Costs

Such products may shift customer concern to reliability and its alternate—maintenance cost. These become increasingly important when the output of any one unit depends upon production from another. For instance, two in a line each having 90 per cent reliability combine to make an overall of 90 × 90 or 81 per cent availability. Then comes maintenance costs. How expensive is it to get at the element that needs fixing? How much does the replacement part cost?

Why did it fail? One answer is given by James Quinn. In speaking of maintenance engineering, he uses the term corrective maintenance and says this

"covers improvements rather than normal repairs. For example, minor changes in design, substitution of more suitable components, or improved materials of construction." [2]

His method of cure is by way of injecting some science into an old-time art. But few companies can approach a solution like Du Pont does. Note, he is doing engineering in the maintenance function that seems necessary to overcome the shortcomings in original design.

[1] Schleh, Edward C., "Management by Results," p. 133, McGraw-Hill Book Company, Inc., New York, 1961.
[2] "The Real Goal of Maintenance Engineering," p. 90, *Factory*, June, 1963.

Customer Specifies

Next are these questions. Will he buy from a different manu-facturer next time? Or will he specify changes in design and buy from the same company? The average purchaser, however might not detect the engineering faults. He would repair and repair. Thus, his inclination might be toward trying another product, thinking his luck might change.

Sketchily, the foregoing describes the eternal triangle made up of customer, salesman, and engineer. Once in a while, this is reduced to a twosome consisting of only customer and engineer. The purpose, of course, is to arrive at clearer specifications. After that, the price is established and, presumably, it covers all the features agreed to.

Three Gaps

Unfortunately, even in the case of the latter, supposedly under-stood design, the overhead costs are not correctly applied. And that's only the beginning of lack of control. The product has to be designed, produced, inspected, and shipped. Then it may have to be proven in at the customer's plant. Still more overhead.

Part of the excess overhead occurs because of three gaps in the processing. The first is in the design. Here the engineer tries to translate into blueprints his understanding of what is required to meet the customer's wishes. The second gap shows up when mechanics try to turn the designs into fabricated materials. This gap may not be much different if parts are bought outside. Al-though at times, inspectors will allow more leeway to home folks than to outsiders. The third gap appears where inspectors at-tempt to reconcile the physical pieces with their specifications.

Drawing Errors

These three gaps exist whether the designs are made up for special jobs or are for regular products. They result from both incomplete and incorrect specifications. Some of the errors creep in because we start too late and rush the engineering. Most, as a rule, are caused by wrong habits.

One example is that often called "tight limits" in the shop. The tolerances are usually loose enough. The trouble is that they are in the wrong place. A pin may have a dimension of 1.0 inch $+ .000$ $- .002$ and its corresponding hole 1.0 inch $+ .002$ $- .000$. Both will pass inspection at 1.00 inch. But the assembler is confronted with a "snug" instead of a "free" fit.

More trouble is created when engineers use words like "must be concentric" or "straighten when necessary." Since neither exact concentricity nor straightness is practically attainable, who's to say what deviations are passable?

Another missing link is in the way dimensions are shown. Often, the mechanic has to add or subtract to get those he needs to make the part. To emphasize this extra overhead, I often say, "Then, we wonder why the $\frac{1}{4}$ inch too long or too short always shows up in the middle of the piece. And while the mechanic is making mistakes in arithmetic, a \$50,000 machine tool is standing there eating its head off in depreciation."

Tolerance and dimension problems are fairly easy to solve. As they are, much rework time will be saved. More important will be the preservation of interchangeable parts. This ideal is destroyed in many assemblies with reamers, files, and hammers. Some day, such "getting by" comes back as more overhead when the spare part the customer gets to fix a breakdown won't fit.

Finish Specifications

Failure to specify also occurs as a lack of definite instructions about surface finishes. When is a surface buffed, or polished, or ground? These terms for processing only partially describe the finish required. Ream, hone, and lap are no more definite. And when the engineer notes "smooth" or puts an f symbol on a surface, the shop has a guessing contest on its hands.

Lack of finish specifications causes an enormous amount of overhead in two ways. One is in the extra work done to "play it safe." These costs are now buried in so-called direct labor. They continue because we seem to accept as necessary all work carrying the label "direct." Just think for a moment about how much contrary proof has come out of intensive value analyses. The other is in time lost in arguments trying to preserve rubber standards, in consequent rework or scrap, and in the incidental costs of equipment, floor space, and money tied up. Some of these costs grow out of customer complaints.

Either way, decisions about finishes and tolerance not specified are often made now by mechanics. These are paid higher wages as a result. Their thinking cannot be done by tapes and computers. Remember, these robots are not equipped for "mind-reading."

Standardize Designs

Many of these extra overhead costs and those of Engineering can be reduced by standardizing designs. For example, suppose a usage of 1,000 of a typical part and a design cost of $500. If there were only one design, then the Engineering cost would be 50 cents ($500/1,000) a piece. On the other hand, if you made four designs, the average usage would be 250 parts per design and your Engineering cost would be $2.00 ($500/250) each.

Beyond this creative cost is a long series of other overhead expenses set in motion by each additional variation. These were explained as setups in Chap. 3 and include costs like

Re-engineering	Setups	Grievances	Paying Supplier
Purchasing	Scrap	Material handling	Cataloguing
Planning	Tooling	Quality control	Storing
Timestudy	Equipment	Inspection	Ordering
Supervision	Floor space	Costing	Order filling
Timekeeping	Inventory	Accounting	Shipping
Estimating	Obsolesence	Invoicing	Customer complaints

Several Designs

Sure, you distribute your risks when you have more than one typical part design. Contrariwise, you can and will correct all of one kind of problem when you have one design. Thus, product reliability increases when standardized parts are used that have been evolved through trial. This advantage is not so likely to be gained when you have half a dozen designs. The same holds true for all the other troubleshooting overhead functions. Our intentions are good. But pressures fix our attentions on handling one problem at a time.

This is also a reason for our multiplicity of designs. The larger number wasn't planned. It happened. Individuals were handed jobs to do. Each may not have known what similar parts existed. Some may have known, searched half-heartedly, and given up. Others may have tried and come up against, "We can't modify that design. There are too many on the market."

All such reasons will have to be set aside if you go in for automation. You have to collect together the quantities now spread among several designs. You may have to combine your runs with those of a supplier or competitor. Some way you must get quantities above a break-even point before you can afford the oft-mentioned cost-cutting tool of automation.

Prior Steps

Between now and then, you can take some prerequisite steps. These will effect gains sometimes attributed to automation. I refer to doing better in specifying tolerances and finishes.

Specifications should be determined from the functional demands upon surfaces. In their design, keep in mind the basic cost-creating part they play as described by Robert Pearson. He said,

> "It is the draftsman who initially processes the part by the tolerances he puts on the drawing. In fact, the draftsman does more processing than the man in the Industrial Engineering Department."

Revise Habits

In seeking improvement, you can break out of the habit Pearson calls "decision by precedent." Somebody did the "thinking" for you, shall we say, many years ago. For instance:

> "From now on plus or minus a quarter of a degree is the standard for this shop . . . 'Then comes the day of reckoning.' We are not competitive. Get that two cents out of the manu-

facturing operation. Buy the material for less. Get the engineers into the factory, etc.! And all the time the reason for the high cost is some ridiculous decision made *many years ago* that adds $20.00 to the costs *today.*" [1]

Precedent Decisions

"Decisions by precedent" save time. Besides they are a form of standardization. Hence, by developing economical "precedents," you cut engineering costs and also save time.

Time seems to be getting shorter in this age of "innovation." It follows that the Engineering Department dare not be too slow. The market may be largely gone before products can be delivered.

Time as well as cost can be saved also through part standardization. Look at these opportunities through Drucker's eyes. He says,

". . . the essence of genuine mass production . . . rests on *uniform parts* which can then be mass-assembled into a larger variety of different products." [2]

This is how you get the combination of features you want in *your* car.

Cheaper Drafting

You can go further to reduce Engineering costs. Two basic ways are open. One is to make use of the many methods for eliminating work such as those explained in "Simplified Drafting Practice" by William Healy and Arthur Rau.[3] Examples are freehand drawing, use of symbols and mechanical aids, abbreviations, and simplified drafting. Many of the illustrations indicate reductions of work ranging upward from 50 per cent. Similarly, lettering cost can be reduced to about half when a specially designed typewriter is used. These are methods of raising productivity.

[1] "Cost Reduction and Profit Improvement," p. 41, Machinery and Allied Products Institute, Washington, D.C., October, 1960.

[2] Drucker, Peter F., "The Practice of Management," p. 100, Harper & Row, Publishers, Incorporated, New York, 1954.

[3] John Wiley & Sons, Inc., New York, 1953.

In addition, the second way affords further savings through the use of less skilled people. For instance, the picture containing the drafting typewriter just mentioned shows a good-looking girl operating it.[1]

Utilizing lower skills is a move in the right direction. It relieves the pressures of the "engineering shortage." Its practical application hinges upon the recognition of a simple fact. This is in knowing that most of us work most of the time doing things that require less than our highest skills. Yet our wages are based on the highest skill required. The situation with respect to managerial decision making was discussed in Chap. 10. Similarly, an analysis of an Engineering Department revealed that only 15 per cent of the time was spent in designing. The remainder, 85 per cent, was given to execution.

These proportions will differ from yours, probably. Yet, considerable savings can be made and more contentment achieved, if engineers are enabled to do more engineering. They can concentrate on working out the ideas. Then they can turn over rough sketches to technicians to be put into usable form.

Some methods for reducing costs must be diligently applied if yours have risen as much as William Byrne, past president of ASME, reports. He writes,

"Vacations, sick leave, coffee breaks, upgrading, labor turnover, print checking and other innovations have fantastically increased the cost of operating a drafting room in the past twenty years." [2]

Free Engineering

Along with these several approaches to overhead cost reduction should go another not often mentioned. It might be described as free engineering. It is free only to those companies that pose as customers and then don't buy. The engineering is paid for by your actual customers and stockholders.

Perhaps management wants to offer such services. Similar

[1] *Mechanical Engineering*, p. 73, February, 1963.
[2] *Product Engineering*, June, 1957.

forms of bait are often used with hopes that customers will be attracted. Great sums are being spent on proposals nowadays.

Nevertheless, these expenses are overhead even if the business is obtained. Therefore, they should be controlled. Like R & D we read so much about, its costs should be separated from those of Engineering. Free engineering is a sales expense the same as samples and martinis. Also, such costs should not be spread over the regular business.

The control needed is a comparison of the profitability of resulting sales with the costs of preliminary engineering. Undoubtedly, an allowance must be made for some per cent of "no shows." In addition, care should be exercised to see that free riders do not repeat often.

A better control will be in effect if you treat preliminary engineering as another product. You can set a price for it. Then, if the prospect elects not to buy your product, you will be paid for your engineering. Under this plan, you could quote a price for your product that was lower by the amount of engineering paid for separately. This is a very appropriate way to quote when quantities ordered may vary.

An alternative but less valid method is to credit the engineering charge against the total invoice if the final sale is made. This is an averaging process. It neglects quantity. Further, it requires your real customers to pay for engineering they did not receive.

These suggested plans, I know, are contrary to "industrial practice." But one time or another, you must choose between fiction and fact. Free engineering comes out of profit unless it is recovered through higher prices paid by your actual customers. This average practice leaves you without effective control over your engineering costs.

Consider Material

Up to this point no mention has been made of material cost. You know, however, that engineers decide what these are to be when they make their designs. Too often, they must err on the conservative side. They will prescribe castings, for example, when estimated sales quantities are below those necessary for tooling to fabricate sheet metal. Or they may be forced into this choice by time shortage.

Later on, increased quantities may prompt redesign. Perhaps, shrinking profit margins will nudge Engineering to take another look. A case in point is cited by Donald Burnham. He reports that Westinghouse bought 5-horsepower motors from half a dozen competitors, disassembled them, weighed the parts, and estimated their costs.

> "We found that on some parts we have the lowest cost. On many . . . some of our competitors had lower costs because they had better cost reduction ideas. . . . These ideas . . . plus our own developments . . . gave us a superior cost position. This program typically gives us 10 per cent cost reduction immediately and another 10 per cent is realized at the next major design change."[1]

Constructive as these savings are, it's much better management to omit elements of cost at the start than to whittle on them

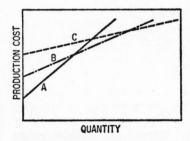
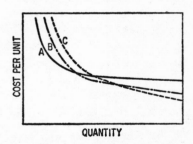

Fig. 63. With better forecasting you can eliminate one or more stages of design, material, and process change.

after parts are in production. And the longer you wait, the more inertia there is to overcome.

When there are options, managers should consider risks before designs are allowed to set. To illustrate, Fig. 63 shows three suitable materials with their costs per unit crossing at two quan-

[1] *Steel,* p. 27, July 17, 1963.

tities. These costs are totals correctly determined for decision
making. "Correctly" as used here is intended to call attention to
Lawrence Miles's statement ". . . that the mere inclusion of
overhead does not bring meaningful costs for value decisions." [1]

The costs in Fig. 63 include tooling and labor because these
are apt to change with shifts in material. The question then is,
"How much are you gambling by making a higher outlay now?"
The amounts may be larger. The risks may be greater. But the
overhead cost control problem is no different from that discussed
earlier as free engineering.

Mill Sizes

In another direction, engineers should give more study to material costs before they fix their designs. Perhaps they do. Yet,
some parts look like they were laid out so as to waste material.

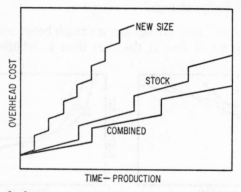

Fig. 64. Standardization with fewer raw material sizes tends to reduce
overhead costs.

At least, the shop isn't told what the engineer had in mind when
he decided upon his particular type of design.

The point is that frequently there seems to be little if any
thought given to the material usage when the drawing lines are
placed on paper. A sixteenth difference in placement might have

---

[1] Miles, Lawrence D., "Techniques of Value Analysis and Engineering,"
p. 44, McGraw-Hill Book Company, Inc., New York, 1961.

saved waste from a unit of material amounting to a whole piece.

Said another way, engineers should remember that materials have fixed dimensions. They have none of the flexibility inherent in placement of lines on paper. Besides, "decisions by precedent" may include factors of safety as large as 200 per cent.

Thus, there is considerable leeway in where lines can be drawn on paper. This flexibility should be used in either or both of two ways. One is to save scrap. The other is to make designs conform with stock materials. The latter avoids adding one more series of costs to overhead. This is indicated by the "New Size" stepped line on Fig. 64. Each raw material size added increases some part of 20 of the 28 overhead costs listed earlier. Scrap is the chief offsetting item. And part of this loss is canceled by the higher price paid for smaller lots.

In contrast, increased usage of a material already carried in stock reduces overhead cost. The reason why is suggested by the curve labeled "Combined."

In this and the other ways discussed in this chapter, Engineering plays a major part in creating overhead costs. Primarily, it establishes these by the types and numbers of designs it develops. In addition, it causes chronic indirect costs by failures to specify precisely what is required. These expenses are not known in the average plant. Getting these out where they can be seen is only a rearrangement of costs. Real overhead cost control begins when you and Engineers know what costs they create and take preventive measures to stop them at their sources.

CHAPTER 15

Reduce Purchasing Papers

"Will you ship us two rating films so we will have them by Wednesday?", asked the Purchasing Agent by long-distance phone. When I replied, "They will have to be sent by air-mail to meet that date," he said, "OK."

In this very simple transaction overhead costs were increased. To emphasize, Olin Mathieson reports,

> "The Packaging Division has to sell 1,600 pounds of corrugated containers to make enough profit to pay for a single long-distance telephone call between West Monroe, Louisiana and New York." [1]

These examples are cited, however, for another reason. This is to point out the cause, namely, too short a time. The buyer phoned me and then specified air-mail in his efforts to overcome his time squeeze. Maybe he was the one who started too late.

Good Service

Instead, chances are Mr. P. Agent was left holding the bag. Either way, he does not have the ability to stop the clock. He is squeezed into the time left between late notice and rigid date. Hence the decision is made to increase overhead costs, if necessary. Too often there is no easy escape from, "We must have it by Monday." Thus, the decision is "Yes."

[1] "Beating Today's Profit Squeeze," Elliott Service Co., Mount Vernon, N.Y., May 8, 1963.

Many people all through the company fail to plan far enough in advance. Eventually, they hope for deliveries yesterday. The result—higher overhead costs in both Purchasing and other consequent steps.

Overhead excesses continue if buyers take on the attitude that "they just work here." The same happens when they look upon themselves as strictly service people. Overhead will increase if, in providing service, they take pride in turning handsprings to show how adept they are in doing the "impossible."

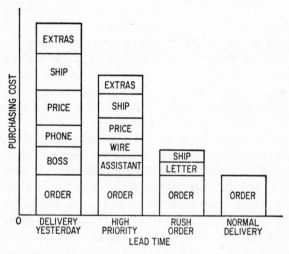

FIG. 65. Costs of purchasing build up as time limits shrink.

To get better control, the first step you might take is to dig out some costs like those shown in Fig. 65. These suggest the kinds of premiums paid to overcome the shortage of reasonable lead time. The extras on top represent equivalents like scrap, caused by accepting substitute sizes or below-standard qualities.

Such cost weapons should be given to Purchasing people so they can begin to fight. You may have to coach or retrain them. If this does not sufficiently correct the condition or attitude, you may have to make some changes.

Lead Time

Purchasing should protest. They should call attention to the higher costs. They should use numbers like $50 rather than emotional arm waving. Otherwise, people will think the buyers are lazy, selfish, or plain ornery.

Here I'm trying to make a distinction like that between inspection and real quality control. The latter goes beyond sorting bad from good to (1) find causes of defects and (2) work to remove causes.

The analogy is that Purchasing is a process involving several kinds of inspection. One is that of inspecting the time element. Purchasing knows when it gets a request to buy something whether or not there is a normal time available for getting the item. Perhaps, however, they have not broadcast this information. It follows that Purchasing should prepare and issue lists of lead times. Such lists should show current normal delivery times for all commonly ordered materials.

These time-tables serve several purposes. Primarily, they are a must for sound production scheduling. Secondly, they afford a way to re-educate the late-starters and hence to prevent excess costs. Thirdly, they supply the gauges for measuring lateness in ordering. Finally, those measures can be used to report to management the occurrences of causes of excess costs in both Purchasing and elsewhere in the chains of events created by purchase orders.

Incomplete Specifications

A second form of inspection that Purchasing should perform is that of specifications. Are these definite? Will the items sent by the supplier be those you want?

They may be, if the vendor writes or phones to ask for more information. This causes more overhead. If Purchasing has to get more specific identification, the excess overhead is inflated further.

On the other hand, your supplier may try mind-reading and ship what he thinks is being ordered. If he does, then another series of excess overhead costs is created. This takes in practically every overhead operation that would be performed with an acceptable product. In addition, you must pay for consultations with the intended user, repacking, and shipping, and then start fresh again.

Lack of specifications may increase overheads in another way. Materials may be received that look all right and may be accepted. Then or later, they will be used. In production, they may go through several stages before problems occur. The color is off. Castings are too big or too hard. The metal cracks in bending. The heat-treatment does not come out right.

Some variations from standards can be detected at incoming inspection. Many get by, unfortunately, because test specs are not available. Since they are lacking, they were not made part of the purchasing contract. Consequently, the company usually must assume the losses.

Often also, losses are incurred because "There isn't time enough to ship on the 13th and try to get in another lot." Here is a for-instance taken from a union contract.

"Defective parts produced by the employee upon specific instructions from responsible supervision, after attention is called to a faulty condition, shall be counted as good production in computing incentive earnings."

More to the point, Fred Peck reports,

"Eighty per cent of quality problems originate during the first 25 per cent of the manufacturing process. That includes purchased parts and services, receiving, purchasing, material stores, and the machine shop." [1]

Such overhead cost leaks should be plugged. One big leak stopper is insistence upon having better specifications when purchasing. While these originate in Engineering, errors of omission would cause less excess overhead if Purchasing were held accountable for inspecting the specifications before buying materials of any type.

[1] *Steel,* p. 20, July 17, 1963.

Value Analysis

Purchasers can go further. One did. Lawrence D. Miles created the method we call value analysis. Since then, the approach has been developed as a highly productive function separated from Purchasing. Yet the originator still says,

> "The purchasing department has the duty and authority to ask reconsideration of specifications or quantity of material, if, in the opinion of the buyer, it appears that the interests of the company may be better served." [1]

One obvious instance that ties together specifications and quantity is non-standard material. The responsibility of Engineering to design using standard materials was discussed in Chap. 14. Just the same, Purchasing should flag requests for new sizes or different specs to avoid adding the overheads created by each variation.

Miles makes it clear that Purchasing is not to take over the Engineering function. Still he says it has the "duty and responsibility to ask reconsideration" when available knowledge suggests alternatives. And there should be many opportunities for taking another look.

Much information about other products, tools, methods, and finishes comes to Purchasing from outside the company. Salesmen are always trying to get business by emphasizing the advantages their products have over their competitor's. These improvements are in finished articles, raw materials and substitutes, equipment, tools and supplies for processing, and all kinds of general items.

In addition, there is a vast amount of skilled know-how in the plants of suppliers, both current and prospective. Some of this comes to the attention of buyers in competitive bidding. More can be obtained when it is deliberately sought.

[1] Miles, Lawrence D., "Techniques of Value Analysis and Engineering," p. 180, McGraw-Hill Book Company, Inc., New York, 1961.

Seek Value

Naturally, the amount of knowledge acquired depends upon how the buyer looks at his job. If he assumes the specifications are the last word, and simply asks for quotes, he tends to shut off suggestions. If, rather, he is more value-conscious, he may start off with, "This is our best guess to date. Do you have some better ideas?" Even this approach is expensive. The mere act of presenting a conclusion, such as a blueprint, tends to turn off the valves of creativity.

Even so, the purchaser should try to make the most of his opportunities as the connector in the two-way communications between suppliers on the outside and specifiers on the inside. In so doing, he can help to reduce many of the overhead costs that are created by incomplete and incorrect two-way exchanges.

Poor Materials

In such efforts, buyers will not deliberately seek bargains. They realize, as Miles says, that "cost and quality have no direct relationship." The smart buyer will distinguish between value and price. He will know that "using cheap or inferior goods to save money is about as logical as stopping a clock to save time." [1]

For example, he will have learned that a lower price per pound of casting may actually result in a higher cost per piece. It usually does. For one thing, the pound is no specification of quality. Besides, the company gets excess pounds by seeking to buy weight.

Concealed in this casting illustration is a basic fundamental of overhead cost control. It is lack of cost facts. As pointed out in Chap. 12, costs of imperfections show up where the work is done. In the instance of excess stock on castings, its removal is in labor cost and in all the overheads incident to "more time." Yet, many accounting departments do not report even the extra labor cost to the buyer. Hence, he does not know the total cost of his pur-

[1] Nielsen, M., "Accelerating Engineering Progress," p. 10, *Proceedings of the American Power Conference*, March, 1962.

chase. And he may continue to buy the same item in the same way.

This is a two-pronged problem. One is the purchase of items that experiences seem to prove were satisfactory. The other is buying wherein mistakes are made. Neither is corrected until, in some way, Purchasing is made aware of excess overhead costs resulting from its work. Buyers cannot exercise control of overhead costs they initiated without "feed back" to guide their decision making.

Paper Starters

Moving into the mechanics of buying, Purchasing can make further savings in overhead costs. The amount depends upon kind and number of pieces of paper issued. One example of saving was the blank check method started by Kaiser Aluminum that "embraces 92 per cent of all its orders" (Fig. 52, Chap. 10).

You and I can't tell from that statement how much paper work was saved in Purchasing. Maybe none. Still we know that Accounting usually wants a Purchase Order as authorization for paying money. Thus the key that unlocks this chest of gold can be an accounting rule.

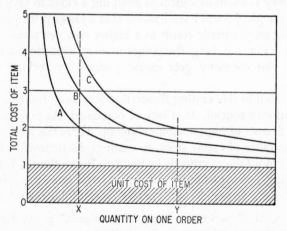

Fig. 66. Total cost of any purchased item depends upon both the amount ordered and the overhead cost of the whole purchasing cycle.

What regulations apply if you go out to buy something for cash? How much cash can you spend in any one purchase? If you sent out for that same item must you issue a P.O.? These questions are calling attention particularly to C items. Observe on Fig. 66 that buying a small amount, marked X quantity, may double, treble, or quadruple the cost of an item to your company, depending upon the overhead steps involved in the complete purchasing cycle.

Many Papers

Here are two contrasting methods of purchasing. In one company, a study of small orders revealed many for one item each from one company on regular dates. Our conclusion was that a clerk went through an inventory record and wrote an order for each item that was at or below minimum stock. In the other, a maintenance supervisor goes over his stock of supplies periodically and makes out one request for all anticipated requirements. What systems or methods can you devise or utilize to cut out most of your sheaf of papers?

If there must be a P.O., can it be some kind of blanket or open order? If you use this method, does it require also another piece of paper to get more of the same? Or can you send the supplier a schedule of quantities and dates of shipment for a month, a quarter, or a year?

Two Directions

Your overhead cost control is two-directional as indicated by Fig. 66. One is in going from quantity X to Y. This reduces unit overhead cost to one-third. The other is in changing from system C to A. Again, in this cooked-up example, the unit overhead cost is cut to one-third.

What are all the operations in overhead that are started every time Purchasing decides to buy something? Are P.O.'s made up and sent out? How many copies are distributed? Are competitive bids sought? Are salesmen interviewed? Do engineers get in on the discussions?

These are but a few of the many bits of overhead cost initiated by Purchasing. It sets in motion a whole series of overhead operations in both trying to buy and in committing the company to pay for goods.

Usually, pieces of paper are started through the "mill" when a purchase is made. Remember, however, that paper is cheap, relatively. The big cost is in all the handling and subsequent operations performed because of the paper. If you can eliminate the paper, you may remove practically all of the related overhead work. If you must have the paper, then keep in mind that it creates overhead. In this case, control depends upon curtailing the number and extent of operations performed in processing all copies.

CHAPTER 16

Improve Production Flow

We have come a long way in customer relations

". . . since that day W. H. Vanderbilt uttered his famous (or infamous) dictum, 'The public be damned.' . . . today, the trend in management philosophy toward 'The public be served' concept is seeping down through all echelons of management —even unto the very workers themselves.

"And this is good, for it is meek and proper that all of us know whence cometh our provender—and realize that the money we find in our pay envelopes traces its lineage back to the company's customers—and thence back to the customers' customers." [1]

Probably, most people in your company "know whence cometh our provender," if they stop to think. But many I have known do not quickly reply, "From our customers," when I ask, "Who gives us our paychecks?"

Customer Cycle

My question is designed to correct the notion that production is turned out "for the Sales Department" or "for the Company." Take an example in reverse. Many people including managers seem to think that increases in production gained through installations of wage incentives and methods improvement will automatically go out the door in bigger sales.

---

[1] Greene, Sam T., "Parables for Management," p. 51, Frederick Fell, Inc., New York, 1961.

Similarly, supervisors and middle managers hesitate in answering the question, "How do we *earn* overhead?" Too many have the vague idea that overhead is earned some way in the Accounting function. When I get them to recognize the difference between applied and earned, some say, "When we get a check from the customer."

Then I try to make the basic point of this chapter. It is to strive for the lowest practical time interval between receipt of the customer's order and deposit of his check.

In this direction, major changes must be made before the average company can operate as stated by du Pont, namely, "The customer wants delivery tomorrow, and in our business he gets it."

Total Control

Delivery tomorrow requires "Total Production Control"—plagiarizing A. V. Feigenbaum's book title.[1] Overhead steps that hold up the customer's order or the goods bought must either be eliminated or carried on concurrently. Also, generally, products have to be both standardized and in stock. This condition is suggested by Fig. 67a.

Even "specials" can be shipped promptly when production-minded people decide, "That's the way it's gonna be." Two companies I know have stocked blank sizes. The dimensions of these were determined from studies made of occurrences in prior orders. These blanks are turned out in production runs. Then when the "special" dimension is ordered, the only process time is that of removing a few thousandths or tenths.

These folks have unearthed the patterns that exist in specials. As a result, the manufacturing time cycle that takes place after the order is received is limited to modifying. This step appears in the middle column (Fig. 67a) under the title "Specials." You can see, however, that the 90 to 95 per cent gain in manufacturing time might be lost in overhead steps before or after modifying.

[1] Feigenbaum, A. V., "Total Quality Control," McGraw-Hill Book Company, Inc., New York, 1961.

Standard product	"Specials"	"Tomorrow"
	Interpret	Interpret
	Credit	
	Production Control	
Made	Modify stock	
for	Inspect	
stock	Pack	
	Ship	Ship
	Bill	
	Collect	

a. If you have products that can be made in advance, do you still have too many overhead steps that can slow up delivery?

Prepare	Make	Release
Interpret	Inspect raw	Inspect
Check credit	Transport	Pack
Design	Mill	Ship
Purchase	Drill	Bill
Plan	Assemble	Collect

|←——   Customer Cycle   ——→|

b. How many overhead steps do the order and the materials bought go through before the customer gets delivery?

FIG. 67. Study the steps in your time cycle to see how many can be eliminated to speed up delivery.

For example, consider the time taken by the order handling described by Donald Burnham. He says

". . . one Westinghouse division had 57 people handling an order before it reached the shop: 25 people maintained files involving the order. Now only four people and one file are required on one order." [1]

Single Items

Granted, many companies do not go much farther in preparation than to carry likely raw materials. Their usual customer cy-

[1] *Steel,* p. 28, July 17, 1963.

cle abbreviated might look like Fig. 67*b*. For instance, I have been in many plants where Purchasing bought items just as specified on the bill of material. The buyer treated the order before him as though it were the only one in the plant. Twenty minutes or twenty hours later he would buy another six or eight 1⅝- by 6-inch bolts.

Such a habit is expensive. It may be practiced though because of some inventory control policy. On the other hand, there are three other business factors that should be studied. First is the important one of delivery. This becomes the only advantage your company may have when competitive quality and price are about equal.

Second is the whole series of overhead costs generated by the Purchase Order. This was dwelt upon in Chap. 16. And not many folks have figured out how much money is spent in buying some one thing, or a dozen.

Third is the lack of study of commonness or standardization. The efforts that Engineering should make to utilize common designs and materials were discussed in Chap. 14. Those that should be developed by Production Control will be outlined here.

Probably the reason more has not been done in this phase is because few plants have real Production Control. Too many work on the shortage principle. Stock chasers, pushers, or expediters are used to "personally escort" the missing pieces to their destinations. Again, this is an application of the one-at-a-time idea. Being a bit more organized, some plants use the minimum-maximum method of inventory control.

Find Patterns

Both of these systems disregard the existence of commonness. Therefore, you can reduce overhead costs by utilizing the mass production principle in purchasing and in processing. To gain these advantages, you should search for repetitions in both phases of Production Control.

Start with your material requirements. Ask yourself, "How

many different items do we make from each one of our specific materials?" One good way to identify these repetitions is to set up material code numbers. Then all part numbers made from a given unit of material should be recorded on one card. An example is shown in another book.[1] Alongside each item is put the decimal equivalent that the part takes of one material unit.

Then each planning period, you post forecast quantities beside the part numbers on the material code cards, and extend. In this way, you collect together all the material of each kind needed. After comparing these quantities with raw stores inventories, you can inform Purchasing of your total requirements. In turn, Purchasing will consider lead times and market prices and order accordingly.

Process Standardization

The same analysis should be applied to processing. For instance, foundry men have always tried to melt the amount of each type of iron needed to pour the molds to be made each day. Millmen have sought to compound the batches necessary to supply the extruders with the several mixes specified.

Sure, these are simpler processes than your manufacturing may be. Even so, you should take advantage of the parts of your production cycles that are common to more than one product. This general idea has long been used in producing assemblies common to several final products.

Every instance you can utilize of commonness of material or of process affords two gains. One is in reducing the overhead costs that would otherwise be created by the larger number of distinctions—orders, schedules, setups, scrap, and recordings, to name a few.

The other gain is in "turnover" or its equivalent—return on investment. This comes from shortening the customer cycle a small or large amount. The amount you cut out depends upon how much you anticipate his wants by preparing ahead of time.

[1] Carroll, Phil, "Profit Control: How to Plug Profit Leaks," p. 146, McGraw-Hill Book Company, Inc., New York, 1962.

Broken Promises

Those parts of the customer cycle discussed up to this point were stressed first for two reasons. One is that they may have major influences on delivery times. The other is that few managers think of the work outlined as belonging to Production Control.

Usually, this function concerns itself with manufacturing only. Such limited view may be all right if the production cycle is not part of your customer delivery promise. This can be the case when all your products are made for stock.

When instead, length of process time bears directly on deliveries, you must look at all phases. Failures to deliver when promised create many overhead costs. Typical examples are

Overtime	Expediters	Telephone
Extra setups	Partial shipments	Sales calls
Scrap–rework	Air express	New customers

You may want to interpret "Expediters" as meaning Vice-Presidents. One told me he spent 40 per cent of his time answering customer phone calls.

The occurrences are multiplied when Sales makes promises without verifying their reliability with Production Control. Also as indicated on Fig. 67b, customer cycles can be stretched out on both sides of your production cycle. All three time phases should be reduced. In so doing, you will cut out steps that are increments of overhead cost. In addition, you should insist that Production Control be responsible for delivery time promises.

Better Scheduling

This latter shift may force better scheduling. That is no reason for hesitating. Rather, it is a way to make worthwhile savings in overhead. Perhaps the best negative example was that shown in a recent TWA ad. It portrayed a gondola freight car filled with silver dollars. And the punch line read, "Your capital doesn't earn a dime in transit."

So it is with your work in process. Your money is tied up. In addition, floor space is occupied, material is rehandled, and damage is incurred. The solution is to shorten the elapsed time.

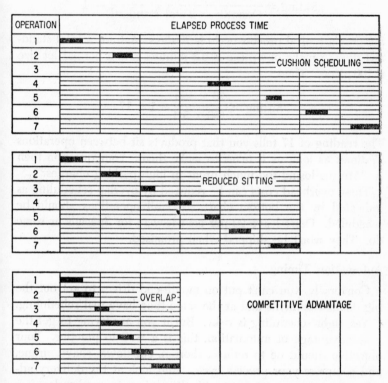

Fig. 68. Reductions in process cycle can give you the competitive advantage of better delivery.

Time taken to process in many plants is illustrated by the top Gantt chart on Fig. 68. It is labeled "Cushion scheduling" because large margins of time are allowed between operations.

Less Sitting

The middle chart shows a reduction in this safety factor. The tag "Reduced sitting" was chosen to emphasize the overhead cost leaks you should plug. To get a measure of amount, apply this simple test.

$$\text{Sitting} = \frac{\text{Process cycle}}{\text{Quantity} \times \text{Total standard}} - 1$$

Suppose a typical process cycle is 20 days. Assume a total standard time to make one piece is 5.3 minutes and a normal lot size is 100 pieces. Then

$$\text{Sitting} = \frac{20 \times 480}{100 \times 5.3} - 1 = 17$$

The reading of 17 tells you that products sit between operations 17 times as long as it takes to make them. Your question then is, "Are we losing too much profit in high parking charges?"

These overhead costs can be reduced by overlap scheduling as indicated by the bottom chart. And all operations should be scheduled. Don't leave 20 per cent leeway for Specials as some do. They won't be shipped when promised.

Automation Timing

Conversely, you can't put on month-end drives to get out the big dollar shipments and at the same time have real scheduling.

Yes, tight scheduling is risky. But if you are trying to get the time advantage of automation, this is a way to practice. Your objective should be to reduce, shorten, cut down, shave, prune, and compress your process cycle. And look at the delivery advantage you can gain along with the savings in overheads.

Precise Timing

Of course, the tighter you shrink the elapsed time, the more precise your timing will have to be. Work must be supplied at the rate it will be done. If it is fed in faster, the product waits. If slower, the people wait. This says that Production Control must keep a close watch on productivity rates—operation "efficiencies."

Further, you must guard against the tendency to think that old-time principles dressed up in new names are cure-alls. PERT [1] is an example.

Practical managers regularly tackle the big, difficult, complex, troublesome parts of an assembly first. Yet these are not often the causes of failures to ship on time. Commonly, they're trifling items like 5-cent lock washers.[2]

The obvious fundamental of timing, where you have assemblies, is that 100 per cent of the pieces must be there to complete them. And note carefully. This applies with equal emphasis to assemblies of products on any customer's order.

Timing that permits shipping your customers everything they want when they want your products depends also upon internal commitments. Material, supplies, blueprints, machine repairs, and the like must be delivered when promised. Consequently, you must see to it that Production Control is properly supported by all the functions it relies upon.

In controlling these functions remember that any stretching of lead times they may do "to make sure" will raise overhead costs and lengthen delivery cycles. Therefore, the factor to stress is reliability. This means the real chore is to develop better management.

Level Loading

Better managing in Production Control itself requires more control and less "stock chasing." The basic job is to fit an uneven customer demand into a relatively fixed capacity we call the factory. The disparity to be overcome is suggested by Fig. 69.

Unless the sales curve is leveled, overhead costs go up. In peak periods, you have added expenses like customer disappointments, overtime, hiring, training, learning, and scrap. The alternative is excess capacity. During low production levels, you

[1] Program Evaluation Review Technique.

[2] Carroll, Phil, "Wanted: Five-cent Lock Washer," *Supervision*, October, 1960.

may have excess costs like sales drives, waiting, make-work, and reduced efficiency. Offsetting these are the money costs of inventory and of warehousing.

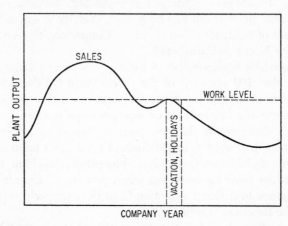

FIG. 69. Comparison of variable customer demand and semi-fixed factory capacity.

Where the balance points are will differ among companies. However, peering ahead a little bit will prompt you to include the probable increases that could accrue from higher equipment costs, technological obsolescence, and the much-talked-of annual wage.

Buying Habits

Considering all the angles, especially the costs of customer ill-will, chances are you will seek uniform work load. To achieve this state, Production Control will have to translate sales forecasts into production schedules. The extent of conversion will depend upon how detailed and precise in time your forecasts are.

Since sales predictions are often too general for scheduling purposes, Production Control will have to uncover the patterns of buying habits. One way to find these is to plot sales quantities of major volume items. The quantities by months should be converted to per cents of annual sales. When these per cents for two or three years are plotted, patterns should stand out. "History repeats itself."

Knowledge of these patterns will enable your planners to shift peak demands for production into valleys. Thus the work load can be leveled with respect to capacity bottlenecks.

More than that, cumulative Gantt charts (Fig. 61*b*) can be made of both forecast sales and planned productions. Against these may be plotted actuals. These comparisons will signal important changes of trends in time for corrective steps to be taken.

Running Forecasts

To narrow the margins of error, you should try to get running forecasts. An example is 6 months' forecast by months. One month is added each month to replace the one just past. Also, the intervening quantities may be revised.

Such forecasts have planning advantages. Primarily, they provide a formal way of notifying Production Control of probable changes. For instance, suppose some sales campaign is in the making. Most likely, this will shift buying habits of your customers for the time being. As a consequence, you could create ill feeling instead of good-will by being unable to deliver after persuading people to buy. Obviously, the wise course of action is to give ample notice of change to Production Control.

Control Forms

From the foregoing, it may not be apparent that there are overhead savings to be made in the Production Control function itself. To illustrate, it may not be clear that stock chasers are not necessary. Not only are they excess baggage, but also, the more you have, the more evidence there is that you do not have Production Control. To use numbers, I set up a real scheduling plan in one plant with only one person added in the office and six expediters dropped in the shop.

Besides wages, you save excess setups and related scrap, labor, and lost capacity caused by zealous expediters. The extra setups these fellows caused were so costly in one plant that we separated all such setups for special control attention.

Similarly, good scheduling can eliminate lots of paper work. For instance, you don't need production orders. This is a carry-over from job costing. The order number was necessary to identify the proper pile to dump costs into. This labeling is not required with modern cost methods. Anyhow, when you supply foremen with correct, up-to-date schedules of what and when to run, they don't need any more papers.

Lot Tickets

Lot tickets should disappear also. One explanation was just given. The more important reason is that runs should not be broken up into lots. Theoretically, but not actually, every lot calls for a series of setups. In turn, these increase related overheads as do also the lot tickets.

In essence, minimum-maximum control has the same effects. Besides, it fails to adjust for seasonal buying habits as illustrated by Fig. 69. Planned as distinguished from routine scheduling is essential if you are to maintain control of inventory while economically meeting peak and valley demand. Keep in mind then, you can eliminate the overhead costs that production orders generate when your scheduling is really working.

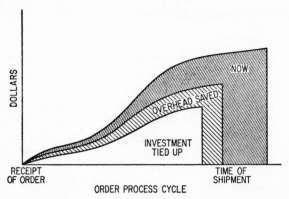

Fig. 70. Production Control can reduce overhead costs of both interferences and time cycle.

Investment Control

Bringing all the details together, you should think of this function as one of investment control. Much of the money tied up is in your plant, equipment, material, and process labor.

Your purpose in using this money for manufacturing is to make profit. But in this phase, profit is roughly the difference between excess of price over cost and the time cost of money. It follows that profit will increase as you cut the time multiplier.

Two general ways have been outlined. One called "Total Production Control" emphasized the shrinking of all steps in the time cycle from receipt of the customer's order to the deposit of his check. The gains are indicated on Fig. 70 by the darkest area.

In this shrinking process, some overhead steps will be eliminated. So also will overhead costs be saved by using better methods of Production Control. This second way of reducing time and expense is shown in lighter shading.

These stages of progress are portrayed as happening with a single order. This is the only device I could think of to show the gains to be made. Just the same, I believe the diagram reveals the major advantage sound Production Control affords in the control of your overhead costs.

CHAPTER 17

Study Maintenance Causes

James Quinn tells us,[1]

"Since maintenance is a 'cause and effect' situation, eliminating the cause obviously can be more significant than improving the effects. Traditionally, however, evaluation of maintenance operations is often limited to how well we are taking care of the effects."

You cannot gauge by tradition and also get control of the major overhead expense we call maintenance. William King cites an illustration. He writes,

". . . it is among the old-ways-are-best group that we find some of the worst culprits against cost reduction. There is the production superintendent, for example, who waits four months for a special stamping press. When it does arrive, usually at four o'clock on a Friday afternoon, he declares that his entire program will be shot if the machine isn't running by eight o'clock Monday morning. No, he can't wait for the job to be done on straight time; bring the men in and work them around the clock Saturday and Sunday. After all, it is maintenance that is increasing the overhead, not him."[2]

Moving Costs

King's mention of shifting responsibility brings in a second phase of maintenance cost control. This has to do with substi-

[1] Quinn, James D., "The Real Goal of Maintenance Engineering," *Factory*, p. 93, June, 1963.
[2] King, William O., "Profit Improvement and the Plant Engineer," *AMA Management Review*, p. 49, February, 1963.

tuting replacement for repair. In such decisions, Ray Reul offers this caution,

"In order to avoid making investments which will not be profitable and to locate and select from those available to us, those with the greatest possible yield, we should endeavor to use the best possible techniques for predicting performances." [1]

Reul is concerned primarily with new investments. But the point is that costs are of two kinds that are kept in two different piles. One is called Depreciation and is a bookkeeping amount. The other is named Maintenance and consists of labor and materials.

On top of this division of control, we are adding another complicating factor. We are substituting machinery for direct labor. Examples of increased capital investment per employee in 5 years are

American Telephone & Telegraph	$28,000–$47,000
Standard Oil of New Jersey	$54,000–$77,000
Swift & Company	$ 8,000–$11,000

These dollar amounts have in them two offsetting modifiers— volume of business and number of employees. The fact remains that maintenance costs are being increased by adding equipment.

Maintenance Budget

Such a complex of costs cannot be controlled by using ordinary budgets. One obvious reason is that your measure of volume shrinks when you substitute machinery for direct labor (Chap. 1).

Of more importance is the basic purpose. You want maintenance carried on in order to keep equipment running. Really, it's the production you are after so as to make deliveries on time. With prompt service assured (Chap. 16), your aim is to increase turnover so as to make greater returns on investment.

[1] Reul, Ray I., "Calculation of the Rate of Return on Investments," *Tappi,* May, 1960.

One way of looking at the whole picture is to note the *multiplier of turnover* in the following.

"Daystrom's formula for return on investment is computed by using earnings as a per cent of sales multiplied by turnover. . . . This earning as a per cent of sales reflects the division manager's success (or lack of it) in keeping a satisfactory lid on costs. And turnover measures his success in parlaying the capital entrusted to him in sales volume."[1]

From this business point of view, there are at least two elements that must be considered before control can be effective.

1. Comparison of downtime losses with costs of maintenance, replacement, or spare equipment.
2. Determination of effectiveness and efficiency of maintenance.

Other alternatives will undoubtedly be weighed. Should you make or buy? Would it be cheaper to lease equipment? Will new equipment enable you to increase production?

Equipment History

Whatever maintenance is done will tend to increase with age, use, and misuse of equipment. Thus, a primary lever in control is a record of repairs made to each machine. In time, this will indicate when you can no longer afford to patch certain machines.

Meanwhile, the record should show that some machines are more troublesome than others. This history is vital in considerations of the best types of replacements to buy. Further, it should reveal that some parts require most of the repairs or replacements. Here are examples of A conditions (Fig. 39, Chap. 8).

"McKinnon Industries found that of some 6,000 machines, only 199 showed annual maintenance costs over $1,000. Further breakdown showed that a low of 1.2 per cent of the machines

---

[1] Nicholson, Scott, "The Crisis in Corporate Control," *Dun's Review and Modern Industry,* July, 1963.

in one division caused 14 per cent of the costs, as compared to a high of 5 per cent in another division causing 51.1 per cent of costs. Company-wide, 3.33 per cent were causing 25 per cent of total maintenance costs." [1]

Corrections	Saving
Changing type and location of limit switches reduced effects of cutting oil splatter............	$ 7,800
Changing steel specifications and type of maintenance reduced forge hammer rod breakage.....	10,000

Maintenance Types

These two changes are examples of maintenance work that James Quinn calls corrective. These are efforts made to remove causes. He lists corrective first among four types of maintenance he names and describes.

Corrective—making minor changes in design, substitution of more suitable components, or improved materials of construction

Predictive—using sensing, measuring, or control devices to determine whether there have been significant changes in physical conditions of equipment

Repairs—doing maintenance work as the need develops, or "as required" especially noncritical equipment

Preventive—undertaken before the need develops to minimize unanticipated interruptions or major breakdown only when
Corrective maintenance cannot be justified
Predictive maintenance cannot be applied
Repair maintenance effects cannot be tolerated [2]

Each of these types and combinations has different costs. In this respect, they are like alternative choices of tooling or meth-

[1] Watson, John A., "Know Where Your Maintenance Dollar Is Going," p. 50, *Factory*, December, 1962.

[2] Quinn, James D., "A Discussion of Objectives in Maintenance Engineering," International Plant and Maintenance Engineering Conference; Alexandra Palace, London, June 17, 1963.

ods for production. Similarly, some cost more than others for the moment but should have lower long-run costs per unit of output.

Engineered Maintenance

With choices available, maintenance cost depends upon those choices made. Thus, control of this overhead cost is largely determined by the skills of its managers in getting and using facts. As William King writes,

> "Indeed, a top-flight plant engineer has enough information right at his finger tips to enable him to cut over-all maintenance costs by a third." [1]

Major cost reductions like "a third" come from three general improvements in managing—and a spark plug. The better managing might be described as

1. Deciding how often maintenance is to be done
2. Specifying what type of maintenance to apply
3. Planning when and how the work is to be carried out

The igniter or controller of what is done is work measurement.

Deciding Frequency

All four phases determine costs. In maintenance as in all overhead expenses, frequency is the multiplier. This cause was mentioned in Chaps. 7 and 8.

Note, for instance, that Quinn placed preventive maintenance last in his list of four methods. Further, he specified "only when" as taking precedent over repetitive costs that may not be worthwhile. In this way, the attempt is made to control maintenance cost by reducing unnecessary frequencies.

Then he specifies the other form of preventing breakdowns he calls predictive. This sensing, like "see your doctor once a year," again can be expensive or nominal according to its frequency.

[1] King, William O., "Profit Improvement and the Plant Engineer," *AMA Management Review*, p. 49, February, 1963.

Both preventive and predictive types of maintenance are forms of insurance. Their costs should be managed. The amounts you pay should be balanced against the losses you might incur if you didn't insure. Further, the risks are being changed by customer demand, corrective maintenance, equipment purchases, and in-line developments. Hence, frequency decisions must be modified from time to time if you are to achieve control of maintenance costs.

Work Specifications

Beyond deciding how often, and in part influencing, is the management job of work design. For instance, correcting faults in machine construction should reduce frequency of repair. Yet, correcting as compared with replacing or repairing a part will create a different cost at the time, and later.

The element of cost control entering here depends upon who makes the decision—mechanic or manager. If, as D. B. Hagen cites, you hand mechanics work orders like "faucet is leaking" or "furnace not working properly," they must decide what to do and then make the repairs. Such decisions bring in three cost factors. One is the type of repair made. This stems from the analysis of cause of failure. A second is extent. This grows from method of working and decision as to how many other things should be done at the site. The third is determined by how long the repair will last.

Lack of specifications has been the largest single cause of high maintenance costs in my experiences. For instance, walking to and fro consumed 25 per cent of the total in one case. Furnishing scooterbikes or trucks would have cut this per cent. But that is remedial.

The cure was to specify also how many men and what tools and materials were required. This is to reduce the waiting time of everything and everybody that would occur if someone had to go back or send for a "monkey wrench." Hence, a big part of maintenance cost control may be gained by utilizing "engineering" as outlined in Chap. 7.

Work Standards

When jobs are specified, work standards can be set more easily. Their cost-reduction advantages were discussed earlier. So were their control values.

In maintenance work particularly, you need to learn why performances on standards are not up to expectancy. Skipping over matters of ability, men fall behind when they have delays or extra work to do that was not allowed. Typical causes are shown on Fig. 71.

Cause	Wait Time	Extra Work
Tools...................	Lack Faulty Breakage	Faulty Breakage
Material...............	Lack Faulty Breakage	Faulty Shortage
Specifications...........	Lack Faulty Breakage	Faulty Incomplete
Scheduling.............	Lack Incorrect	Incorrect
Workmanship...........	Poor Incomplete	Poor Incomplete

FIG. 71. There are many kinds of time losses revealed by the applications of work measurement.

These extra times are not averaged into good work standards. Consequently, mechanics should be given credit for them. Either way, you have measures of the skill and degree of supervision. And as Ralph Geil reports,

"Work measurement forces maintenance foremen to do an extremely good job of planning, scheduling, material and data procurement." [1]

This same point is made by D. B. Hagen in different words. He writes,

"When the foreman can make job assignments on the basis of work content he is in a better position to reduce the amount of overmanning. On small jobs he can break up the 'buddy system' and on large jobs he can assign the right number of men." [2]

As a by-product, work standards aid greatly in charging, recording, and estimating maintenance costs. A simple method of prorating was shown on Fig. 57, Chap. 11. In recording, work standards provide more exact descriptions of work done. Just to estimate costs for deciding the most economical choice of alternatives alone, work standards might pay for themselves.

Services Supplied

In maintenance, much of the work is done for quite obvious reasons. But in all phases of service work, there is lots of opinion. Janitorial is an example. Taking care of appearances like washing windows, mowing lawns, and painting aisle lines are others. Internal trucking is similar.

These are not controllable by work standards except as to cost per unit. The number of times work is repeated is the big gap that must be closed. What makes this phase of control difficult is lack of tangible worths to weigh against costs.

Yet, maintenance costs of services of these types cannot be controlled until someone decides how often. Once frequency and degree are determined, work standards will afford the same type of control over delays and added work as explained earlier.

[1] Geil, Ralph, "Straight Talking on Maintenance," *Factory,* p. 98, March, 1963.

[2] Hagen, D. B., "Maintenance Improves with Work Measurement," *Mechanical Engineering,* p. 51, October, 1962.

Schedule Sequence

Too, work standards with performance measures are essential to sound scheduling as outlined in Chap. 16. In maintenance planning, they have added advantages. They help in deciding when and how to do a maintenance job.

To illustrate, one plant had a high-class mechanic with an oil-can going to machines to inspect their conditions. When he came to certain presses, he would stop as many as six operators working as a group. After some discussion, his schedule was revised. He visited such operations during the lunch-hour.

Point No. 1. In the control of overhead costs, all of them, schedule maintenance work that can be planned to be done when it will not interrupt the flow of goods to customers and the time of people producing them.

In another case, a stand-by mechanic held up eight operators while he tinkered with a labeling machine. This delay was reduced by providing spare labelers. Then when one acted up, it was yanked out of the line and replaced by another in good working order. Similarly, you have read of line operations set on bedplates. Faulty machines can be lifted out by cranes and good ones set in their places.

Here is a third example.

"A complete spare assembly of modules is kept only a few feet from the N/C machines. Once the fault is located, a complete module can be plugged in. The defective module is returned to the shop for repair and subsequent testing."[1]

Point No. 2. Whenever possible, make repairs "external" to the process cycle, as timestudy men would say. In so doing, you reduce the overhead costs of delays to production and deliveries, and for all the people related to them. Study Fig. 72.

Utilize Waiting

Go further. Recognize that stand-by maintenance men may be kept busy by repairs as little as 20 per cent of their time. There-

[1] "Numerical Control Skills," *Factory*, p. 55, December, 1962.

fore, work should be delivered to them for two reasons. The obvious one is to reduce maintenance costs. Part of these savings can be spent profitably for the purchase of spare units to reduce process downtime.

The second reason is not apparent to the casual observer. It is the tendency of men to stretch the time of repair work when they have been forced to kill time in waiting. They want to make

(a)

    a. Overhead costs of goods and people are increased when your production cycles are interrupted by maintenance.

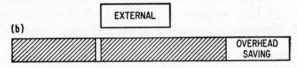

(b)

    b. Maintenance work can be taken out of your process cycle when spares can be substituted.

Fig. 72. Maintenance costs should be raised whenever practical to make repairs concurrent with your process cycle.

the most of their opportunities to do something constructive and to demonstrate their skills. Such additions of time, remember, are increasing slightly all your overheads of money tied up and people waiting. You can lessen these by bringing in other important jobs to be done effectively and on time.

Planned Work Load

Scheduling work for maintenance is very much like that for production. Jobs create variable demands as customers do. And your maintenance crew has a relatively fixed capacity similar to your factory. The problem is to level the peaks and valleys.

One way has been suggested. This is to reduce fire department calls by corrective and predictive maintenance.

Another method that some managers are beginning to use is to develop more versatile mechanics. This is necessary. There are too many different skills required in modern maintenance work for strict specialization. Subdivision cuts down the number of men in each type. This restricts both planning and expediting of repairs. Also it increases time lost in waiting for work.

A third approach is to classify jobs into degrees of priority. In this process, you set up a backlog of fill-in work. Watch this carefully. It must bear a proper ratio to your work force. Otherwise, (1) you get behind or (2) you raise costs by making jobs last.

A fourth plan is to use a different work week. The continuous-operation plants must, in some degree. This is another illustration of doing maintenance work "external" to the process cycle so as to avoid the overhead costs of delays in production.

After you have exhausted these and other approaches you think of, use outside contracting to take off peak demands.

"For example, a fair-sized plant in the New England area can spend as much as $30,000 for snow removal during a tough winter. Should the plant engineer invest in the equipment and manpower to do it with his own forces or should he contract the job out?" [1]

Proper Stores

When you provide a suitable backlog, you gain time for procuring or making parts. Again, however, you must balance costs. On one hand, you can carry too much inventory of spare parts or you can increase their costs by rushing through too many purchase orders. An alternative is to pay three or four prices by making parts you could have bought "off the shelf." On the other hand, you can be the creator of excess equipment tied up. More of this later.

The important factor concealed in the foregoing is that you do

[1] King, William O., "Profit Improvement and the Plant Engineer," *AMA Management Review*, p. 48, February, 1963.

not have a lead time in emergencies. For this reason and that of good planning, you should maintain proper stores of spare parts. Caution. Check them before you stock them neatly in bins. Don't feel confident that your insurance is "paid up" until after you know they will fit.

By way of emphasizing the probability of getting non-interchangeable parts, let me recommend that you reread Chap. 14. Then think of your part in the control of overhead costs. You do not wish to be the cause of delaying the receipt of your customer's check. Nor do you want to raise maintenance costs by making the parts fit during a breakdown. So be prepared.

All such problems will come to the surface when you utilize good work measures. But their corrective advantages can be lost. It is necessary, therefore, to record causes on your equipment history. The old saying applies—"forewarned is forearmed."

Excess Capacity

Finally, as mentioned several times, the high costs of excess capacity should be watched. These expenses are ballooning. As Millard Faught puts it,

> "How much per swallow does a coffee break cost management if the worker has left for 15 minutes a set of tools which frequently cost as much as a vice president's annual salary? And do not forget the downtime costs in nonproductivity from this same set of tools if the work week of their user amounts to only 24 hours plus one; or nine months out of every 12." [1]

Acting to offset this trend H. W. Bridgford worked out with his union a unique schedule. He reports,

> ". . . the plant equipment in Anheim will be utilized for 147 hours out of a 168-hour week instead of just 80 hours for two shifts, as under the previous contract. Since the half-hour

[1] Faught, Millard C., "Time Income: Hottest Bargaining Goal," *Factory*, p. 81, August, 1963.

lunch periods are staggered, facilities will be used 21 hours a day, with three for clean-up and maintenance, seven days a week . . . ."[1]

A glance at Fig. 73 will show the overhead cost reduction he made by avoiding the expenses of expanding. When you already have the excess capacity, your overhead cost is high in the relation shown.

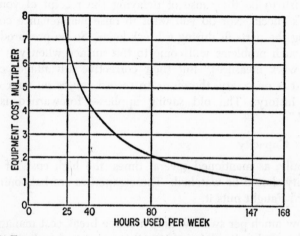

Fig. 73. Equipment costs per unit of output increase rapidly as hours utilized decline.

Besides, it is a brake on your earned return on investment. Its avoidance or removal is equivalent to a boost in profits as far as your showing is concerned.

Toward this end, you should maintain reports of equipment utilization. These will bring out all sorts of time interruptions. In addition, they will show up the presence of imbalance. This overhead leak is generally unknown. One reason is that it creeps in with shifts in product mix, changes in design, and improvements in methods. Usually, we correct in some way when these

[1] "Four Days On, Four Off," *Business Week*, p. 120, February 23, 1963.

alterations create bottlenecks. But we tend to overlook the growing idleness of facilities.

Be on the alert then to control this overhead cost. It can mount up because it serves as a cushion to take up the shocks of equipment breakdowns. Too much protection can make you insurance-poor.

CHAPTER 18

Decrease Transportation Expense[1]

Your products are useless to your customer until he receives them. Said another way, your customer is actually the end point of your "production line." The space gap between your plant and your customer is filled by transportation in some form. This movement of goods is a major element of overhead cost.

Shipping your products and all the others turned out by American industry costs $50 billion a year. This is ". . . better than twice the net profits compiled by all American Corporations last year."[2] In and out freight cost is the third largest expense in many companies, surpassed only by labor and materials, and yet, many managers have little more than vague general knowledge of distribution costs.

To get a quick look at the potential benefits of better control of this expense, compare 10 per cent of your freight costs to your net profit for last year. Is it equal to 20 per cent of your profit? If so, your cost-to-profit relation is like that of many companies. Thus, a saving of just 5 per cent of shipping expense would have a substantial impact upon the profit showing of your company.

Physical Distribution

Toward this end Henry Lefer writes,

"If you want to save money for your company, try to back off, look at all the costs involved in getting your product to the

---

[1] This Chapter was contributed by Phil Carroll, Jr.

[2] Transportation—The $50 Billion Battle, *Dun's Review and Modern Industry*, June, 1961.

customer, see how one cost affects the others, then rearrange the distribution elements so you get the best possible service at the lowest possible cost." [1]

All the costs you should analyze include those of transportation, inventory control, warehousing, packaging, material handling, and a portion of administrative overhead. To reduce their total, you might raise one of these costs, but in the process lower one or more of the others. It's the total cost of distribution that you are endeavoring to control.

Unfortunately, there is no single solution that will result from a carefully executed analysis of your company's product distribution. The variables are numerous. For example, to get answers you can rely upon, you need data of many kinds such as the following:

1. Tabulation of outgoing shipments by date, weight, and geographical area
2. Tabulation of incoming shipments by date, weight, and geographical area
3. Lead times allowed to fill customers' orders
4. Rating of the ability of your sales organization to change buying habits of customers
5. Realistic sales forecasts
6. Costs of maintaining inventories in your plant and outside warehouses
7. Lists of carriers available—plane, train, boat, for-hire trucks, private fleet—considering service, speed, and rates
8. Locations of possible warehouses
9. Other data peculiar to your own problems

With such information, you could simulate alternative methods of distribution into a given market until you found the optimum method—greatest service at lowest cost. Any such solution is correct only for a time. So you must be prepared to alter your methods to keep pace with your changing conditions. That's

---

[1] "Centralize Distribution? Yes, says Singer," *Handling & Shipping*, May, 1962.

why the application of linear programming on high-speed computers is the only feasible way to get solutions in many cases. But the answers won't be any better than the skills of those who ask the questions.

Transportation Cost

One of the vital questions hinges on the costs of shipping. In most companies, transportation is the most important single element of product distribution cost. Because of this, it's no wonder that shipping, long the control responsibility of middle-managers, has come to the attention of executives. With $50 billion at stake, many managements are beginning to take an upgraded approach. It is not only the cost considerations that have spurred recent surges of interest, but also the problems of customer services.

However, these efforts pay off. Savings can be tremendous. In some cases, they have been, according to Murray Harding, ". . . as high as 40 per cent after adoption of new methods based on thorough-going research." [1]

Piggyback Shipping

One new method that offers great cost reduction possibilities to many companies is the railroads' piggyback plans. Piggyback combines the flexibility of over-the-road trucks with the low-cost long-haul characteristics of the train. This is done in five different ways.

Plan I calls for the railroad to carry the trailers of common carriers.

Plan II puts the railroad in the trucking business, offering door-to-door service to shippers.

Plan III calls for the railroad to haul piggyback shipper-owned or leased trailers at a flat charge, whether loaded or empty.

Plan IV calls for the railroad to move shipper-owned trailers on shipper-owned flatcars.

[1] Harding, Murray, "Physical Distribution Theory & Practice," *Traffic Management,* p. 20, January, 1962.

Plan V puts the railroad and the common carrier in partnership, giving joint service to shippers.[1]

Plans I, II, and V usually offer the shipper very little, if any savings in freight costs. But, he can expect to receive faster service with less damage. Shippers that can utilize plans II or III will realize the benefits of the other plans. But, in addition, they may save as much as 50 per cent of their transportation costs, although, to reach the full potential of plans III and IV, you must coordinate your incoming freight with your outgoing, since the charge for returning empty trailers is the same as it is for full ones.

Container Handling

A refinement of piggybacking that has interesting possibilities is containerization. You can load your trailer at your warehouse in Chicago, drive it to the railroad yards, transfer the body (container) from the chassis to a flatcar, move it by train to the docks at San Francisco, load the body into the hold of a ship, have it taken to Japan, reload the container on a trailer chassis, and deliver the good to your customer's door in Tokyo. All this without having to rehandle the product, and for a single rate.

Piggybacking is probably still in its infancy, but it shows great promise of cutting costs. Shippers that have used this means of transportation are enthusiastic. Therefore, even though it may not now fit into your distribution plans, keep an eye open for future developments. The chances are some will be worth your consideration.

Regulated Carriers

While these developments go on, the railroads and the for-hire truckers are wasting much of their energies fighting among themselves. Much of the turmoil arises from trying to take business away from each other. Meanwhile, many companies have tired of high cost, and sometimes poor service, and decided to haul their own products.

[1] All subject to revision at any time.

Often, the regulated carrier's worst enemies are their own customers. Because of this, many have begun determined drives to find out how they can provide you with better service at lower costs. For instance, some carriers are equipped to study your entire distribution system, acquire special equipment, and, in general, adapt themselves to your particular needs.

Hence, by getting your carriers to sit down with you and spelling out your problems, probably you can come up with better service at lower costs. If this doesn't get the reductions you want to achieve, you may want to try "rolling your own" trucks.

What Choice

The choice between common carrier and private fleet methods involves an argument that has been waged for years, usually from prejudiced viewpoints. And, nothing would be gained here by adding a few words to the millions that have already been said. Besides, the optimum combination of cost and service probably lies in the knowledgeable use of both. The exclusive use of either can create profit leaks that often pass undetected.

In the matter of service, for example, your traffic manager may hold onto customer orders too long in an attempt to build a payload for one of your trucks. On the other hand, a common carrier may take as long as 10 days to deliver your goods, generally with more damage to the product. So, you want to consider the various alternatives, analyze all the costs, and select the method that provides you and your customer with acceptable service at low costs.

If your plant is in Richmond, Virginia, to make an illustration, you may service customers in nearby states with your own trucks. But, should you transport products to your scattered customers in Texas? You have many choices.

1. A pooled load on your own truck with each order delivered to your customers' door, using a backhaul of beans to help reduce costs.
2. A pooled load on your own truck delivered to a public warehouse or common carrier for distribution to your customers, again using a backhaul.

3. A combination of 1 and 2. Delivering orders along your route with your own truck and releasing the remaining orders that are off your route to another carrier for delivery.
4. Maintain a warehouse, public or private, in Texas and deliver inventory to it with your own truck, or common carrier. Then distribute from your warehouse by common carriers.
5. A pooled load by common carrier, broken down into individual orders upon arrival in Texas.
6. Ship each order individually by common carrier.

The right answer today will not necessarily be the right one the next time. Since your most profitable freight picture will change, you must have available cost information that will enable you to make right choices with regularity.

Private Trucks

To get cost information good enough to operate your own truck fleet successfully may require a change in your accounting. A recent survey of 300 companies that roll their own fleets revealed that only 13 had reliable cost information.[1] This is further evidence that most managers have ignored the transportation phase of their business. This is no longer permissible, with freight costs rising and profits falling.

Hence, it seems to me, the first thing you ought to do is gather up all the costs involved in the operation of your trucks. Figure 74 suggests a possible breakdown of expenses. Note that there are some "hidden" costs included such as management time and office expense.

Many common carriers argue that companies would become disenchanted with private trucking if they included *all* costs in their analyses of their operations. But, quoted carrier rates don't tell the whole story either. You still have many "hidden" costs when you use for-hire truckers. Some are processing freight bills, tracing shipments, slow delivery, filing claims, and auditing bills.

[1] Survey conducted by The Texas Transportation Institute, Agricultural and Mechanical College of Texas, College Station, Tex.

FIXED EXPENSES

Interest on borrowed capital............................ $_____
Interest on equity in equipment........................ _____
Depreciation on trucks and trailer..................... _____
Depreciation on garage and maintenance equipment...... _____
License fees... _____
Property taxes... _____
Federal highway use taxes.............................. _____
Insurance.. _____
Paint and lettering.................................... _____
Truck and trailer accessories.......................... _____
Washing and polishing.................................. _____
Garage supervision..................................... _____
Garage expense (heat, light, telephone, etc.).......... _____
Fleet supervision...................................... _____
Management time allocated to fleet operation........... _____
Office expense caused by having fleet.................. _____
Payroll taxes and fringe benefits...................... _____

TOTAL FIXED EXPENSES.................... ═══════════════

OPERATING EXPENSES

Fuel... _____
Tires (repair and replacement)......................... _____
Lubrication.. _____
Antifreeze, tire chains, etc........................... _____
Maintenance parts...................................... _____
Maintenance labor...................................... _____
Maintenance costs in outside shops..................... _____
Road service charges................................... _____
Toll road fees... _____
Rental charges for substitute equipment................ _____
Drivers' salaries...................................... _____
Drivers' payroll taxes and fringe benefits............. _____

TOTAL OPERATING EXPENSES............... ═══════════════

TOTAL FIXED AND OPERATING EXPENSES....... _____
LESS BACKHAUL INCOME...................... _____
TOTAL NET EXPENSE FOR FLEET...............

COST PER MILE $_____
COST PER 100 POUNDS _____

Fig. 74. One form of analysis of trucking expenses that gathers together all known costs.

To make correct decisions, therefore, you must compare like things—*all* the costs for private with *all* the costs for common.

While you're at it, compare your expenses with the rates offered by a leasing company. It may be that it can provide better equipment at lower cost. Too, many a financial man would prefer leased equipment even if the cost was slightly higher because he can make productive use of the money by investing it in other phases of the business.

Loaded Miles

Whether you own or lease your trucks, the success of your "truck line" will depend upon the ratio of loaded miles to empty miles. Private carriage can save you money. However,

". . . even when the cost advantages are clearly visible, they vanish almost overnight if the private trucker can't avoid empty backhauls." [1]

So, when you operate your own fleet, you find yourself in a two-way business. Still, there are only two things you can legally backhaul.

1. Raw materials, packing materials, machinery, office supplies, and the like that you use in your own business
2. Agricultural commodities that are exempt from ICC rate regulations

As a result, many fleet supervisors find themselves in a profit squeeze. Some slip into the "gray area," using illegal backhauls to reduce their costs. Very often managers are unaware that such violations are going on. Sometimes, they wink one eye and turn their backs. The most common of the illegal practices are

1. Leasing of both vehicle and driver usually on a trip basis. If the "lease" covers a one-way trip, the driver is "free" to make another deal for a backhaul.

---

[1] "Shippers: Rolling Their Own Pays Off," *Dun's Review and Modern Industry*, June, 1961.

2. Buying a commodity to get a backhaul, and selling the load at its destination.
3. Hauling non-exempt commodities with no attempt at cover up.

If private carriers persist in balancing their budgets with illegal backhauls, they run the risk of being regulated into oblivion.

Backhaul Income

Anyhow, making your fleet operation profitable by returning home with payloads doesn't just happen. It takes tight coordination between sales, purchasing, production control, and your fleet supervisor. Simultaneously, you must serve your customers promptly, roll your trucks loaded, and yet keep low your inventories of materials, supplies, and finished goods.

If loading the trucks to capacities becomes the stronger motive, inventories will be high. William Mitchell tells us,

"This can get to be expensive when you consider that, in many industries, the cost of carrying inventory runs as high as 18–24 per cent of the cost of goods sold." [1]

Keeping the right balance will require constant control. When purchasing cannot come up with a backhaul, you must try to locate a payload of an agricultural commodity. Many companies use brokers to help them locate such backhauls. But, because of stiff competition for these loads, the rates are low. Yet, if you can recover out-of-pocket expenses, it may be all you need to make the trip profitable.

Many sales people argue in favor of opening up new markets or of cutting prices because of favorable backhaul situations. This is dangerous for a number of reasons.

1. You may change vendors and have different backhauls.
2. Your vendor may stop allowing customer pickup, as some companies have done.

[1] Mitchell, William G., "A Creative Approach to the Question of Private Carriage," *Handling & Shipping*, p. 39, December, 1962.

3. Your vendor may move to another location.

4. Your customer may decide to pick up at your plant.

So, rather than create a situation that may change into a profit leak at a later date, *all* of the backhaul income should be used to offset the total fleet expense, as shown in Fig. 74.

To maintain control, I would set up two separate backhaul income accounts, namely

Backhaul income—company purchases

Backhaul income—exempt commodities

To the first you would credit the value of each load at the *equivalent common carrier rate*, and charge the appropriate freight-in-purchases account. Then your purchases are costed independently of your "truck line." Also, the price will be the same when, because of the schedule, you must bring your purchases in by common carrier. To the second, you would credit the gross income for each load, picking up any brokerage fees in its own account.

Compare Costs

Even though specific backhauls should not be credited to specific trips for the purpose of reflecting low rates on certain sales, each trip should be compared with common carrier rates to determine the most economical way to ship the order. The multi-variable chart shown in Fig. 75 is a convenient device for getting a quick answer to the question, "Should we haul the order on our truck, or can our common carrier do it for us cheaper?"

This chart considers six variables. These are round-trip miles, cost per mile of a variety of vehicles, payload in hundredweight, number of stops, cost per stop, and value of backhaul. The specifications for our sample trip are, 1,500 miles, at $.30 per mile with a $150 backhaul, 30,000-pound payload, and six stops at $5.00 per stop. The composite rate for the trip is $1.10 per 100 pounds. How does this compare with the carrier's rate?

Incidentally, the chart demonstrates the tremendous importance of the backhaul. As you can see, the rates tumble as the backhaul

Cost / Mile: Number of miles 1,000	1,500	2,000	Dollar value of backhaul											Payload in hundredweight									Cost / Stop: Number of stops 3	6	9
.20			100	50	0									400	300	200							3.00		
.30	.20			150	100	50	0								400	300	200						5.00		
.40		.20			200	150	100	50	0							400	300	200					7.00	3.00	
	.30					200	150	100	50	0							400	300	200					5.00	3.00
	.40	.30					300	250	200	150	100	0						400	300		200			7.00	5.00
		.40						450	400	350	300	200	0							400	300	200			7.00

Dollar value of backhaul											Rate in 100 pounds								
400											.27	.28	.30	.32	.35	.39	.43	.46	.59
300											.35	.36	.38	.40	.43	.47	.51	.54	.67
	400										.40	.41	.43	.45	.48	.52	.56	.59	.72
200	300	400									.52	.53	.55	.57	.60	.64	.68	.71	.84
			400								.65	.66	.68	.70	.73	.77	.81	.84	.97
		300									.69	.70	.72	.74	.77	.81	.85	.88	1.01
	200			400							.77	.78	.80	.82	.85	.89	.93	.96	1.09
			300								.85	.86	.88	.90	.93	.97	1.01	1.04	1.17
					400						.90	.91	.93	.95	.98	1.02	1.06	1.09	1.22
		200		300		400					1.02	1.03	1.05	1.07	1.10	1.14	1.18	1.21	1.34
							400				1.15	1.16	1.18	1.20	1.23	1.27	1.31	1.34	1.47
					300						1.19	1.20	1.22	1.24	1.27	1.31	1.35	1.38	1.51
			200					400			1.27	1.28	1.30	1.32	1.35	1.39	1.43	1.46	1.59
						300					1.35	1.36	1.38	1.40	1.43	1.47	1.51	1.59	1.67
				200			300			400	1.52	1.53	1.53	1.55	1.60	1.64	1.68	1.71	1.84
								300			1.69	1.70	1.72	1.74					2.01
					200				300		1.77	1.78	1.80	1.82					2.09
						200				300	2.02	2.02	2.05	2.07					2.34
							200				2.27	2.28	2.30	2.32	2.35	2.39	2.43	2.46	2.59

FIG. 75. Chart providing a quick way to determine a trip cost rate for comparison with a carrier's rate.

increases in value. Also, it shows the relative unimportance of the number of stops.

Set Rates

Thorough analysis of your trucking costs will reveal a pattern similar to that of common carrier rates. That is, a relatively high constant cost per hundredweight, with an almost constant additional cost per mile carried. A plotting of your costs will look something like Fig. 76.

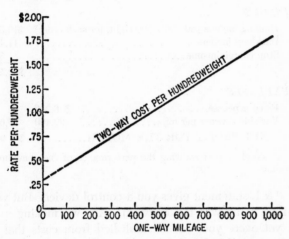

FIG. 76. Curve showing the rate per hundredweight rising as distance hauled increases.

In this illustration, the constant cost per hundredweight is $.30 with $.15 per hundredweight for each 100 miles. With such costs known, you are able to set rates for your "truck line." You can establish a rate for each point your trucks serve. Or you may prefer to set rates by zones. For instance 0 to 100 miles— $.38, 101 to 200 miles—$.53, and so on.

Further, you would be well advised to set a separate charge for each stop to be added to your basic rate. Of course, in establishing your rates per hundredweight, you would not include any expenses that went into the buildup of your stop charge. Keep in mind that the backhaul income was used to reduce the trucking expenses. Hence, *all* your rates are lower because of your back-hauls.

Decrease Costs

Now that we have rates for our "truck line," we are able to measure performance. Perhaps, the simplest way is to prepare a weekly or monthly profit and loss statement. Figure 77 is a simplified illustration of the form this might take.

INCOME

Hauling income (rate/cwt × weight, for each order)		$19,520
Backhaul income...............................		11,400
Stop charge income............................		580
		$31,500

EXPENSES

Fixed expenses........................	$ 8,200	
Variable expense per mile..............	22,400	30,600
NET PROFIT FOR THE MONTH..........		$ 900

Fig. 77. A simple report showing the performance of the company's trucking operation.

The P & L statement gives you a control device. But you must go further to answer the question, "Are we making a profit?" Worse yet, were your rates established from costs that are too high? You may be showing a profit on "loose" rates. To explain, your truck costs are too high, according to General Motors. They report, "GMC research teams have yet to complete a study without finding a savings potential *greater than 20 percent.*"

This booklet[1] lists seven profit leaks you can close up. These are

1. Lack of direct attention to fleet productivity by top management
2. Lack of exacting vehicle selection
3. Lack of planned vehicle replacement

[1] "Seven Common Profit Leaks in Truck Transportation," GMC Truck and Coach Division of General Motors Corporation, 1962.

4. Lack of systematic analysis of useful records
5. Lack of strong maintenance policies
6. Lack of clear standards for performance
7. Lack of skillful dispatching[1]

These seven profit leaks fit the same pattern of management errors we've been "harping" on for many years—failure to plan, failure to specify, failure to follow up. To the seven, I would add another profit leak. It is

8. Lack of coordination between salesman, purchasing agent, and fleet supervisor in their efforts to serve customers

Now, I'm not much of a mathematician. But to me the potential saving of "greater than 20 per cent" found by General Motors is well worth going after. To make this more apparent, let's couple their finding with the earlier statement that on the average, transportation costs a company "better than twice the net profit." In simple arithmetic, 2 × 20 per cent says that if you will critically study your "truck lines," you should be able to increase your company profit by 40 per cent.

"Milk Runs"

Going further, there is another variation you should investigate. If you operate your own trucks, your practice may be to pick off the truckload orders, and leave the LTL for the common carrier. This is a mistake. There is more money to be saved in the small shipments than in the truckloads. Incidentally, if you take all the prime traffic, the common carrier who may have offered you a commodity rate because of high volume between points will probably be forced to revert to a higher rate when he loses the volume. Thus, the higher rate charged for the small orders you give to the common carrier could cost you more than you saved on the truckloads you hauled on your own trucks.

My reasoning on the less-than-truckload shipments is based on the same cost relation that exists between the production run

[1] "Seven Common Profit Leaks in Truck Transportation," GMC Truck and Coach Division of General Motors Corporation, 1962.

and the small order specials. Everybody wants high volume production runs. Truck lines are no exception. They offer low rates on truckload shipments because nobody seems to want the small orders. Yet, there is more profit to be made on specials than on high volume business. It just takes more management—more planning, more specifying, and more follow-up.

To handle LTL shipments, one method that is used successfully by many companies is the "milk run." In this practice, your truck is scheduled to travel a more or less set route weekly, biweekly, or monthly. Your salesmen "educate" your customers to the merits of regular deliveries. They may even use some form of incentive to cement their cooperation.

Then your purchasing department lines up backhauls close to the ends of the "lines." When everything clicks, you have a profitable operation because the common carriers' rates are high for this type of business. Consequently, "milk runs" provide your "truck line" with high potential income. The possibility for profit is great since the number of stops your truck makes has relatively insignificant cost (Fig. 75).

As an example, one company operates a fleet of 16,000-pound straight trucks on "milk runs" within 200 miles of its plant. Savings of 20 per cent of common carrier rates are passed on to the customer. Yet, the company makes a 15 per cent profit on the operation. This is done with backhauls on only half the trips.

Major savings can be made by the exercise of control over your overhead costs of transportation. To gain these as improved profits calls for the coordinated efforts of all related functions together with the directed attention of management.

CHAPTER 19

Complete Your Cycle

If we agree that a chain is no stronger than its weakest link, then every operation in your overhead cycle should be studied. Those already discussed were singled out for only one reason. They have been, in my experiences, the major causes of excess overhead costs. Keep in mind, however, that my viewpoint is prejudiced by job-shop exposures.

Perhaps some operations herein outlined are even more important in your overhead controls. I hope not. I like to think that my emphasis has been reasonably well placed. Regardless, we should mention other functions that are links in your customer cycle.

Incoming Inspection

The start of your production hinges upon the receipt of material. Time losses here can add to your overhead cycle and customer appeasement costs. Pressures used to overcome time lags at this stage increase other overhead expenses. Hence, better scheduling is required to maintain low cycle time and minimum overhead expense. Your better planning should take place in Production Control and Purchasing.

However, there may be one other roadblock to overcome. This is incoming inspection. The importance of getting acceptable materials was stressed in Chap. 15. Those you buy should be correctly specified. The prime reason is to avoid the overhead costs of corrections or wastes within your plant. These follow

247

your taking in of sub-standard materials when time does not permit you to obtain replacements.

Of course, you must have correct and complete specifications if you are to check incoming materials in Receiving. Your alternatives are two. The costly one of default is to let your production people discover the errors when they start working with the materials.

Qualify Suppliers

The constructive one is to "qualify" or "certify" your suppliers. This is done by first making sure they understand your specifications and how you will inspect for conformances. Then you have to be assured that they can produce materials that will regularly pass the agreed-upon tests. Finally, you must verify their reliability in sending you only those materials that meet your specs. When these conditions exist, you can accept incoming products with little inspection and delay.

This approach is sensible. Your respectable suppliers will ship only after they have verified the quality of their products. They want to retain your business and your good-will. Too, they want to avoid the many overhead costs caused by rejections.

It is logical, therefore, to cut out as many of your duplicate inspection operations as possible. Save repetition. Save the overheads created by ignorance and misunderstanding of your specifications and tests. Develop your suppliers so they become departments of your plant.

Quality Control

After production is under way, quality control must continue. Here is one expense you should watch very critically. The folks who carry on this function can give the plant away before you know it.

Behind that facetious remark are two vital facts. One is your deliberate attempt to give your customers increasingly better quality. Against that is industry's extravagant lack of definitions of quality. Two phases were stressed in Chap. 14. Considering these facts, quality control efforts I have seen have been built largely upon existing rubber measuring sticks.

As a consequence, much of the work was wasted. What was worse were the costs of repeated arguments. These came mostly from resentment of what seemed to be the imposition of QC standards.

To control this expense, several steps are necessary. The first is fundamental. You must see to it that Engineering establishes standards for both tolerances and finishes. It will determine certain specifications for appearances in consultations with marketing. Until all these are clearly established, you have no reliable way to inspect production for conformity.

Such standards should be economically sound. This is a special study related to your own products.[1] It can be very fruitful if my many experiences afford any indication. I have often said, "We wear out the pieces by repeated inspections before the customers get them." To me, this suggests an exorbitant price for insurance together with all the extra costs of "playing safe."

Whatever your specifications are, they govern time standards for shop operations. Then if more work is required at any time to improve quality, the plus amounts should be reported as excesses. This method was explained in Chap. 12. It is the best way I know to keep you informed of quality being added that was not in the price quoted.

Define Control

The next step is to insist upon an understanding of real quality control. It is not a sorting of good from defective. It is not an accumulation of statistics. It is like any other control—it is removal or correction of the causes of defects. When this is done right, the production system will again repeat within its limits. Under these conditions, sampling can be used with major savings in inspection costs.

[1] Juran, J. M. (ed.), "Quality Control Handbook," 2d ed., Chap. 1, McGraw-Hill Book Company, Inc., New York, 1962.

Quality Maintenance

In some respects, Quality Control is like Maintenance. Basically, its function is to maintain quality. Therefore, similarly, its work load varies with age or state of equipment, training and skill of operators, length of runs, and product mix. In product, I am including the major variable of quality specifications.

To get a fix on this expense, first you must get the statistical adornments whittled down to useful proportions. In the main, the data I have seen being accumulated was basically used in attempts to make decisions that Engineering failed to complete.

Next you instruct and follow up to get the determinations of causes. Their corrections will require the full assumption of their responsibilities by Purchasing, Engineering, Production, Maintenance, and perhaps Sales.

Inspection Budgets

After the major problems are solved, you need to establish measures of work required of Quality Control. These should reflect the effects of two variables. One is a project type of research work undertaken to find causes of major increases in defectives.

The other is maintenance expense. It is a series of time costs set to gauge the Quality Control cost of each run of each product. As a starter, I would apply this measure to final production counts. One reason is simplicity. The other is that assembly catches the errors.

If your process is drawn out over several periods, use a running average trend. Don't go to the vast detail of measuring by parts unless (1) Quality Control expense is a big per cent of overhead or (2) the fluctuations from period to period exceed reasonable limits.

Control Setups

Many problems of Quality Control originate with improper machine setups. That's why we say, "Make sure the Inspector checks the first piece." This preventive form of inspection should be rigorously enforced.

In addition, you must control the costs of the setups themselves. These are often a big factor in manufacturing overhead. Whether these are made by operators or setup men, they should be measured and put on incentive.

FROM	TYPE	50 X 60 1	2	3	4	5	70 X 90 1	2	3	4	5	70 X 120 1	2	3	4	5	70 X 162 1	2	3	4	5
50 X 60	1	0	33	40		48	28	40				30		48			36	40	53	58	69	69
	2	30	36		48	53	33	44	48	53	58	36	44	53	58	63	40					
	3			40														53	58			
	4	33		44			36					40					44	58	63			
	5																					
70 X 90	1	28	33	40	48	53	0	44				30	44	48	58	63	36	40	53	58	69	69
	2	33	36	44			33	40	48	53	58	36		53			40					
	3			48																		
	4	36	40		53	58	36	44				40	48				44					
	5																					
70 X 120	1	28	33	44	48	53	30	40	44	58		0	44	48	58	63	36	40	53	58	63	69
	2	36	40	48	53	58	36	44	48	53		40	48	53			40			69		
	3								53	63			58				44					
	4	40	44				40		58													
	5																					
70 X 162	1	30	36	44	48	53	30	40	48	53	58	33	44	53	58	63	0	53	58	63	69	69
	2	36		48		53	40	44		58	63	40	48				44		58	69		
	3			44	53	63			53	58	63			58	63	69						
	4	40					44	48				44					48		63			
	5																					

FIG. 78. Change-overs from one job to another are charted like mileages on your road map.

One very important reason is that there is no consistent relation between direct labor and setup. Two factors upset any relation. Primarily, it is because you get no production while the setup is being made and vice versa. Secondarily, the setup itself is a variable. The work done to set up a specific operation depends upon how much or little of the prior setup can be utilized. We would understand this fact if we called them change-overs.[1] See Fig. 78.

[1] Carroll, Phil, "How to Chart Data," Chap. 20, McGraw-Hill Book Company, Inc., New York, 1960.

Typical Standards

But as pointed out in earlier chapters, setup standards will help you get control only of the work done. Not its frequency. Here again, you have to work out product factors. These will be quite easy to compute when you have setup standards.

Typical standards are established for cost estimating purposes. These are recorded on Production Control operation sheets for scheduling purposes. Totals can be built up for cost control use by parts, sub-assemblies and final assemblies, giving proper considerations to quantities run. These totals will be excessive. They will have to be reduced by finding the relation between average actual and typical setup standards.

From these figures, you can work out product ratios. These must be computed for several different volumes. Obviously, the setup is fairly constant regardless of the number of pieces in a lot. Hence to get your control figures, you would divide setups for Product A, for example, by low, medium, and high direct labor volumes for Product A. You could plot these answers to get factors for in-between volumes.

Then each period, you would compute your standard costs or budgets for setups. These would be product volumes times product ratios. You would add these to get totals for comparisons with total actuals.

If you needed more precise control, you could get it. Your first step would be to identify setups with products when they were made. Then, in any period, you could collect actual setups by products to compare with standard setup for those products.

Tool Costs

Setups usually involve tools. Your tool costs may be large or small. They may be charged to customers, written off as expense, or even capitalized. They may be purchased or made within your company. And finally, they are comprised of initial and maintenance costs. Hence, their control is a complex of variations.

To get under way, I will use the term tools to mean jigs, fixtures, punches, dies, patterns, molds. Toolmaker is to include all who make them. These are today's developments from Eli Whitney's "thing-a-ma-jig" designed to turn out interchangeable parts.[1] They create constant type costs expended to get into production. When charged to your customers in lump sums, they are controlled and out of overhead.

Those charged to overhead should be controlled better than they usually are. Many times, we say, "We gotta have tools." This is true of patterns, for example. How would you make a casting otherwise? Then, having made that decision, their costs are generally forgotten. The same is often true of tools made because production is impractical without them.

As an intermediate degree, we make tools to eliminate the excess labor costs of whittling. Lastly, there are many devised for improving methods. Usually these are justified—in essence, controlled. Rarely, however, is there any follow-up to verify the correctness of the estimated pay-offs.

Three Leaks

There are three leaks in this process that should be plugged. One is to check estimated savings to see if they were realized. This could be a simple routine with good timestudy in operation. With sound standard data, they could be ascertained as soon as the new method was measured. The second chance for loss is in the difference between guesstimated and actual cost of tooling. The third is the quantity multiplier.

To get control of these expenses, you should devise a two-part system. The first portion is to check estimates. Those who do the crystal ball gazing continue to assume they are correct until facts are presented to check against. Besides, there seems to be an abundance of optimism in good production managers. The other part is to check accrued quantities.

Both checks are necessary. Like all other dollars spent, their full costs should be returned with profit. In theory, your prices include amounts for tools that should have been computed on the

---

[1] Kettering, C. F., and Orth, Allen, "American Battle for Abundance," p. 19, General Motors, 1947.

basis of quantities to be sold. Until these quantities have been exceeded, you have lost money on these portions of your overhead.

Fictitious Ratios

Some such control is the only type you can rely on. Ratios are fictitious. You spend your money for tools before there is any production to measure by. When productive labor accumulates, your tool costs have already been written off. Thus, any overhead rate or budget measure of tools is a comparison of costs of tools you haven't used yet with production from tools paid for in the past.

The only current comparison of value is that of tool maintenance. These costs occur because of use—production. And while you may sharpen and repair tools only after runs are completed, the time interval between use and maintenance costs may be short. When this is true, ratios will apply. Even so, you need several.

This was explained in Chap. 1. Briefly, the more tools you have, the less labor is required. That's why you make tools. So to get realistic ratios, you must classify your degrees of tooling and compare their maintenance costs with their corresponding labor outputs.

Artistic Tools

But don't stop here. Look critically at tool costs themselves. Many I have seen are much too expensive. They are works of art. They are built to last 100 years. Some weigh several times too much. And no two are alike.

One explanation could be, "We're learning every day." The real reason is that the toolmaker is the designing engineer also. In addition to putting his personal preferences into the tool, he creates major variations in direct labor.

Concealed Overhead

At least, you should standardize basic designs to achieve minimum labor time in using your tools. This will give you two controls of overhead. One is the obvious reduction of time now wasted by tool-makers in creating individual designs.

The other is explained in Chap. 2. It is the overhead cost of extra work done because of differences in design. If "Load"– "Unload" is .290 minute for one jig and .055 minute for another on a like operation, the .235-minute difference per piece is not

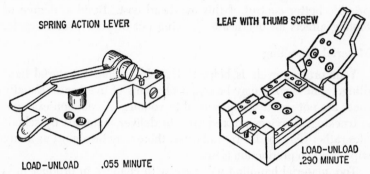

FIG. 79. Standardizing designs will reduce differences in tooling handling that are overhead costs.

added output. It is inflated cost. Regardless of how such variances are now recorded, your best method for controlling these overhead costs is to eliminate them at their sources. Pictures like those shown in Fig. 79 will help. Your basic problem is to change viewpoints of tool designers from structural concerns to production (profit) interests.

Measure Toolmaking

Additional savings can be achieved by work measurement. Beyond the gains made through increased productivity are three more quite worthwhile. One is the better utilization of skills. Much work usually done by toolmakers can be turned out by machine operators. In one instance, considerable work was transferred to turret lathes in the shop.

The opposite is gain No. 2. Harry Heywood moved "cats and dogs" from direct departments into the tool room. His purpose was to increase the flow of higher quantity production in the shop.

The third advantage is improved accuracy in tool cost estimates. This is important if your plant uses lots of tools and makes many methods improvements. Both are often decided according to break-even points. And there are several determined, in part, by degree of tooling. For this reason, better estimates provide better control of this overhead cost. Besides, degree of tooling affects all overheads growing out of your process cycle.

Material Handling

Your process cycle is helped along by prompt "material handling." These costs may be major elements of overhead. Usually these are not strictly proportional to volume. A common example is trucking. Services are required to deliver materials by schedules rather than loads. In dull times there may be almost as many trips as when production is up.

Too, material handling will vary with changes in product mix. To illustrate, let me cite an extreme case. In this plant, an overhead crane was used to assist in the assembly of one product. While holding parts in place, it could not make lifts for any other operations.

One important control of lift-truck expense is trip standards set from timestudy. These standards should be allowed only for loaded trips. When this method is used, you find you have a surplus of trucks you can sell.

From recordings made of trips, you can work out material handling requirements of your several products. Then by analyzing peak and valley trips, you can find the effects of volume. From these two sets of factors, you can develop realistic budgets for expense control.

Casting Cleaning

Before lift trucks take products to Shipping, one or several operations are performed in foundries that deserve special mention. They are called Casting Cleaning. Their costs are large and are dumped into overhead.

Often, the work done in this series of operations is greater than the sum of molding and core making (direct labor). It is wrong to treat these costs as overhead. Primarily, the work is not related to the pound or ton measure used. Of more importance are the errors made in costing and hence pricing.

Therefore, the proper way to control the major part of this expense is to measure it on a piece basis and change it to direct labor. The remainder should be gauged by classified time standards set for types of work, preferably based on piece count. This remainder should include only those operations whose time costs per piece would be insignificant in comparison with molding, core making, and cleaning.

Ship Promptly

Shipping is usually the department where your products start on their journeys to your customers. For this reason, the work should be scheduled and followed. You don't want any part of your delivery cycle lost in failures to ship promptly. And it can be, especially if Receiving and Shipping are one department. Remember, manufacturing applies pressure to "get material in." In contrast, frequently there is a letdown once the completed products are delivered to Shipping.

As a control device, you should get a daily report of days late in shipment. This can be a simple tally sheet. It can have as column headings numbers of days late. Under each is placed a corresponding count of orders shipped.

Granted, the delays in shipping may have been caused way back in the Sales Office where the orders were received. Yet, only as they go out the door has the internal cycle been completed. Thus, it is important to maintain a check on lateness in shipping. If the reports are unsatisfactory, you will want to trace back to causes by using intermediate transfer times. But don't increase overhead except momentarily by putting in another system. Your only interest is in removing roadblocks. Your goal is to achieve the shortest economical customer cycle.

Standard Packages

Your shipping operation may consist of one or several parts. Often, goods are packed as the last operation in manufacturing. Under this condition, labor and material are usually charged as direct costs. If so, they are better controlled than if they were thrown into overhead. Said the other way, you should try to move from overhead to direct such packing costs as can be practically applied.

In this between stage is an excellent place for many companies to make overhead savings. The opportunity lies in going to standardized packages. The gains may be of two main types.

1. Savings in purchasing, accounting, handling, and floor space, to name some, by using fewer container designs
2. Reductions in selling, accounting, order filling, and shipping by selling standard package quantities

Incidentally, one company saved more in freight than in packing materials when it changed from boxes and barrels to corrugated paper cartons.

Perhaps you can take the next step and introduce standard pallet loads. One shipping operation I observed used four-, five-, and six-high pallets. These quantity arrangements had been determined from studies of demand. The point is that a lift truck loaded a six-high at no more cost than a four-high. And all the paper-work operations were reduced one-third also.

Order Picking

Your products may be too small for pallet loading. Besides, your customers may buy as they would in a grocery store—some of several items. Whether these are in standard packages or broken lots, the order is "picked." This operation has in it a pattern you can use for controlling what is done. It is apparent in algebra as

$$\text{Time per order} = \text{Constant} + X \text{ items} + Y \text{ pieces}$$

The constant includes all the work done because of the piece of paper we call a customer's order. In one case it involved cutting a stencil for addressing. The X is really walking in that every item has its location in the stock room. The Y is counting pieces of each item.

One glance at the equation tells you that the way to control overhead is to increase items and pieces per order. This was the approach outlined in Chap. 3. It's only there that you see the physical result of the 12 or 100 steps in the overhead process that started with the salesman.

After you improve the order size, you can go further by re-arranging your store room to reduce walking. One big department store put its bins on wheels. Then the items advertised could be brought next to the truck-loading conveyor. Meanwhile, you can get correct or rough standard times for each of the three elements. Applying these to actual outputs will enable you to maintain control of the work being done.

Shipping Measures

If none of these approaches fit your conditions, then you must construct some measures. Your best tool is timestudy. For one thing, some critical looks at the work will reveal that many improvements can be made. For another, you need better gauges than total labor, tons, or sales dollars.

Studies will give you means for classifying shipments in typical groups. Here I think of the great differences between packing for shipment by truck versus preparing for export.

You should try several convenient measures. Three might be

Product	Ship. Hours	Mfg. Hours	Labor S/H	Pounds Weight	S/P	Sales Dollars	S/$
A	10	100	.10	50	.20	$375	.027
B	5	70	.07	100	.05	400	.013
C	12	50	.24	30	.40	250	.048
D	20	180	.11	75	.27	700	.029
E	15	40	.37	60	.25	140	.107
F	30	90	.33	25	1.20	230	.131

Fig. 80. Determine factors to use in maintaining control of overhead expenses in Shipping.

those shown on Fig. 80. In shipping hours per manufacturing labor hour, you might choose three groupings. Under pounds and sales dollars four are indicated. The number you choose depends upon three factors.

1. The error in measurement caused by the use of an average for a group.
2. The per cent that shipping is of the total overhead.
3. The separation you want in product groups on your P & L statement and other reports of profitability.

Having determined the measures, you multiply each one by its group total for the periods. This is just like computing the standard cost of goods sold. Only in this and similar cases, you compare the total of your extended standards with total Shipping —hours or dollars, whichever is convenient or more correct.

When goods are shipped, manufacturing usually feels that its job is done. Shipping does conclude the internal cycle. However, there are other elements of overhead cost that are related. Several of these will be discussed in our next chapter.

CHAPTER 20

Investigate Related Costs

Up to this point, the discussion of specific functions has been directed toward their effects upon your customer cycle. That is the primary sequence of efforts underlying your enterprise. Unless this cycle is completed in time agreeable to your customer's wishes, your firm may have more vital problems to solve.

While I think your first concern should be to shorten your customer cycle, costs must be kept in control. Those most directly involved have been outlined in previous chapters. There are others, however, somewhat outside the basic cycle, that should be touched upon.

Indirect Materials

Essential to your operations are certain materials classified as indirect. Their costs are put in overhead for any of three reasons. Usually it is because their costs are small relative to direct materials. Examples are small rivets and screws. A second reason is difficulty in computing direct costs. This is true of weld rod and plating. A third are types like foundry sand that, in the main, are reusable.

Controls of such material costs should be approached from a factual basis. First, determinations should be made that they are insignificant. These should not be opinions distorted by laziness or seeming difficulty. A common illustration of this laxity is Casting Cleaning described in Chap. 19.

You should start with some practical limit of error as explained in Chap. 4. The test is per cent error in apparent profit caused

261

by error in computed cost. To illustrate, take material as 40 per cent of cost and profit as 20 per cent. Then a computed material cost of 35 per cent would make it appear that profit is 25 per cent. This error of 12½ per cent (25/20 − 1.0) may be too much for competitive decision making.

The error is in the difference between an average applied by an overhead rate and a correctly calculated cost. Your error will be reduced when you set up correct product overheads[1] (Chap. 8). Still, you should find out how far the product average is from calculated amounts. In other words, prove by testing extreme cases in your groups that your errors are within acceptable limits.

Cost Separation

Now let's not confuse costing with controlling. Said more emphatically, don't confuse pricing with accounting. For instance, you can have some of your welding rods in direct and the remainder in indirect.

For control purposes, you should put them together. You want to measure how much was used in comparison with standard amounts built up from product factors multiplied by volumes of output. Then the accounting separation for direct from overhead can be done by calculated proportion.

Your factors should be determined within the departments where the major portions of your indirect materials are used. The corresponding product direct labor times can be collected as shown on Fig. 22, Chap. 5.

Incentive Control

A direct form of control can be very effective with certain types of materials or supplies. Acetylene, weld rods, hones, grinding wheels, and other high-usage supplies are examples. When their costs per day approach the wages of their users, consider dual incentives. Suppose for ease of discussion that your incentive plan is expected to afford 30 per cent earning op-

[1] Carroll, Phil, "How to Control Production Costs," McGraw-Hill Book Company, Inc., New York, 1953.

portunity. Assume also that normal acetylene costs per day equal wages per day. Then, in my opinion, it is sound engineering to base half the incentive per cent on control of supply consumption and half on productivity. This is simply a way of assuring economical costs of productivity. It is practical. It tends to discourage the deliberate wasting of materials when this adds to incentive earnings from increased productivity.

Operation Supplies

Like Indirect Materials, Operation Supplies may be small or large expenses. Some companies use tremendous amounts of steam, water, or air. Others spend huge sums for "perishable tools," cutters, grinding wheels, and the like. Many buy large quantities of hand tools, measuring devices, and similar aids to production.

In general, expenses like these are among the few that are closely related to production volume. But to assume their costs are proportional is a mistake. In the first place, your past experiences may be bad. Supplies may have been wasted. Some may have "walked off." In the second place, some products take more than others. Also supply costs themselves may be high or low.

Recognizing that two times zero is still zero, your costs of supplies may be too small to bother with even if they were doubled. In contrast, many firms need better controls. And the degree should be in proportion, obviously, to the size of the expense. Unfortunately, few firms I know have gathered any data suitable for setting control limits. The best I've seen is the variety of tool crib checks.

Supply Factors

Giving the mechanic a new drill, reamer, or file in exchange for an old one does roughly maintain a relation between tool usage and production. But the boss can't tell from totals how much of a rise or fall in tool costs was due to a shift in product mix. If the variation isn't enough to worry about, let me add one caution. Don't blame the foremen for increases until you know whether they are caused by changes in product mix or laxity in control.

If your supply costs are only moderately large, you can get a fairly reliable control by using factors. These could be supply costs for each major product per standard direct labor hour. You might get these for just the departments consuming the bulk of your supplies. These rates might be worked out by a mathematician using simultaneous equations. Consumptions could be converted to product or plant totals by the relations of departmental product hours to total product hours.

If, instead, your supply costs are huge, then you need more precise standards. You should assign a clever analyst to this task. He should find out what the costs are of every major supply per unit of product output. These would be like standard costs —what your costs should be. Not what they are.

These would be extended each period by volumes of output to get standard costs of supplies. The extensions could be made separately for each major supply. Comparisons of actuals with standards will be measures of control. Variations in product mix will be accounted for correctly.

Reducing excess usages may require some retraining. For example, some men run cutters too long before changing. Once the edge is gone, cutter wear increases rapidly. One sharpening may cut away the stock that should have extended over three or four. This is quickly learned when you set standards for cutter sharpening. From applications of these standards, you can locate excess tool wear. Reports of existing practices in one plant brought about substantially more savings from curtailed tool wastes than from gains in tool sharpening productivity.

Product Development

Also outside the main cycle, but hopefully its sustainer, is the creative function we call Product Development. Like tools discussed in Chap. 19, developments of new designs are setup costs. Their costs are largely spent before you have any production to "absorb" them. It follows that current volumes of output of other designs are not measures of such costs.

Your controls have to be like those sketched for tools. One phase might be called the project method. This is simply a comparison of actuals with estimates.

Your chief control is in the second phase when you compare quantities sold with those estimated both in numbers and in time periods. You need this latter control to avoid innovating your company into bankruptcy.

True, you must develop new products and new designs just to stay even. You must offset the declines in profits of existing products suggested by Fig. 60, Chap. 13. The time and degree of decline depends upon the relation of supply to demand. As Robert Schultz puts it,

> ". . . *the profitability of any expansion program must not be judged in terms of current prices, for it is a reasonable assumption that the price will be lower when the new capacity goes into operation.*" [1]

He is talking about plant expansion. But output expansion caused when you or your competitors bring new products onto the market has much the same effect.

Two Tests

Thus, there are two elements of control that new designs create. One comes from timing. Are you moving into an untapped market? Or are you expecting to take a share of an existing demand? The other relates to quantity already mentioned. A new design may simply replace sales of other designs. If sales are spread thinner, you may not get enough to recover your development costs, let alone make profits.

Few of us can predict how customers will react. Yet, you must establish controls that will help to trim the tops off of Sales

[1] Schultz, Robert S., "Profits, Prices, and Excess Capacity," p. 77, *Harvard Business Review*, May–June, 1963.

optimism. Consequently, your fundamental test is, "Did we sell the quantity we said we would in the time periods we agreed to?"

Misplaced Aptitudes

Until your products, new and old, are sold in sufficient quantities, your planned profits are not likely to be achieved. In selling and in the resulting operations, your profits can leak away unless the productivity of your people is at or above levels figured in your costs.

Productivity depends in a large measure upon the attitudes and skills of your people. These, to some degree, result from the selections made when you hire them. We know that new employees tend to adopt the "style of the department they work in." On the other hand, we recall that "a rotten apple can spoil a barrel." Thus, part of your success in meeting consumer demands is assured or deterred by the men and women you employ.

One of the chief stumbling blocks in many firms is the square peg in the round hole. People are taken in with little or no attempt to find out what aptitudes they have. If those hired are supposed to be skilled, we tend to be swayed by extent of prior experiences. Most of us erroneously conclude that long servitude makes for high skill. We fail to understand that 40 years' experience doing wrong things is bad rather than good. Unfortunately, we have locked in by seniority agreements many who would be happier and more successful in jobs across the aisle.

Poor Supervision

What is worse, some managers have euchred themselves into positions where senior employees must be offered openings in supervision. Here, we have several problems mixed together.

First, as one speaker said, "We have no right to balk at this stage. The mistake was made 20 years ago when we put him in the groove." He is right, if the contract was written that way. At the same time, he is pointing out what may have been an error in hiring.

Second, unless you can promote from within, you stifle initiative. But again, long experience in work operations does not give an individual the different abilities he needs to manage success-fully. Therefore, the primary phrase is "skill and ability being equal." It is not "seniority shall prevail." However, the meaning of "skill and ability" should be spelled out to include "potential to both learn and carry out supervisory responsibilities."

Third, you must recognize past mistakes and take steps to cor-rect them. Now, I know there have been arbitrations, threats of strikes, and perhaps walkouts, in protests of testing. Job security is at stake. Nonetheless, if existing talents are not adequate for future needs, you must build up your individual skills. You must get into your contracts some way to retain and promote exclusive of seniority.

The points raised here, while stated in terms of contracts, apply just as emphatically to non-union employees—shop, office, or sales. Whether they turn out work or supervise, they must have sufficient aptitudes and interests to succeed or they will be dis-satisfied. No amount of wage and fringe benefits will make them happy.

Peaceful Co-existence

"Peace at any price" seems to be the guiding principle in many industrial relations contests. The higher prices paid are overhead as are the costs of arguments that precede them. All time paid for but not worked is overhead just the same as idle capacity.

So is all paid-for time spent in negotiations, grievance pro-cedures, and arbitrations, together with all paid for time of stewards and officers carrying on union business. And the list of fringes and trimmings continues to grow longer.

Besides the obvious, many plants pay out major sums every year in concealed and defaulted ways. Chiefly, these are caused by actions postponed, compromises made, and precedents con-tinued. Most I have seen are in so-called direct labor. Con-sequently, managers do not recognize their costs as overhead. They are, however, when you define direct labor as equivalent to good salable pieces (Chap. 2). The extras are higher costs—not more output.

Exactly the same types of excesses are in overhead operations.

They occur and continue because they are people costs. Think also of the pressures exerted and decisions made toward equalizing the fringe benefits of blue- and white-collared groups. Now, seemingly, the decision is to give salaried people the gains granted to the hourly folks.

Such added costs won't disappear if we look the other way long enough. They must be noted first. Then computed. Knowing how much they are, skilled managers will be prepared to reduce or eliminate them in future negotiations.

Educate Supervisors

Getting agreement in negotiations is just the beginning. Frequently, managers will "sweat blood" to gain or regain certain rights only to have them given away by faulty administration. That's how the problems come into being. Therefore, changes must be made if the cycle isn't to repeat itself.

The place to start is with the supervisors. They do the things many times every day that conform or conflict with the contract. They and others hear about the conflicts. Are they conflicts? Or are they efforts to make additional gains not granted in the agreement? Too, how often are concessions being made—overhead costs being raised—when actions taken appear to conform because there is no evidence of conflict?

Answers to these and many similar questions must be given to your supervisors. They must be taught the meanings of the contract—not the words. They must understand the principles and their many implications. How else can they correctly apply them to the hundreds of incidents that occur daily?

Trouble Begins

Yet, it's when they run into conflicts that control of these overhead costs begins or is put off. So much depends upon whether supervisors are backed up or overruled. Often, too many outsiders are overly cautious for fear of "rocking the boat." They look at the incident as though it were isolated from the principle. Some even say, "That's only a trifle. Why get upset?"

If some compromise is effected or the supervisor is overruled, he may give up trying. He thinks in terms of black or white. He doesn't know about "gray areas." If he has made an honest mistake, he must be shown why or where he made an error. Otherwise, he is apt to think he was overruled. But when he is backed up, he knows that he is doing what management wants done in abiding by the rules (contract).

Right here is a very important determinant in the control of your overhead costs. Control is action. And the actions you want require changes in habits and practices. For these to be constructive, the first line supervisor—in the office or in the shop—must get his people to carry out the new procedures.

That brings us to an understanding of authority. It is explained by Chester Barnard this way,

"If a directive communication is accepted by one to whom it is addressed, its authority for him is confirmed or established. It is admitted as the basis for action. Disobedience of such a communication is a denial of its authority for him. Therefore, under this definition the decision as to whether an order has authority or not lies with the persons to whom it is addressed, and does not reside in 'persons of authority' or those who issue these orders." [1]

Supervisors Undermined

You recognize that acceptance of instructions depends upon many elements. Momentarily, it may be the weather or what a person did the night before. In the main, however, the thorough and skillful carrying out of instructions stems from respect for the supervisor.

Respect is undermined when events seem to prove that the supervisor is not running his department. Even he makes this evident if he hedges or appears uncertain. Most of our current trouble was brought on to a large extent during the big drive for unionism. Lawyers, Vice-Presidents, and Personnel Managers took over.

[1] Barnard, Chester I., "The Functions of the Executive," p. 163, Harvard University Press, Cambridge, Mass., 1940.

My opinion is that the supervisor's position and standing must be restored. If he is incompetent, that condition should be corrected. The supervisor directly in charge of those who do the work is the manager who actually controls costs. Your best-laid plans become operative only when the people who must carry out their mechanisms do so both correctly and completely.

Thus, all the controls discussed in this book are of value only when they are made to work effectively. This occurs when supervisors know how, are skilled, and are expected to do the jobs they are paid for. Those chores expected of them are assigned by their superiors. That gets us to the question, "How concerned are your managers with the continuing success of your company?" Toward that subject our next chapter will be directed.

PART THREE

How Managers Should Apply
Controls to Improve Profits

*Systems are lifeless. To be effective, systems must
be applied by managers and used to direct the energies of the people in the organization toward achieving its goals.*

CHAPTER 21

Organize Manager Tasks

According to Claude Carson,[1]

"Today's biggest problem for any individual firm is to build an organization which can keep its mind on making a profit in the face of everchanging operating conditions, and still have time to plan for the future."

Whether developing good managers is the biggest task or not, it is a vital one. You see in nearly every description of an executive's job some prescription "to develop successors." Certainly there have been a great many executive and manager development "courses" put on by companies, associations, and colleges. Supplementing these is an expanding group of consultants, sometimes called "pirates." These experts help to save the costs of development by enticing skilled men away from other companies.

Status Conflict

The need for successors exists for two reasons anyhow. One is to fill the age gap created during the depression. The second is to develop or obtain men with the skills demanded in our space age. All this furor, especially when "crown princes" are anointed, tends to make some feel that they are more important than their jobs.

Feeling important and needed is essential to our mental well-

[1] "Management Problems in 1963," *Harvard Business Review,* January–February, 1963.

being, the psychologists tell us. But when this becomes the end instead of the means, the company loses. Note how Edward Schleh points out this trend.

"Personnel, accounting, engineering, or legal—each group wants to raise its status. Unfortunately, this drive does not always take account of the needs of the enterprise so much as the personal desires of the individual specialists. At times they have developed 'professionally accepted' methods antagonistic to the objectives of the firm, with a negative effect on the company." [1]

Organization Fences

Seeds of this condition were sown when we created specialized functions and gave them names. Growth was nurtured when we developed budgets for keeping track of their expenses. As one consequence Schleh observes,

"In some firms employees feel they are to carry out administration instead of to work out creative solutions for problems. Managers carefully follow the budget but do not necessarily cut long-range cost. The logical corollary is that people want to know 'what they should do,' and then wait for directions." [1]

Partially suggested by Schleh's comments is the restrictive influence of organization charts. Seymour Tilles thinks these cause such interferences that he says,

". . . *most organizations would probably contribute enormously to their own progress if they burned their existing organization charts and manuals.*" [2]

Using Tools

I'm not agin' status seekers, budgets, organization charts, or manuals. I do think, however, that the preceding quotes point

[1] Schleh, Edward C., "The Decline of Corporate Initiative," *Business Horizons*, p. 64, Indiana University, Spring, 1963.

[2] Tilles, Seymour, "The Manager's Job: A Systems Approach," p. 79, *Harvard Business Review*, January–February, 1963.

to a serious weakness. There is too much conformity. Yet, the question I ask is, "Do these conditions exist because of the management tools we provide or because of the training we give the men who use them?" In this use, training means designed education or slipshod catching on.

By way of making my point, let me tell of two comments I heard several years ago. One was in a talk given by Tom Turner. He said in essence,

> "I do not believe in boxes on organization charts. They leave as undefined many borderline tasks that don't get done. Too, I'm looking for men who will grab for opportunities to do the in-between jobs that others neglect."

The other was stated by Joe Juran in an address before the SAM in New Jersey. He emphasized the lack of point credits in position evaluation for necessary interdepartmental work and collaboration.

Now there is a third factor. It is mixed in the decentralized-centralized switching. But very few analysts have more than hinted at the need for some major realignments of functions. This was mentioned in Chap. 9. It was touched on again in the discussion of teamwork in Chap. 10.

Manager Team

All these deficiencies should be corrected. At the same time, you want to make progress in the control of overhead costs. Putting these together, we might recap the basic objectives as being:

1. Get managers to keep their minds on making company profits.
2. Realign functions to reduce borderline gaps and to expedite work flow.
3. Shorten customer cycle to gain competitive advantages while reducing the related overhead time and complaint costs.
4. Reduce system, paper-work, and function overheads that either obstruct the customer cycle or do not pay off.

One approach is to assign a group of managers the task of reducing your customer cycle. When you induce them to concern
themselves with serving customers, their self-interests are out-
weighed by profit-making alertness.

The managers put on the team should be those responsible for
the major time segments of your customer cycle. They are the
men who have to make whatever corrections are to be achieved.
Besides, the experts tell us, managers strive more diligently to
meet standards they have a part in setting.

Cycle Portions

To get under way, you can ask these managers to get the time
portions of the complete cycle they are responsible for. They
might begin with one of your major products. The cycle they
analyze should be from the time the order is taken until the
customer's check is deposited. These should be time facts ex-
tracted from a sample of recent transactions. If facts are not
available, begin anyhow. Let them use their knowledge to provide guesstimates to work with while sample times are being
processed.

When these times are laid out end to end, you have a check.
How does the total compare with the average time represented
by your turnover?

Then your managers should discuss all those time portions that
seem excessive. Naturally, each will think his is "the best I can
do." Even so, the others will ask why some portions are so long.
Out of these inquiries should come many suggestions for shrinking the cycle.

The next question becomes, "How does the proposed cycle
time compare with the turnover goal you have set?" This measurement may show that further reductions are to be made. This
may require another type of approach. Let me cite a homely
example. When I buy a shirt, almost without exception I become
irritated. What bothers me is the time I'm forced to wait while
the sales girl writes up her book. Usually I say, "Give me my
change and shirt so I can go. Do your bookkeeping afterwards."

Critical Path

What steps are now in your cycle that can be pulled out and done later? This is simply a general application of the idea called "external" work in Chap. 17. It is the paralleling of work alongside the "critical path" determined in the glorified Gantt scheduling process currently named PERT and CPM.

The basic difference is this. With PERT and CPM, the critical path of the longest or determining process is known. The other processes or components are brought along in parallel. Here instead, you are working toward a "critical path" of customer cycle that is the shortest practical time. You achieve this path by removing from past procedures every time element that is not required in time sequence.

For example, can the primary cycle be continued with one copy of whatever you use while secondary work is done with others? Also, how far along the cycle can you progress while a customer's credit is being checked? This reminds me. Years ago, the son of a prominent Cleveland industrialist was learning the business. He was in charge of Credits and Collections. At the end of the first year he proudly reported, "Dad, our bad debts were reduced to one-half of one per cent." He was chagrined when asked, "Son, how much more profit would we have made if it had been five per cent?"

Horror Exhibit

Next, you might set up what Charles Edgar named a "Chamber of Horrors." This was an exhibit of all system forms used, showing all copies. These were connected and interconnected with colored ribbons to show all their procedural steps. As you can imagine, this took up several walls of a normal-sized conference room.

When it was completed, those interested were invited to study the exhibit. After the initial commotion subsided, questions were asked. Many investigations were made before some could be answered. Forms were being used in departments that their managers didn't even recognize.

Many sessions followed. "Why?" was asked repeatedly. Managers found answers and reported. From this series of meetings came a lot of constructive changes in routines, many redesigns to achieve more useful forms, and a large number of eliminations of both forms and copies.

Paper Vehicles

Sometime in a study like that just described, the customer cycle time should be brought in. The purpose is to connect the two ends. Pieces of papers are the vehicles in the early and concluding parts of your customer cycle. In addition, they may aid or impede the flow of physical materials. For instance, do you insist upon a requisition to get bolts from the stock room? You'd wait a lot longer than you now do for delivery of that shiny new car if Chevrolet assembly lines requisitioned parts.

Study of the interrelations between time cycle and paper work should bring out further time savings. Some will come from outright eliminations. Others will be gained through finding more ways to parallel paper work and process cycle.

In addition, these analyses should reveal overlapping or obstructing borderline duties. Further examinations may suggest the need for realignment of functions. Such changes should be made when they will improve results. Remember, there is nothing sacred about the existing organizational arrangement. Chances are it is chiefly the result of happenstances.

Form Analysis

Efforts to compress your customer cycle should be continued until it is reduced to or below the turnover goal established. After this objective is reached, the managers should be requested to concentrate on the forms themselves. They should be told about the order costs described in Chap. 3. They should be informed about profit leaks in C items. Then they should be asked to analyze methods and make suggestions for profit improvement. Don't be surprised if someone recalls that Sears doesn't use customer order forms. As you know, they even return your letter in the box with the goods you ordered. So it is possible to send items to customers without typing a handful of forms.

Keep reminding the responsible managers that major overhead costs are in paper handling—not in paper costs. Hence, they will reduce overhead expenses when they eliminate pieces of paper. Repeated analyses will develop understanding. Your managers should eventually see the distinction between people and paper. People get things done if we keep to a minimum the paper interferences.

Fourfold Purpose

In the foregoing, nothing has been said about staff help. The omission was deliberate. The team method was proposed for achieving the fourfold purpose outlined earlier. It is the managers who set the pace for their subordinates. It is the managers who must be profit-minded if their supervisors are to be. It is the managers who are to assume new or changed responsibilities if progress is made.

Staff men can take on none of these managerial functions. Sure, they can do legwork. They can perform certain tasks better than managers. That is to say there's no reason for avoiding the assistance of skilled staff people.

Be careful, however. I know from many experiences as a consultant how willing some managers are to "delegate." They will hire a consultant to put in a "system." They will perform all the niceties of making him feel at home, giving him a comfortable place to work, and then leaving him to do the job. Sooner or later they kiss him goodbye. Then they begin to wonder what they got for their money. In time, they may criticize him when some snag occurs in "his system."

Not enough managers realize that the consultant took the know-how with him when he left. They didn't acquire very much because they let him do the work. The same thing can happen in this case if the responsible managers get all the staff help they want. It's only one more step to turning the whole job over to them.

Here we're talking about evolving a system. However, this is only the vehicle. It's a very important one. But its values of reduced customer cycle and lowered overhead costs are reflected in improved profits only to the extent the managers "make things happen." Therefore, keep in mind that the system will work better when the managers devise it and make it work.

CHAPTER 22

Increase Conversion Value

M. S. Moyer writes,[1]

"The marketer is not as much engaged in selling a product as in finding adequate outlets for the engineering and production skills of the company."

He says as Charles Kettering does that,

"The product of a factory is just a packing crate in which people working there ship out their labor and get money in return for it." [2]

The labor skills both men refer to are commonly called conversion. Some prefer the term "value added." This process has made us the greatest industrial nation in the world. Other nations, even some states in our own country, have come to realize that they must have more industry in order to "develop."

Indeed, turning out production seems to be the primary goal of many companies. This is natural. It has been the basic drive in our country ever since our colonies decided to make rather than buy. It was our production achievements during two major wars that made us the "arsenal of the world."

[1] Moyer, M. S., "Is Management Conflict Avoidable," *The Business Quarterly*, University of Western Ontario, Summer, 1962.

[2] Boyd, T. A., "Professional Amateur," p. 201, E. P. Dutton & Co., Inc., New York, 1957.

New Conditions

Now conditions are changed. We have trained and equipped nations abroad to help themselves to recover from the devastations of World War II. As a result, we have "foreign competition." This will become more severe when the Common Market has its own pipelines filled. And we dare not forget Nikita Khrushchev's threat to bury us.

Already, we have suffered some losses in export sales. The explanation given by *Business Week* is that our country's pro-

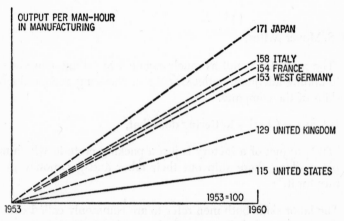

FIG. 81. Productivity has been growing more slowly in the United States, as shown in *Business Week*, p. 67, June 24, 1961.

ductivity has lagged behind. Our rate of increase is the lowest of several shown on Fig. 81.

To be competitive, we must improve productivity or its equivalent—reduce costs. Our prices for like qualities have to be in line. How else can we provide jobs for all those who want to work? We can't solve our unemployment problem "by taking in each other's washing."

While nations abroad have been building competitive strength, we have been fighting among ourselves. First, we went through many rounds of wage increases as unions strove to gain power.

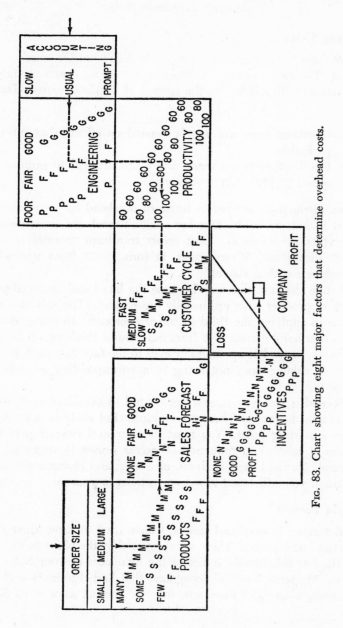

Fig. 83. Chart showing eight major factors that determine overhead costs.

286

Then we blamed each other for causing inflation. This spiral was halted momentarily on Friday the 13th by presidential action.

Consequently, as the experts say, "Our environmental conditions have been altered." An attempt to show the major external influences is made in Fig. 82.

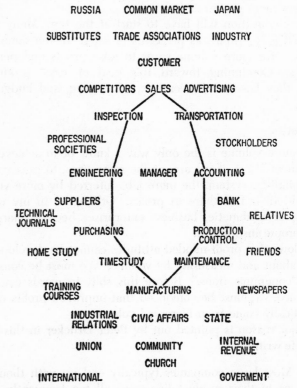

Fig. 82. Diagram suggesting the many external and internal influences that bear on your customer cycle.

Goal Choices

Carried from outside into the company is another change. This is one of attitude. Currently, we appear to think chiefly in terms of security. Conformity seems to take precedence over initiative, creativity, and risk taking. These are brakes that can slow down earnest endeavors made to ease the profit squeeze.

Coupled with this is another carry-over—wholly constructive but misdirected. It is the premise that the company's goal is to turn out production. This idea mixed with conformity may account for the repeated discussions lately of the need for making employees more profit-minded.

Such re-education will have to start at the top. Many presidents still judge profits as per cents of sales. In the same vein, they press for more volume so as to raise profits and per cent showings. Continuing toward this goal of more production (sales), they base sales incentives, advertising, and budgets on volume.

More Jobs

Still, more volume is the only way I know of to achieve "full employment." Yet, if we are, at the same time, to preserve our free capitalistic system, the more jobs inferred by more volume must add their full share to profits. Otherwise, in my understanding of arithmetic, business enterprises become more like philanthropic institutions.

It follows that profit-minded attitudes cannot be developed by talking about and measuring by volume. We must be consistent in our "communications." Before this shift in words can have acceptance, we must be convinced that improved profits do not automatically come from increased volume.

A major reason is pointed out by Peter Drucker in this statement. He writes,

". . . Most large companies typically end up with thousands of items in their product line—and all too frequently fewer than 20 really 'sell.' However, these 20 items or less have to contribute revenues to carry the costs of the 9,999 nonsellers." [1]

[1] Drucker, Peter F., "Managing for Business Effectiveness," *Harvard Business Review,* May–June, 1963.

Wrong Costs

You and I may draw different conclusions from Drucker's comment. Therefore, to keep us together, let me set down my interpretations with relation to the control of overhead costs. These are

1. Overhead costs are largely wasted on efforts that are not profitable.
2. Overhead costs are more nearly proportional to number of orders (9,999) than to volume.

These deductions are put in terms of overhead for two reasons. First is that, probably, Drucker couldn't reach his conclusion if our costs were correct. Cost errors transform themselves into profit distortions. Wrong costs, in turn, result from spreading "overheads with a shovel."

I state the case this way because the labor and material portions of product costs are usually quite exact. The mistakes are made in applying the third factor of overhead. In these allocations, our habit carries over from our volume thinking. It blinds, however, instead of opening our eyes to the fact that each added unit of volume does not bring in a corresponding amount of profit.

Second is that you cannot get control of overhead costs until you know its causes. These are multiple. But analysis is no more than a starting point. You must measure and reward performances in relation to reduction of excess causes in order to get control. To the extent analyses, measures, and rewards are fully utilized, you will bring about corrections in your product costs.

Eight Factors

Returning to overhead causes, I have tried to show their connections with profits. These are suggested by the chart in Fig. 83.

The left side mainly indicates the influences of your Sales efforts. My term "mainly" recognizes that both Products and Incentives, even Sales Forecasts, may be internal as well as Sales

factors. Even so, the four left-hand causes indicate the kinds of orders to be filled. In contrast, the right-hand causes typify what is done internally with those sales orders.

Of course, you may have factors more dominating than some of the eight I show. Also, any of these eight may have more effect in your company than indicated. Nevertheless, this picture will reveal more clearly, I hope, two fundamentals this writing has attempted to bring out. These are

1. Volume is not the primary cause of overhead costs, and
2. Control of overhead costs is a major factor in profit making.

Profit Leaks

That overhead cost directly affects profit is evident from several points of view. One is its size. It is the largest element of cost in a typical division of Westinghouse. According to Donald Burnham, the three components are in the following percentage relations.[1]

Direct labor	11	1.00
Material	42	3.82
Overhead	47	4.27
Total	100	

A second factor is also emphasized by these figures. It is that the overhead portion is high because most of our cost control efforts have been concentrated on direct labor. Here is another by-product of volume thinking—get out the production. By the same action, indirectly, we tolerate a bit of "never mind the cost." Doing "whatever you have to, but ship on time" extras raise overhead costs.

A third is stated by a German industrialist who had made a tour of U.S. plants. He said,

"Don't blame all your profit troubles on the wage differentials of your foreign competitors. As a matter of fact, we could pay our workers the same wages as yours and still be competitive.

[1] *Steel*, p. 27, July 17, 1963.

The difference is that we have fewer managers, and they get more done." [1]

A fourth is the logical conclusion you can draw from the first. It is that you can make more progress with a given amount of effort in the part of costs that is both biggest and least analyzed.

Separate Overhead

The cost we call overhead varies greatly from plant to plant. The main difference results from the type of industry. For example, we think of a process plant as being mostly pipes, tanks, and instruments. There are very few, if any, direct labor people. In contrast, we see fabrication as having machines and benches with many direct labor people.

A second difference arises from the degree of use made of management "tools." Consequently, that portion of cost called overhead depends somewhat on definition. For instance, as stressed in previous chapters, extra work done by direct employees may now be classified as direct labor. Added work that does not result in equivalent, salable pieces is extra cost rather than extra production. All such cost should be classified as overhead for control purposes. The reason is that it usually arises from work that management failed to complete.

You know that, as a rule, it is both better and cheaper to have any one finish a job while he is at it. Too, there is always the probability that the specialist in any phase of work will do the job more cheaply. Therefore, from the standpoint of control, it is advantageous to record as overhead every cost that does not represent real production.

Packing Crate

Looked at in this light, you may have more overhead cost than is now apparent. What is more vital is its control. You are spending the money now. You want to spend more, if necessary, to achieve the highest practical return on your invested capital.

[1] "Make Jobs Pay Their Way," *Nation's Business,* September, 1961.

At the same time, you want to cut out expenses that do not pay off.

Therefore, it is the whole conversion process you must study. It is "value added" you are selling, as suggested by the opening quotes from Moyer and Kettering. Thus, it makes no difference whether the cost is in your left or your right pocket except—in the final analysis, only salable pieces can earn overhead.

Luxury Costs

From this viewpoint, the make-up of overhead is pictured in Fig. 84. The proportions are not indicative. The four blocks across the bottom represent major causes of overhead.

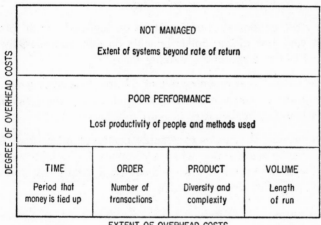

FIG. 84. Graphical picture of the main causes of overhead costs.

All of these are increased by the degree that performances are less than you consider attainable. These additional costs are represented by the horizontal block in the center.

Both of the foregoing are inflated by whatever luxuries you may have in your systems. Luxuries, suggested by the top block, are refinements of all kinds, not obligatory, beyond the basic systems that pay their ways. Some of these are niceties—things you'd like to have—lovely lawns, oriental rugs, shiny windows, and the like. That's your choice.

Your primary concern is with reductions of paper work and related expenses incurred in handling *C* items. These are created mainly by using the system for such customer cycles that was designed for major sales orders.

In all cases, however, you should cut the tops off of systems that are more ornamental than productive. Each system should return its profit on the money invested. You should strive to overcome the mesmerisms pointed out by Peter Drucker. "Our civilization suffers from a superstitious belief in the magical effect of printed forms." [1]

Note also that systems you can buy may not be the answers either. Three instances are revealing.

". . . the general decline in return on invested capital proves that very few of the dollar benefits on automation really accrued to the corporations making them." [2]

"The score: 18 companies out of 27 aren't saving enough on computers to cover what they are putting in; the other nine are obtaining handsome returns on investment." [3]

"Let me say that I am reasonably confident none of us here will live to see the day when a company faced with weighty problems, will send its officers away on a fishing trip and call a meeting of its electronic brains." [4]

Basic Causes

Starting again at the bottom of Fig. 84, Time refers to all costs created by your customer cycle. This is depicted as the inner

[1] Drucker, Peter F., "The Practice of Management," p. 133, Harper & Row, Publishers, Incorporated, New York, 1954.

[2] "Who Profits from Automation," *Forbes*, June 1, 1963.

[3] "Only One out of Three Pays for Itself," *Business Week*, p. 152, April 13, 1963.

[4] Rockefeller, David, "Managerial Work and Human Progress," 13th International Management Congress, New York, September 16, 1963.

system on Fig. 82. It is your life stream—your reason for being in business. Its costs depend upon a combination of rate of turnover and its inverse—customer complaints. Remember, however, the by-product. Better deliveries can help you get more sales.

Next is Orders. This represents the sum total of overhead setup costs created by sales and production orders. These costs are fairly constant regardless of quantity (volume).

Alongside is Products. Again, these are like setup costs. Also, they affect Order costs. Such overheads are more costly for some products than for others. For example, some products require more overhead operations. Also, Engineering, Sales, Tools, Equipment, and other costs may be expanded with each product added or redesigned.

Orders and Products overlap. You have orders for products. So you should separate costs due to development of products from costs created by orders for them. Then you can establish different degrees of order costs to reflect product differences.

Last is Volume. It does cause some overhead expenses. These are suggested by the phrase "length of run." For instance, tools need sharpening and machines require maintenance when you use them. Even so, Volume is placed last for two purposes. One is to stress further the error of measuring overhead in terms of volume. The other is to emphasize the probable greater effects of Time, Orders, and Products upon your overhead costs.

Budget Measures

Recognizing these influences is necessary to getting control. Your measurements of effects must be closely geared to causes. In this direction, budgets should be based upon the work required by the causes.

As Arch Patton says,

". . . budgets developed by many companies are often not supported by qualitative and quantitative objectives for the individual executives who help to attain these goals. The individual members of the management group thus find it difficult to identify themselves emotionally with company goals, for they are unaware of their own vital share in attaining them." [1]

Let's discuss further the terms "qualitative and quantitative." The meanings of qualitative that I think apply here are two. One is the Time element. Most functions of overhead will cost you less rather than more when you reduce your customer cycle. Thus, it is highly desirable to point your manager's efforts toward serving your customers promptly. Doing work on time is to me a form of quality.

Second, it should mean doing the work assigned both correctly and completely.

Quantitatively also has several meanings. One is to use measures that directly gauge the work to be done. Another is a corollary. Your budgets should be cut to exclude inefficiencies and adornments as their amounts are reduced.

Managerial Action

Proper measures of quality and quantity are only instruments of control, as you fully realize. Yet, they are fundamental. As Douglas McGregor states, "Measurement is . . . the key to equity in administering economic rewards." [2]

Said in reverse, "Whom can you count on to really manage your operations?" This includes making all the changes indicated by your analyses of overhead costs. You know, as Erwin Schell so often said, "You can have change without improvement, but you cannot have improvement without change."

Sometimes, you will be forced to say as Tom Marshall did, "I'm not paying you to tell me why it can't be done. Your job is to come up with ways and ideas that will help me solve the problem." Too, perhaps you will think as Charlie Thomas put it, "They lack a sense of urgency."

In these efforts of developing managers who get results, you

[1] Patton, Arch, "Developing Executives to Beat the Profit Squeeze," *Business Horizons,* Indiana University, Winter, 1962.

[2] McGregor, Douglas, "The Human Side of Enterprise," p. 92, McGraw-Hill Book Company, Inc., New York, 1960.

will find measures like those shown in Chap. 6 to be helpful. In particular, proportional gauges similar to those in Fig. 32 will aid considerably in sorting the "men from the boys."

Rearrange Duties

There will be arguments. The number and intensity will be governed mainly by the extent of realignment you make in functional duties. But as M. S. Moyer states,

> "Honest conflict between members of the company team is neither unhealthy nor avoidable; it is an inherent part of getting the company job done. Management should recognize that its role is not to ignore, deplore, or eliminate reasonable conflict between subordinates, but to limit it, harness it, and direct it along constructive lines—in short to *manage* it." [1]

His "limit it, harness it, and direct it" carry two meanings that apply to our subject. The first is to strenuously oppose the costly building of alibis. As Harry Levinson explains,

> "The subordinates amass reams of data on all kinds of obscure questions just in case someone should ask for some isolated bit of information. Endless hours of countless staff people are devoted to compiling reports whose sole purpose is to prove that the executive is 'on top of' his job." [2]

Such tactics raise overhead costs. Still, conflict must be resolved. In your efforts to "harness it, and direct it," you can use two gainful methods.

Numerical Goals

First is to set up your company goals. In this step, you may want to take a cue from James Black. He advises,

> "Your best bet is to know your own business, operate it imaginatively and originally, and avoid placing too much reliance

---

[1] Moyer, M. S., "Is Management Conflict Avoidable," *The Business Quarterly*, University of Western Ontario, Summer, 1962.

[2] Levinson, Harry, "A Psychologist Looks at Executive Development," *Harvard Business Review*, p. 72, September–October, 1962.

on statistical reassurances about what other companies are doing." [1]

Naturally, you will make more progress when the goals you choose are long-range. Then, you ought to break these into annual or even shorter time objectives. And express them in numbers. For example, you might say, "Before vacation time comes in July, we want to

1. Take 10 days out of our customer cycle time.
2. Increase sales order quantities to eliminate the bottom 20 per cent of current *C* orders.
3. Shave off 50 per cent of our system costs of handling small orders.
4. Cut out 10 of the unprofitable items in our line."

With specific goals that managers understand, you can more effectively apply the second method. This is to talk, remind, cajole, persuade, emphasize, stress, and insist. The point is to harness and direct energies toward the attainment of goals.

Outweigh Selfishness

By persistence you establish priorities. As some psychologist said, "You can't overcome resistance to change. But you can pile enough advantages on the other side of the scale to outweigh it."

The problem is somewhat like that every foreman faces. On one side are all the desires of his men. They want more money, better training, and upgraded jobs. On the other are concerns of his boss—more production, better deliveries, and lower costs.

The successful foreman satisfies both. Yet, in a pinch, he must give preference to his boss's requests. So must higher managers. They will pay more attention to company goals when those are stressed. This will allow less time for empire-building.

And when promotions are given to those who produce measured results, your company goals have "teeth in them."

[1] Black, James M., "Management and Risk-taking," *Management Review,* p. 4, August, 1962.

Leadership Required

Managers want to get ahead. Many have wrong definitions of success. That's beside the point. Those men you can count on recognize that their futures are limited or enhanced by the profit-making results of your company's operations.

In addition, they look for signs of progress. They know that to just coast along on an even keel may signal decline. The more intelligent men may act on such signals and depart. They're in a hurry. They may figure, "We've got only 30 years left to make names for ourselves."

Your potential future managers are alert. They know what is happening in other companies. They read technical journals. They go to professional society meetings. They attend many courses—manager development and others—often because they are sent by company officials.

These exposures to progress are very advantageous when men see that their companies are keeping abreast. They understand, even if they have never heard, that "nothing succeeds like success." Most are quite willing to take their chances with a company that appears to be "going places."

It is important, therefore, that your managers see ample evidence of enlightened management. This can be readily observed when you constructively attack overhead costs. One reason is that many managers are in the departments being worked on. Word will travel fast to all others. Some managers in Manufacturing and Sales may say, "It's about time." Even so, all your up and coming managers will be enthused with the prospects. They will work diligently to achieve the goals set for them in a company where the boss is determined to increase values to customers and to prosper with them.

Index